2023

from the arena

an entrepreneur's journey

the story of pigsback.com

written by Michael Dwyer

edited by Gavin Daly

To old friends: Alf, Gerry, Nick and Jenny

Contents

About the Author

Michael Dwyer is originally from Dundalk in Co Louth, Ireland and lives in Monkstown, Co Dublin, with his wife, Karen. They have three daughters Kerry, Nicky, and Ella.

Michael graduated from Dublin City University in 1985 with a degree in International Marketing and Languages. He spent 15 years in marketing positions in the international food industry before launching Pigsback.com, one of Ireland's best-known digital businesses, in 2000, close to the peak of the dot-com boom.

In February 2019, after almost two decades of immense volatility, Pigsback.com was sold for approximately €25 million.

from the arena is the story of Michael's entrepreneurial journey, based mainly on his journals.

These days, Michael invests in and advises start-up and scaling businesses, mainly high-tech companies. He has time to enjoy his wide-ranging interests, which include art, writing, horse racing, poker, running, the outdoors in Connemara, and family.

Introduction

When you hear the sound of the cannons, walk toward them - Marcel France

Founding and running Pigsback.com was a 20-year rollercoaster ride.

Having turned my back on a lucrative corporate career in 2000, the financial and emotional stakes could scarcely have been higher. If I was brave in following my dreams, I was foolhardy in equal measure, but, ultimately, survival is the name of the game.

This book is my account of those dreams, their consequences – professional and personal – and of the measures it took to emerge intact 20 years later. This story is for entrepreneurs, aspiring and practising. I hope it bears witness to much that is difficult – if not impossible – to teach entrepreneurs. In the real world of start-up businesses, overnight wonders are few, global successes and so-called 'unicorns' even fewer, and case studies of perfect strategy and execution almost non-existent.

Entrepreneurs try to anticipate trends and market movements, often with thorough research and planning. But the future is a slippery creature, defying prediction. Inevitably, they face unanticipated and sometimes unanticipatable challenges. The business plan is then cast aside, together with all its reassuring data, certainty, dotted i's and crossed t's. Only then do entrepreneurs find themselves in the real world, where the measure of success is how they evolve with their teams to face this new reality.

Yet the world of start-ups remains sexy and alluring, perhaps suggesting to some onlookers that it is an easy path to easy money. Nothing could be further from the truth. Enterprise is a test of staying power, optimism and creativity. It is a huge personal challenge, too, physical and mental; unchecked, it will ruthlessly extract its toll on entrepreneurs, their partners and families.

In 2010, I first came across Theodore Roosevelt's famous speech "Citizenship in a Republic", which he delivered to the Sorbonne in Paris 100 years earlier. I was immediately struck by parallels between entrepreneurs and "the doers of deeds" in the famous passage from Roosevelt's speech known as *The Man in the Arena*. The entrepreneur "strives valiantly... knows great enthusiasms .... [and] spends himself in a worthy cause", but most will stumble and fail. Deep reserves of resilience and adaptiveness will be called on as markets, people, and entrepreneurs' own imperfections come repeatedly to test them.

Amid the demands of my enterprise and journey, I turned to writing what became a sequence of more and more regular journals. The entries addressed the mix of opportunities and challenges I was facing at a given time, both professional and personal. These journals became an entrepreneurial record, which is reflected here. Just as importantly, the writing process was cathartic, my bridge over the frequently troubled waters of trying to grow or just manage a business, helping me to unburden, reflect and unknot my challenges.

I was conscious too of the historic times these were. Pigsback.com was founded at the tail-end of the dot-com boom and found its feet as mass adoption of the internet was gathering pace. New brands were emerging with entirely new ways of communicating and doing business. Less than a decade later came the global credit crunch and recession, triggering Ireland's prolonged economic depression from the late 2000s. Even in the short few years since selling the business, there have been yet more challenges for entrepreneurs to contend with, from Brexit to the Covid-19 pandemic, to the war in Ukraine, to the dark clouds which are gathering over the global economy just as I pen these final words.

I hope that by sharing my story, prospective entrepreneurs may be better prepared. Some may even opt against this route for the right reasons.

Bringing this book together was far more difficult than I imagined. I enjoyed writing most of the early notes – mainly by hand – but the subsequent editing was more onerous: 'Why is this worth telling?' I asked. 'What gives me the right to publish a book?' I've always respected professional writers and their craft; that respect has sky-rocketed after my own struggles. But I like completion, and I got there in the end.

So, whether you know lots or little about business and enterprise, I hope you find something of interest and value in these pages. Buckle up and enjoy the ride.

Prologue

It could have been his deathbed. My father lay in intensive care in the cardiology unit of Louth County Hospital in our hometown of Dundalk, just south of the border between the Republic of Ireland and Northern Ireland. He looked shook, a greyness about him that made him appear a lot older than his 67 years.

A day earlier, he had suffered a heart attack and cardiac arrest. It was touch and go.

As we conversed, a little and slowly, he pointed to the cover of a business magazine. It was headlined 'The Dotcom Boom', depicting a giant wave looming, bringing with it opportunity and threat.

"Will you do anything about this?" he asked. As always, his finger was on my pulse.

I always felt there was an entrepreneur in me. My father did too. But there I was, 15 years into an ostensibly successful career in the food industry – a few years more than ideal – and beginning to feel that the time to get out on my own was running out.

It's like seeing a drawbridge rise in front of you with every passing year, progressively cutting off the world of free enterprise. It rises even more in those years of lifetime commitments: marriage, children, mortgage, and a more expensive lifestyle that you somehow get used to and grow to expect.

I was hard on myself, my internal voice dismissive of corporate success. 'A corporate career is soft and relatively free of risk,' it would say. 'There are resources at every turn to support you and get the best out of you. It's all too easy, and you take for granted that chunk of money that lands in your bank account like clockwork every month.'

But I knew that I would find it hard to forgive myself if I failed to act on my dreams, to at least have tried. In my nightmares, I heard myself rationalising in my 50s and 60s: 'I always wanted to, but the time was never right. I couldn't afford to take the risk.'

I credit my upbringing in Dundalk in the 1960s and 70s for sowing the entrepreneurial seeds in me. As a hub of the Great Northern Railway until the late 1950s, Dundalk was an established industrial town, at various times leading in coach- and container building, tobacco, brewing, footwear, and later electronics.

It was home too to leading entrepreneurs in those years and since, including Neily McCann of Fyffes in fruit, Larry Goodman and his ABP Food Group in meat, Martin Naughton of Glen Dimplex in electrical appliances, Jim Aiken in concert promotions, and Fintan Gunne, who brought his local estate agency to national prominence.

They were risk-takers who made things happen, and they reaped the rewards. I wanted to be one of them when I grew up.

Dundalk is known locally as 'The Town', a name which implies a special place at the top of all towns. I always assumed this to be a nod to the success of Dundalk FC, the so-called Lilywhites, who we fervently supported in the late 1970s and early '80s during the successful management reign of Jim McLaughlin.

My father, Alf Dwyer, first set foot in Dundalk in 1960, stepping onto the platform of Clarke Railway Station. He was a young taxman on secondment to assist with the new Pay As You Earn or PAYE system. My mother, born Eleanor ('Elma') Kelly, just 21 years old, soon joined him. They were warmly welcomed and immediately took Dundalk and its people to their hearts. My father's experiences on the committee of the Cork Film Festival and as an amateur actor and compère would stand him in good stead. He joined the local Genesian Players, a talented drama group, and the founding committee of Dundalk's international drama festival, taking his turn as president in 1970. From those first days in Dundalk, he would never stray too far from the beating heart of the community, the cultural and commercial life of The Town.

My mother gave birth to three boys in as many years: Harry, John and me, and later to Valerie and Geraldine. Our parents nurtured the solid values of honesty, kindness, education and hard work – but also enterprise. We were brought up to admire the entrepreneurs in our community, and to respect the risks they took and the opportunities they created for themselves and others.

Dad led by example, initially promoting music and comedy acts such as Frank Patterson and Niall Tóibín in his own time. Harry, John and I sold the concert programmes as people arrived; sweets and drinks at the interval; and vinyl records and cassette tapes at the end, more than happy to take a commission.

As kids, we took every opportunity presented for extra pocket money, from strawberry picking in the summer to gardening and babysitting jobs to collecting refunds from bottles. My pal Chris McCann and I tried our hands at a little shop for the peak weeks at the tennis club, our second home for summer months, selling Mars bars and cans of Coke. Between discussions of new business ideas – most memorably, Chris's proposed twist-top Coke can – and our efforts to attract the girls for a game of Spin the Bottle, we ate and drank as much as we sold.

On a trip to the local Cash & Carry, we looked at the prices on the outer boxes, did our sums and were very happy. But when we got to the checkout, Vat was added, wiping away our profit margin and our smiles. Our pleas for clemency amused the check-out staff. It was an early lesson in the ubiquity of taxes.

In 1981, at the age of 49, my father left the Revenue Commissioners, going out on his own as a tax consultant, advising corporate clients on the more complex staff taxation issues like benefit-in-kind. He described his early struggles as "the pains of enterprise", a rite of passage, which he overcame, and he would go on to build a successful small practice.

At the CBS, our classroom doubled as the school library. It was there that I found a book by Padraig Pearse on educational reform called *The Murder Machine,* in which he rallied passionately against the system of education. He wrote: "Education should foster; this education is meant to repress. Education should inspire; this education is meant to tame."

Well, that wasn't going to happen on my watch. I sought expression over suppression, favouring debating teams and drama, discourse (and argument) with family and friends, reading, sport, music, and romance. I thrived in the English- and Irish debating teams as my mind opened to bigger ideas and how to present them. With just a year left until the Leaving Cert exams, I decided to indulge my growing curiosity for Economics. Business subjects were not available to me on the CBS curriculum, so I bought the textbook and went about teaching myself. My C grade in Economics was average enough, but I had found a passion, enthralled by the economic challenges facing Ireland, which was quickly moving from the traditional agricultural economy to one based on manufacturing and technology.

As my Leaving Cert approached in 1981, I learned of a new course in a new college, Languages and International Marketing, at the National Institute of Higher Education (NIHE), now Dublin City University (DCU). This spoke straight to my soul. Off I went to meet 25 other individually-minded students, to walk this untrodden path together. I loved languages but wasn't quite sure what 'international marketing' was. It sounded about right for the times and quite entrepreneurial. That was good enough for me. Still only 16, I was immature in many ways for the third-level world I was entering, but I liked the freedom college gave me, particularly in the pursuit of the extracurricular. It was a time for growing up, learning, leisure, discourse and debating, friendships, relationships, discovery, travel and summer jobs. The more intimate NIHE, in only its second year, suited me.

We studied for a year abroad, quite the novelty in 1983; some went to France, but for me, it was Dortmund University in West Germany, as it was then, the Berlin Wall still standing, with communism on its knees on the other side. Brands and branding

16

became my chosen academic focus and the subject of my thesis. A new passion was awoken in the fusion of creative intent with words, symbols, and colours. With the right execution, mere brand names and logos could be imbued with layers of meaning and emotion, giving them the power to win the loyalty of customers, thus creating lasting financial value for the companies who owned them.

I was learning about a fast-changing retail scene too, where the big supermarket chains and 'discounters' were getting bigger and where own-label strategies could pose an existential threat to weaker brands. Only strong brand leaders that were both innovative and well-invested in their marketing seemed to have protection and real control of their audience.

Then we graduated, and for all my marketing, branding, and languages, I accepted a job trading meat for a company based in Belfast. It didn't last long, but long enough to witness both sides of life in the troubled Northern Ireland of the time. There was warmth, wit and friendliness for the most part, but dangerous sectarianism bubbling not far from the surface too. I was learning a lot in this world of trading but was never really at home in the meat industry. I had enough other troubles to contend with in Belfast, from bomb scares on the train to a close shave with sectarianism on a night out. The final straw was an arson attack on the home I was staying in on the grounds of the meat plant. That night, I reached out to one of my good college friends from Belfast, Peter Lynch, stayed with his parents and listened to his Dad's sage advice.

The next day, I handed in my notice.

Next up was W & R Jacob plc on the Belgard Road in Tallaght, where there were ample branding and export opportunities to get my sweet tooth into. Jacob's was founded by Huguenots who partnered with Quakers and was run by Protestants who benevolently managed the mainly Catholic workforce in its great factory. Then the business hit the rocks in the early 1970s, over-stretched by the move to a modern facility in Tallaght, west Dublin. And now the O'Donnells and McConnells shared the executive rooms with the

Bewleys and the Hendersons, and the Poffs and Pims were happy to take a back seat.

It was the marketing director, Denis Henderson, who offered me a role and taught his new pupil all he knew about brand manuals and advertising agencies and product costings and navigating committees.

The 1980s and early 1990s were a colourful time in the world of media, and the annual Jacob's Television and Radio Awards was a shindig worthy of the series Mad Men. An invitation-only black-tie event, it alternated between the then high-end Burlington and Jury's hotels in Dublin and was broadcast live on RTE Television to a huge national audience.

It fell to Jacob's marketing department to organise the event, and I soon found myself in the middle of it all. The separate panels for the television and radio awards were made up of the respective press critics of the day, and I looked forward to the banter and deliberation between the likes of Eamon Dunphy, Colm Tóibín, Gene Kerrigan and Declan Lynch. Denis ensured that we all understood our roles: *it was not our position to offer an opinion.* There was only one exception in my time when Declan Lynch, frustrated at the other critics' ignorance of Irish racing, turned to me for a view on Ted Walsh's punditry on RTE. That was an easy one for me. Ted was new to TV but brought a cheeky turn of equine phrase, together with a passion and knowledge of racing that combined to lift the experience for armchair viewers. I readily gave Ted the thumbs-up. It was a fan's perspective but helped get Ted over the line with a few lengths to spare.

Progressively, as I recorded a few small wins at Jacob's, they gave me more rein for my ideas. About enough to get me in trouble!

When the Republic of Ireland football team, managed by Jack Charlton, qualified for the World Cup for the first time in 1990, Ireland went into a kind of mania. Like so many brands, we decided to launch a TV-supported on-pack promotion at Jacob's. But unlike most brands, I wasn't having any of the obvious ideas like scarves and flags. I wanted something more original and of much more impact.

I was struggling to find a solution when I took a random call from Noel King, whose name I knew as a soccer player and who was just starting down the road of a successful career in management. We met in Bewley's Café on Grafton Street in Dublin for a cup of tea and a bun. Noel unveiled his idea for an inflatable shamrock and why he felt it would be popular. Inflatable bananas were all the rage, so why not own the trend with our national emblem?

I loved it. It was innovative and exciting, and already I had visions of terraces of Jacob's inflatable shamrocks rallying the Irish team and supporters. Noel very cleverly left me and Jacob's to figure the rest out. We shook on a one-off fee for the idea, which would become known as 'Shake a Shamrock'.

Denis and I met with the Football Association of Ireland (FAI) and completed a deal, making Jacob's an official FAI partner, with access to Jack Charlton for a TV ad. Buoyed up, I commissioned a sourcing company to have the shamrock manufactured in Asia to an agreed timeline.

At the Belgard Road plant, manufacturing of the promotional stock was ramping up, and several million packs of Kimberley, Mikado and Coconut Creams were ready to go with their shamrock packaging. What our shamrock sourcer produced as a prototype, however, was more like an inflatable crucifix – a sign, I thought, of what might be lying in store for me.

"They don't have shamrocks in China," he apologised.

I was up the proverbial creek without a paddle and needed to catch a break soon. There was no internet to research suppliers, so I really was in a bind. As I looked around me, I knew this one was on me and me alone. I also realised that I was the only one in the whole organisation taking this kind of risk and that, for better or worse, this was in my nature. I felt fear rather than regret as I strove for a solution.

Just as I saw a lid being prematurely placed on my career in biscuits, I got a call from Donie Butler, the commercial manager at the FAI, to say that he had received a flyer with inflatable products. I quickly ascertained it was from a small manufacturer in the suburbs of Manchester, which was producing inflatable items for British sporting events. I was on a flight the next morning to check it out.

I was met by a man of Pakistani origin who warmly welcomed me and inspired confidence straight away. His team had a very acceptable prototype ready for inspection on the day. For their trouble, they got an order for 10,000 inflatable shamrocks at a fair price, paid upfront. I was in no position to haggle. He proved to be a reliable supplier, and I was back in favour.

To launch the inflatable shamrock, a group of college friends volunteered to distribute the shamrocks with me at the next Ireland home game, a friendly against Wales. They were happy to work for a free match ticket, dinner and a few pints.

The delighted fans immediately got the idea and had the shamrocks inflated by the time they took their positions on the terraces. What an impact! There was an unforgettable blanket of green on the south terrace of the old Lansdowne Road.

We were off and running. As soon as Jack Charlton took to the screens of Ireland in a cheap but highly impactful TV ad, we were home and dry:

"Shake a Shamrock in Italy. We always knew you were out there, now, thanks to Jacob's, we'll know where," declared Big Jack in his distinctive Yorkshire accent and the Shake a Shamrock stock moved through the trade like wildfire.

As a nice touch to round off a good promotion, Jack agreed to do a Q&A and to sign autographs in a packed Jacob's staff canteen. I loved the fact that such a big initiative could also have a staff dimension.

As I introduced Big Jack, my stock among the workers grew, even among the hardened union activists who weren't accustomed to recognising any value coming from upstairs. Jack was generous to a fault with his time and sincere participation. He clearly loved the joy and lift he brought to everyone in the factory.

A young journalist, Matt Cooper, wrote a piece for the *Sunday Tribune* with the headline 'Shamrocks Inflate Jacob's Sales'. How right he was: Shake a Shamrock put a veritable fire under Jacob's sales that summer.

I had taken a bigger risk than I appreciated, had a look over the edge, but found a solution and got rewarded with a unique and successful promotion. It was risky, but I liked that, and it stirred the spirit of enterprise in me.

An emerging name on Irish national radio, Joe Duffy, also came to Jacob's canteen for his first *Worker's Playtime* segment for the Gay Byrne Show on RTE Radio 1. It was a visit that would ignite the relaunch of Chocolate Kimberley. More about that later.

Then the French company BSN (now Danone) pounced, paying 50 million punts for Jacob's. That put *a schpring* in the board's *schprong* – to bend an old Jacob's tagline – but it put a target on the door of the Dublin factory too.

Une invitation soon came my way: three years in Paris. *Magnifique,* I thought.

We were a small marketing team in Jacob's, led by Denis. I was the marketing manager while Karen Scanlan and Gabriel Cooney filled the brand management positions. We worked hard and played hard. I remember coming down the stairs to greet Karen ahead of her first interview for a marketing assistant role. She cut a very professional and friendly figure and, to my eye, a most appealing one. There was a spark that day, a mutual one, she confided much later. I went through the interview process diligently, of course, with Denis chaperoning. Karen's studies had been similar to mine, business and languages, in her case, at University College Dublin (UCD) and the Smurfit Graduate Business School, where she had excelled. Like many marketing students, she was enthusiastic in her choice of career, creative, a trend watcher and of an entrepreneurial spirit.

When it was time to leave for France, Jacob's workers invited me to their Social Club to say goodbye. That meant a lot to me. Karen came with me. That meant a lot too. There was just enough time for the romantic spark to ignite before I left for Paris.

In one of our final projects together in Jacob's, Karen and I worked on the launch of Danone's LU biscuit brand in Ireland. McConnell's advertising agency developed a radio ad focusing on the relationship between Monsieur Lefèvre and Mademoiselle Utile, the 'L' and the 'U' of the LU brand name. Something was in the air when we approved a radio script declaring in a strong French accent: "zey met, zey married, zey made … biscuits." *A labour of love*, one might say.

Off I went to Paris, making my way to my hotel near Les Invalides, with the Eiffel Tower, Pont Alexander III, the Grand Palais, the Musée d'Orsay all nearby. It's a long way from The Town, I thought. I had an intense week of one-on-one French language instruction.

At just 25, I had my team, France's best from the *grandes écoles*, and budgets that ran to multiples of what I was used to in Ireland. If I was apprehensive, I was buzzing too: it was a challenge made for me.

My French colleagues appreciated my linguistic efforts while enjoying my pronunciation gaffes. At a company conference, 'cutting the costs' or *baisser les coûts* came out as *baiser les culs*, a much ruder statement altogether. They laughed out loud, stamped their feet and clapped my back. I was well in.

My budding relationship with Karen needed wings, and she soon joined Danone in the International New Product Development department. And what good fortune we had to have Paris as our playground for three fun-filled years with some close friends around us. The city was a joy, with its cafés, restaurants, cinemas, grand boulevards and chic culture.

On October 14th, 1994, Karen and I got married in Porterstown Church in Dublin with friends in attendance from Dublin, Paris and The Town.

Next up was London with Danone, where our first daughter Kerry was born in 1996. We lived in Richmond, with the Thames flowing through it, its great park nearby and a Parisian feel to crown it. I had agreed to a spell working in Key Accounts, negotiating with the hardened buyers of Tesco and Sainsbury's. I loved being at that coalface and living on my wits. Sales sharpened me up a bit and rekindled the entrepreneurial flame in me.

But before I would go it alone, Green Isle Foods came knocking in the spring of 1996. Green Isle was an emerging star of Irish food, famed then for its Goodfella's brand in frozen pizzas and its Donegal Catch brand in frozen fish. Initially, I worked from London and ran the gauntlet to and from the head office in Naas and the UK sales office in Manchester: w*elcome to Green Isle. A challenging culture*, I had been told. Indeed, I struggled under a much more aggressive senior management style than I had ever encountered. My induction period seemed to be more about challenging me rather than encouraging me; sowing doubt rather than offering support. I was unsettled and particularly vulnerable during this so-called *probation period* (a particularly one-way arrangement, I thought then and since). It wasn't at all helped by a trigger-happy *performance letter*, essentially declaring: 'Michael needs to do better, or else!'

Bruised and worried for my career and family, I made myself a promise: 'I'll do whatever it takes to keep my job, for now, and stay as long as it suits me and as long as l am learning, but with my next move, I'm taking control of my own destiny and setting up my own business.'

Karen and I decided that a move back to Ireland would be best; indeed a move to Naas, Co Kildare, where Green Isle was (and is) based. It was a move that suited us as a young family. I was no longer rushing in and out on brief visits to the head office. There was time for the casual encounters in the corridor and canteen, those little building blocks of relationships and confidence. Almost overnight, it seemed, I gained control. I would join the Green Isle board as group marketing director not long after and would go on to do that job for another three years with the full weight of support of an excellent and evolving team around me. This team would put its own positive mark on the company's culture before long.

The work was engaging and stimulating too. In 1999, I led a project to develop and test a new pizza range and brand for European markets. It would be the major move by Green Isle into France and perhaps later into other continental European markets. Northern Foods, by now Green Isle's parent, had given clearance for the feasibility study. I connected with my old Danone network, striking a deal to license France's leading pasta and pasta sauces brand, Panzani, as a parent brand. This elevated us into a different league of credibility at both trade and consumer levels. Our brand *Ristozzia by Panzani* could scarcely have got a more positive reaction in consumer research and market tests. All the indicators were positive, but Northern Foods was spooked by the investment and instructed us to take a pull at the last minute. "A risk-management decision," they said, but they had let this one go on way too long. Embarrassed and gutted for my team and our partners, this time, I had enough.

"No," they said.

"No more," I said, "it's time."

The Journals

1

Out of the Deep Pan, into the Fire

November 1999

I spent the 25th in meetings with Sainsbury's in London, doing the customary sparring with the retail buyers of frozen foods. Relaxing on the Aer Lingus return flight to Dublin, I read the closing chapters of Seth Godin's new book, *Permission Marketing*, whose simple thesis I have enthusiastically embraced since I first picked it up.

With internet adoption increasing, there has been a gold rush towards online advertising, but the parameters of this new medium are still evolving. Where consumers traditionally interacted with advertising through print, broadcast and billboards, brands can now insert themselves into people's digital lives in so many dynamic ways, but some of the early executions are shocking.

Godin warns against any advertising that is uninvited and that interrupts us while we surf the internet or check our email. Worst of all are the instances when we click by mistake on the corner of a graphic – if at all – prompting an utterly unwelcome ad to pop up, taking over the screen and hijacking our attention. These 'pop-ups' and banner ads are intrusive and may actually be doing more harm than good for the brand being advertised, says Godin.

The brands that do these things are now nuisances, who either don't understand or don't care that this "interruption marketing", as Godin calls it, is bad for them too. The way of the future, as laid out by Godin, is a mutual "permission-based" and very transparent contract between consumer and brand. It goes like this: 'I know I am signing up to your service. I am not being hoodwinked. I know what the service offers and how frequently I can expect to be communicated with. In return for that, I give you certain data. You promise to safeguard my data and not to sell or rent it, ever. I can withdraw easily at any time.' I think Godin has nailed it and this new approach will stand the test of time.

As this permission marketing concept continued to distil in my head during the flight home, an idea suddenly came to me. I reached for my copy of the *Irish Independent* newspaper, the only piece of paper handy at the time, grabbed a pen and scribbled out my thoughts: *"Develop a hub on the internet to bring brands and consumers together in a way that works for both, using offers as the key attraction. Create a kind of club of brands and consumers that has benefits for both: consumer access for the brands and special offers for the consumers in return. Brands can now reach out meaningfully to consumers and build trust."*

I've called the concept *I'llTryThat.com.*

———◆———

Customer acquisition is the art of persuading new consumers and households to come on board to try a new product or service. It has always been and is likely to remain the key challenge for marketing teams around the globe. There's a growing trend towards the use of introductory or *trial* offers to win over new consumers. I'llTryThat.com will play to this trend, using the internet to bring brands and consumers together in a personalised, targeted and permission-based way, with special offers at the core of everything. We'll be the gatekeepers, building this club of members (the consumers) and brands, safeguarding the consumers' or *members'* data and ensuring the relevance of everything put in front of them.

Companies or brands will pay us for this access, and they have marketing budgets to do it. I can think of many examples straightaway: online retailers or travel agents need new clients; hotels need to fill bedrooms, often last minute (a website of that very name, LastMinute.com is making waves in Britain); sellers of fast-moving consumer goods (FMCGs) need consumers to trial their products; restaurants and spas need to fill off-peak hours.

We'll happily bring all of their special offers to our members. In the food industry, we organise in-store tastings, but this is becoming more expensive and difficult to control as supermarkets increasingly flex their muscles. But with *I'll TryThat.com*, we can bring coupons to our members to perform the same task.

And why not do online research? If we recruit members, there must be a way to survey them on behalf of brands. The possibilities seem endless.

For now, all I have are scribbles on a newspaper inspired by a book. Not a computer in the equation! Could this really be it? I certainly hope so and struggle to remember any good idea that ever came to me from a spreadsheet.

———————•———————

I have been working hard on two other very different ideas, but this is the best. The first idea is to create an Aqua Therapy Health Spa and Resort, similar to Nirvana Spa just west of London, with a bit of inspiration from Champneys in England too. Ireland is becoming more prosperous and is underserved in this aqua therapy and health spa area.

I have visited Nirvana and researched equivalents all around the world, thanks to the internet. I've even commissioned an architect's concept drawing and have a site in mind for the resort. But I'm not convinced. I wonder what in particular I bring to the project by way of relevant experience and skills, and there's the small matter of the very considerable amount of capital required to boot.

The second idea I have been exploring is a strategy development tool, which I've called MAPPER, an acronym for Mission, Analysis, Projections, Pivotal Question, Ensuing Strategy and Resources. It's good, but it's an attempt to improve on another such strategy development tool and training course in the market. It makes me feel like a consultant, which isn't enthusing me. It's a 'me-too' as opposed to something completely original, which also bothers me.

Buzzed up formulating these new ideas, I scribbled down my criteria in an effort to think more clearly:

1.   Play to my strengths and experience

2.   A big market opportunity

3.   International potential

4. High entry barriers

5. Control and ownership of the consumer (so no franchises or licences)

My gut says I may be there now with I'llTryThat.com. The chance to be part of the fast-emerging wave of change that is the internet is exciting. It was only a few months ago that my father pointed to the dot-com headline while lying in intensive care. Thankfully, he pulled through, but his words of encouragement have borne extra weight in the circumstances.

My parents embraced change throughout their lives with so many new things that we now take for granted: from the electrification of homes to early communications in the form of radio and home phones. Our first phone number was particularly easy to remember, with only four digits: 5244. Then came television, black and white in the 1960s (with knobs to pull or twist to change the channels), and colour in the '70s. Then space exploration, starting with the moon landing, was soon followed by satellite technology. The landscape of TV and communications changed forevermore.

Little did I know that, in the mid-1960s, the US military started working on networking its computers on different sites. They called it Advanced Research Projects Agency Network or Arpanet, and it was the earliest iteration of the internet, a road that would lead all the way to this latest wave of dot-com technology.

Now, every day, new applications are being invented to reshape our future. And here I am, with my idea for one such application and a good one, I think. It feels a bit cheeky sometimes, but then I ask myself: 'why not me? Why the hell not? I've as good a chance as anyone else.'

I'llTryThat is of its time, and I think it can last the test of time. It looks like I am about to commit my future to this new digital world. That short flight home from London could change everything.

———◆———

My good friend and former Jacob's and Green Isle colleague, Gabriel Cooney, gave me a hack to get me going on my entrepreneurial journey. As Gabriel struggled to commit to his idea of a new wine venture called Grapevine, he landed upon a trick: tell everyone you meet that you're setting up the business, and you'll soon be embarrassed into action. "Get it out there on the grapevine," he laughed. Funny the games we play to get ourselves moving. I loved it and called it 'the Grapevine Hack'.

A few weeks after my I'llTryThat epiphany, we travelled with some friends to New York, where I ran my first-ever marathon. Thinking of the Grapevine Hack, I lost no time telling friends I had decided to leave corporate life to set up a business.

"So, have you handed in your notice?"

"No".

"Are you clear on what your new venture is?"

"No."

I laughed, but I felt better.

In New York, I boarded the marathon race bus at the Irish-owned Fitzpatrick's Hotel on Lexington Avenue in Manhattan, bound for Staten Island, seriously doubting my sanity and preparation.

Race underway, we crossed the massive Verrazano-Narrows Bridge into Brooklyn, crossed Queensboro Bridge into Manhattan, up the wide expanses of First Avenue to the Bronx, up Fifth Avenue, and into Central Park on the 23rd mile, not quite home, running on empty, eventually crossing the finish, arms aloft, a medal to savour, a foil body wrap for warmth and a tad emotional.

It was exhausting but exhilarating, and I know it won't be my last. The next day I bought the New York Times. My name might never appear on its pages again, albeit along with 31,785 other finishers.

At the top, it read: *Joseph Chebet - two hours and nine minutes.*

And a long way down the list: *Michael Dwyer - four hours and two minutes.*

At a post-race drinks reception in Fitzpatrick's for the Irish group, Karen met Gary Keating. Gary and his sister Linda took part in the marathon to raise money for the cancer awareness foundation they had recently set up as a dedication to their late mother. Marie Keating passed away in February 1998 from breast cancer, aged just 51. The Keating family aims to get the message out that an early diagnosis would probably have saved their mum's life and could save many other lives in the future.

Karen played matchmaker, setting up a blind date between Gary and my sister Valerie. She figures they have much in common, starting with a sense of humour. Valerie will need it when she finds out.

New ventures seem to be in the air.

———◆———

Excited as I am most of the time, I occasionally have to pinch myself at where I'm headed. For the most part, I feel excited and positive at the new perspective, new challenges, new possibilities, and, at last, taking control of my destiny. Occasionally, I get very apprehensive thinking of the many challenges entailed in the venture.

Karen shares the dream and is up for the journey it entails, but her father, Gerry, a career banker, is a different kettle of fish. I am 35 years old and have been married to Karen for five years. We have two kids, Kerry and Nicky, and a chunky mortgage. Gerry forthrightly challenged my decision: "are you gambling with your family's security?"

I wouldn't concede it was a gamble but a carefully calculated risk of the type that can be essential to progression occasionally. I watched my Dad take such a risk at the age of 49, leaving the comforts of the civil service to launch his own business. Gerry's career was corporate all the way, but he did rise to the very top of Ireland's financial services world and from a humble entry-level too. In his leisure time, he was a formidable gambler, playing poker or backing his judgement of the form at the racecourse. I had no difficulty empathising with Gerry's perspective but defended myself and my plan robustly. It's not as if I haven't questioned myself and had my own doubts.

As for Karen, she stood her ground with her father, her own entrepreneurial colours nailed firmly to the mast: "It has been Michael's wish to go out on his own in business for as long as I've known him. It's never been a secret. It's what we want. And being married to a frustrated middle-aged Michael is a much more daunting prospect than anything free enterprise can throw at us."

Karen's conviction was no surprise but a relief nonetheless. We are in this boat together. That had probably been ordained since we met. Debate over.

My own Dad is positive (he ought to be), my mother more reticent, focused on the "good job and package" that I'm leaving behind. For the most part, friends and family are positive and are sharing in the excitement with us.

———•———

December 1999

Shortly after my return from New York and just weeks after my first scribbles on the flight from London, I gave my formal notice to Green Isle, fulfilling my earlier promise to myself by irrevocably committing to my new venture. Looking back on my 15 years in the international food industry, I have no regrets:

The six years with Jacob's were an excellent practical grounding in basic marketing disciplines and allowed me to lead key product development and promotional initiatives and to begin to understand and manage risk. And, of course, I met Karen.

Three years in France with Danone broadened my professional and personal horizons when that was needed and professionalised my marketing experience. A stint of about a year with Danone UK, negotiating with supermarket buyers, sharpened my wits and awoke the entrepreneur in me again.

If Green Isle was initially challenging, it was a particularly good school, with top-class talent at all levels. The lessons were rich and broad-based: there was the very rigorous process applied to define the market opportunity at the outset of any project, helping the business to allocate scarce capital; there was the store placed in marrying uniqueness in process development with product innovation as a key source of sustainable competitive advantage; there was the application of category management processes in conjunction with the major grocery multiples in the UK and Ireland, requiring us to be able advisers on our entire category, not just our narrow range of products.

It all added up to a better appreciation for the important numbers in a business, giving me greater insight into the dynamics of profit, particularly the application of margin flow-through, a simple but important concept for any business journey.

It took long enough to build this bank of experience, but it's something valuable to fall back on now.

———————◆———————

It was the American writer Ralph Waldo Emerson who said that "the mind, once stretched by a new idea, never returns to its original dimensions." I feel I am its epitome. I am learning that creating your own business quickly becomes an obsession. I have been thinking of little else, night and day, working on my concept and plan in every spare hour. I am facing challenges I have never faced before, realising now that corporate life is actually quite sheltered.

But this new game is as exhilarating as it is daunting. I feel alive and just get on with what's in front of me, trusting in my experience and instincts to put the team together, raise the money and face each challenge as it arises.

I'm on the internet constantly looking at related business models. There's a Coupons.com business and a big loyalty-points-combined-with-offers business called MyPoints.com, both in the US. The latter seems very interesting and has a lot in common with my initial concept, but it hasn't reached out of America yet. There are also various travel plays, notably LastMinute.com in the UK, established by the already celebrated entrepreneurial duo: Brent Hoberman and Martha Lane Fox.

I'm advancing my concept all the time, and right now am inclined toward the hybrid offers and points model. Karen has come up with the name HelloPoints.com, which I rather like: *Say hello to new products and services with these great offers and earn points.*

The business model will be challenging on several fronts: to develop and run the tech platform; register consumers in the required numbers through our marketing; recruit enough brands through our sales; to raise enough investment. One or two of these might be challenging enough on their own. The picture is becoming clearer, if not easier, on each front, however. It won't be cheap.

———————◆———————

February 2000

We'll need the right help on the tech front, which is beyond my experience and well beyond my capability but I'm already working on specific solutions. Within a nod of my office in Green Isle sits the very talented but largely unacclaimed John McDonald. As a management accountant, 'Johnny Mc' sources and manipulates data like few others can, creating costing systems and reports, well beyond his pay grade.

He has also been the number one fixer of any new device for anyone lacking the patience to wait for the IT team. To my mind, he has special talents but they are going unrecognised in Green Isle. When I told him of my plans, his face lit up.

Since then, a nod is all it takes, and he's into my office. With the door closed, we're off, excitedly perusing the latest twists and turns in the business plan. The technology is all new to Johnny Mc too, so we both know that we need external help to get us going.

One of the very first doors I knocked on in December was that of an old business associate, Leo Kearns of Octagon Technologies, a growing web technology company in Dublin. Leo and I discussed Octagon committing its resources to assist us in getting started with our technology and website in return for an equity stake in the new venture. Leo himself agreed to become a non-executive director, which from someone so respected, is an important vote of confidence.

He took it to his board in January. I could hardly sleep the night before. When Leo eventually contacted me with the green light, it was my first major sigh of relief on this journey. Some of Leo's fellow directors in Octagon – seasoned businesspeople including Tom McCormick, David Moffett and Paul Moore – have also agreed to make additional cash investments in the business. It is very encouraging and helpful in building to my target.

Since the beginning of the year, I've been meeting Leo for Saturday morning workshops in Octagon's offices in Clonskeagh in south Dublin. We debate the business model and discuss funding and Leo updates me on the emerging development project.

He has recommended that the software development work, based on fairly complex database networks, be developed by an emerging Irish company, aptly named New World Commerce (NWC). NWC specialises in marketing and customer relationship management models. Octagon will do all the design work and oversee the NWC relationship until Johnny Mc gets up to speed.

NWC is a very exciting Dublin company with young Irish developers who are bringing lots of experience and great technical skills to the brief. The team, led by Donal Daly, seem pleased to have an Irish project to work on, one their friends and families can watch as it comes to fruition.

NWC has agreed to adapt its core product for us and to license it in what is called an Application Service Provider or ASP arrangement. It is a good and expedient solution, albeit very expensive. We're in no position to develop or manage our own technology at this early stage so it fits well. This part of the project is likely to cost over €600,000 for development and first-year operation. It will be our biggest initial cost. I need to make sure I can pay for it.

———————◆———————

We'll have to advertise to attract consumers to our site, where we'll ask them, very transparently, for their permission to send certain types of emails at an agreed frequency (some weekly, others fortnightly). In return, they'll get offers from the brands they like or might like, as well as chances to enter competitions and take part in online research for rewards and prizes.

The data will be a huge asset for the access and insights it gives us. We're acutely aware that this data is a privilege of sorts and comes with the responsibility to keep it safe and to never, ever rent or sell it. That will be our commitment. So, from the early seeds of Seth Godin's Permission Marketing, we are gradually elaborating our own digital marketing philosophy.

———————◆———————

I've created a marketing committee to get some broader external business and marketing expertise contributing to our cause. Its role is to oversee branding, design, the advertising and promotional plan, PR and early content. We won't be doing anything too standard here. We need bang for our buck in everything we do; we must reach people and excite them.

First on my list was James O'Connor, who in his 20 years in business has brought more energy and ingenuity to marketing promotions than anyone I know in Ireland. James owns and heads Creative Solutions, which I dealt with right back in my Jacob's days. He's what I'd call a "consumer activation" expert, which will be very helpful in acquiring our own audience.

James pointed me in the direction of Willie O'Reilly, the head of Ireland's largest independent radio station, Today FM. Willie is an experienced and well-regarded figure in media circles, so in agreeing to become chairman of the marketing committee, he's offering a noteworthy stamp of approval. He's prepared to use his network for us in order to bring some brands on board too. His reward is by way of an allocation of share options in the venture; cash is too tight, and Willie is happy to take the punt.

Last, but by no means least, is Gary Joyce, who we have appointed to the marketing committee and the board. As co-founder and managing partner of Genesis Marketing & Communications, Gary is renowned in marketing circles for her pre-eminence in the development and positioning of consumer brands. She was one of the key outside figures involved in the creation of the Goodfella's pizza brand, which was transformative for Green Isle.

We know there is a market need: marketing directors and their teams, like me, are frustrated with current internet advertising practices but nonetheless need to be part of this new battleground for consumers. Their brands need to be seen while being relevant and engaging. And they have the budgets! The big question will be how we access these brands. I'm hoping that the advertising and media-buying agencies we typically use as marketers will bring us to them.

Daunted as I am at times, this one is home turf for me. The business model definitely plays to my strengths and experience in that it is a business-to-consumer (B2C) solution involving a business-to-business (B2B) sale to marketing departments, who I know and understand.

———◆———

An old college pal introduced me to a corporate lawyer by the name of Thérèse Rochford, who is working in a mid-sized legal company in Dublin called Whitney Moore. Thérèse is guiding me through the volumes of legal papers, which would otherwise be enough to put any would-be entrepreneur off. I've struggled so far to fill our senior finance role but could do with someone to take on the mounting legal work from the Articles of Association to employment contracts, shareholder agreements, share option agreements, confidentiality agreements, intellectual property applications and more.

A lot of it is quite straightforward, but it's time-consuming, and I find it energy-sapping. But I know this groundwork will serve us well in the future in raising money and managing the company and team, in particular. Anyway, I'm not suddenly going to abandon a commitment to good structure and rigour, acquired (gradually, it has to be said) over 15 years in the corporate world.

———————●———————

There is a huge buzz, bordering on a frenzy, around dot-com. Companies are sprouting up overnight with massive valuations. Some are just rebranding, adding the dot-com prefix, which is odd, but their stock prices respond. Everyone wants a piece of it. It's fever-like. Stock markets have been soaring, and there's a sense of a world changing radically, of fortunes to be made as huge opportunities present themselves.

Headlines abound, and we are all reading them. There's a new language around 'land grabs', 'roll-outs' and 'scaling' as entrepreneurs and their backers are battling to be first in their sectors throughout the world. New stock market flotations – initial public offerings (IPOs) – are launching with each passing week, turning out more young paper multi-millionaires. Some of it seems crazy, but many investors and entrepreneurs can only see opportunity.

It's nearly all coming from the US; the Irish are mostly sceptical onlookers, and there's really only a limited amount going on here. Ireland is late to this game in international terms, with very few new internet offerings beyond the internet service providers (ISPs) and news websites, with Ireland.com, the *Irish Times*-owned site, being the most talked about. But it's beginning to change, so I feel that I better get a move on.

I had a meeting with Damian Ryan, the founder and former chief executive of ICAN, the online digital advertising agency recently acquired by the telecoms magnate Denis O'Brien. I ran through the Powerpoint presentation of my business concept. He offered to buy it, joking (I think), but the positivity was much appreciated.

Irish household internet penetration levels are abysmal at about 15%, and most of it is poor quality dial-up. Although many people are using email, very few surf the internet, which requires great patience at the download speeds. The slow pace of adoption won't deter me. I see the internet transforming our lives – and certainly, the areas of communications and marketing, which are my main concerns right now.

———————◆———————

If I wanted a barrier to entry, I've found it: this idea needs capital. In a small number of weeks, the concept has moved from scribbles on the back of the Indo to a PowerPoint, and now there's an ever-growing spreadsheet to go with it. I've completed market projections, nationally in Ireland and internationally too, coming at it from several different angles. I have cut the revenue projections based on site activity and also based on the projected number of brand campaigns. I've projected membership based on population, internet penetration and the exposure our marketing campaigns will achieve. Forecasting costs is relatively easy after that.

Although the idea has national and international potential, I'm planning to fundraise in two stages. We need €1.8 million in stage one to fund tech costs, brand development and a well-invested marketing plan in Ireland and team costs through to the autumn. That's enough to be asking for right now for a completely unproven proposition.

If we can accomplish our initial objectives, we'll be back quickly to the markets during the summer for a much bigger funding round in preparation for an international roll-out, starting with Britain and possibly France in parallel, which I am already working on.

The clock is ticking, and I'm trying to have the cash in place by the time I drive out of Green Isle for the last time at the end of March. I am already going around Dublin armed with my laptop trying to find a route to the money. I'm learning that there's no rulebook for this sort of stuff and that being so innovative and early-stage, puts many people off.

I know already that banks won't help. Despite appearances, they don't see it as their role to provide early-stage funding. Venture capitalists (VCs) are of little relevance either, as they tend to invest in businesses which have found their feet and are in the development stage or even later in the cycle.

I spent most of January engaged with corporate finance advisors, but they're not biting, promising to "show it to one or two potential investors" and then in no hurry to get back to me. I've also met a couple of so-called 'angel investors', who are hard enough to identify and harder to get on board.

But there are punters out there looking for riskier plays, too, with higher potential returns. They are buying into the dream, the dot-com headlines, and whatever reputation and track record I am bringing to the table. This week I got a call from a family friend and businessman in Dundalk, which tells its own story:

"Michael, I hear you're doing something. Can I get in?"

"But you don't know what I'm doing", I replied.

"I'll back the jockey!" he insisted before committing a worthwhile investment there and then. The same man is a businessman but a punter too, and in some ways, that's how he views this. He's not alone. There are a good few more like him. It's looking like a 'family, friends and punters' funding round. That's what the market is offering up at the moment.

Karen and I always knew that we would have to lead the early funding by example, and we've emptied most of our reserves with a pledge to invest €240,000. I don't know where that figure came from, other than my enthusiasm. It is about showing serious commitment while leaving a small bit of breathing room. On top of that, I won't take any salary until we have launched, and then a modest one, all going well.

Both of our families look like they will take the lead from us. That includes my father-in-law Gerry who, after the initial grilling, is supportive now and agreed to participate in the fund-raising.

The investment of time and resources from Leo and Octagon – as well as the substantial cash investments from Octagon's directors –

form the second-biggest building block. I'm suddenly getting traction, and my financial target is in sight.

————◆————

I've been busy piecing the core team together. It will be some time before Johnny Mc can leave Green Isle, but I'll be ready for him when he does. There's a contract to respect which requires some waiting. In the meantime, he's helping in every way he can, particularly with Octagon and NWC.

My sister Valerie is our first full-time employee. I appreciate the act of faith, as the company is neither incorporated nor funded yet. She has more start-up experience than the rest of us put together, which makes her a huge asset right now. Most recently, she played a central role in sales and PR, as well as board and investor relations, with TCL, a new telecoms business. It was started, developed and sold to the US group WorldCom during her time working there.

Valerie has always been an immensely positive, can-do person who enlivens any crowd and makes everyone feel better about themselves. She's hardly in the door and has already set about putting systems in place from standardising documents (including dictating that 'the company font will be Verdana and only Verdana!'), and preparing templates for board packs, sales presentations and sales proposals.

She's working on a pipeline management process to be used by the sales team and an early customer relationship management (CRM) system on Excel. This is where we will centrally record all communications with clients and have the history to hand for all to see.

James O'Connor recommended Gareth Lambe, a young brand manager at Pernod Ricard's Irish subsidiary, Irish Distillers. It is best known for the Jameson Irish whiskey brand, which Gareth has been managing. It took me all of a couple of minutes to decide I wanted him on board. If I'm confident about someone, I prefer to share that and establish an early bond and trust. It works both ways.

Thankfully, Gareth didn't take a lot of persuading; he's up for a ride on the dot-com train. He is a young man with a lot of ambition and positivity. He's a big win for us, not only as a rigorous marketing professional but as a strong communicator with a very commercial brain.

On the day Gareth left Jameson, his new company car arrived – complete with all the trimmings and extras he had selected – only to be given to his successor. As he walked away from it and from the safety of Pernod Ricard, he must have wondered deep down about the wisdom of his decision. It's one ballsy move which I respect massively.

Our business model will produce lots of data, and Johnny Mc needs someone who can manipulate it and interpret it for us. My sister Geraldine has taken an active interest in the business as a supportive sibling and investor. She recommended what she called "an exceptional talent" in her fellow UCD graduate, David Foody.

I wasted no time in meeting him last week in the bar of the Burlington Hotel. Dave is tall and was a little awkward and unconvincing in his jacket and tie, the shirt opened at the top button, and the tie loosened. He projects nonchalance but is very bright, driven and confident in his abilities. Like Gareth, he's up for a dot-com adventure.

This one is Johnny Mc's call, but Dave has my vote. He has the analytical mind to untangle the data we are about to produce, but he has good business acumen too and an entrepreneurial streak. I don't think he conforms to the identikit profile sought by the big corporations, but we'll take a bit of non-conformity as a trade-off for raw ability and the right attitude. I shook his hand after the interview as if to welcome him on board.

We have decided to bring our creative design resources in-house and have taken on Dave Monaghan and the pony-tailed Stephen Lennon, known respectively and fondly as Dave M and Ste. Together they bring a healthy dose of Zen and coolness to the mix. We knew both of them from Octagon, where they worked together, and they're coming on board with Leo's blessing.

I have been struggling for a good while to fill the critical chief financial officer (CFO) role, and it has been weighing me down. I badly need another seasoned business person around me, someone to oversee accounts, assist in fundraising, manage costs, put the right administration systems in place, take over all the legal work, and, ideally, someone I can lean on operationally.

I recently shared my plans with a Cork accountant named Rory Duggan, a former Green Isle colleague who has since spent some time with Musgrave Group, one of Ireland's biggest wholesale and retail groups. Once Rory indicated he would be up for some start-up and dot-com action, we struck a deal, and his imminent arrival as chief operating officer (COO) has been a huge relief to me. He will be more than a financial controller, contributing across the business, freeing me up to develop the model, go out and get business with the sales team and work on the marketing plan.

Rory, in turn, has prompted us to bring in Alan Gilson, also ex-Green Isle. He initially committed to a year with us. We'll take it happily. It would be hard to meet someone as personable and positive as Alan. He will work with Gareth in managing the sales team; Gareth is looking after the larger corporate clients, particularly in FMCG, as well as his marketing brief. Every start-up needs good humour, and Alan has it in abundance. With his network, he is already winning new friends into our club of brands and supporters.

The initial team feels strong. In all cases, I have either worked with them already, or they have come recommended by people I trust. The back-end creatives and operations team are all experienced in their respective fields, and those in client-facing roles are all capable of representing us very well.

Most importantly, in all cases, there is an excellent 'fit' with our values and with the kind of culture I've envisaged. They are a capable and committed bunch but sociable too, and every one of them is passionate about the new frontiers in dot-com.

I finally got to my funding target of €1.8 million, thanks to a group of five private Irish investors introduced by Karen's oldest friend, Jenny Walsh. Fortunately, they were familiar with this type of start-up investment and quickly committed to the venture.

I feel very grateful to these and all investors who put their faith in me and in this fledgling business.

———◆———

April 2000

Two weeks ago, I finally left a 15-year career in the food business behind me. As I drove out the gates of Green Isle, I felt some sadness at leaving friends and such a professional community behind, but no regrets.

In the short intervening weeks, that certainty has been put to the test.

Shockwaves have been reverberating through every tech and dot-com company with what is already being dubbed 'Dot Bomb', the bursting of the dot-com bubble. The Nasdaq, the bellwether for tech and dot-com stocks, is in freefall. Other global stock market indices are following suit, though not as dramatically as the tech index. IPOs are being pulled, and companies are failing overnight for lack of funding.

Some are failing so quickly that you'd have to wonder whether they ever had real and sustainable business models. Investor confidence in dot-com and tech companies is hitting rock bottom, with investors nursing their wounds and many left wondering how they were ever taken in. I don't think I'm overstating it in saying that this has changed my world. I am much more nervous about the future in this much more negative environment. It's an achievement in itself to have secured what funds I have, but one that will go uncelebrated under the new circumstances.

Of course, I feel our business model is different and is based on a real market opportunity and need. I know I'm not one of the opportunists just leaping on a bandwagon, but I can kiss goodbye to my fancy plans for a big fundraising in September and to an international roll-out any time soon.

Fortunately, I've secured – and mostly have banked – those investment commitments of about €1.8 million. The bulk of that is in cash, though there are some shares issued in return for services too.

I spent a lot of time in February and March planning a launch in France, leaning heavily on my network of contacts there. It concluded with a major presentation in Paris to a professional French investor I had been in communication with for weeks. With recent events, he has run for cover, shutting the door on France for the foreseeable future.

I got one thing out of the trip, however, taking the opportunity on that last visit to run the Paris Marathon.

How things have changed in a few short weeks. Then, paper seemed to refuse anything but the ink of ambition and optimism, which it now rejects in this chastened new world. To borrow from WB Yeats: *All's changed, changed utterly.*

I find myself repeatedly fending off this awful image of me and everyone around me in the venture hurtling towards a nasty crash. I shake it off, but a residual shadow remains. We're well beyond the point of no return. I carry the weight of other people's money heavily; of expectations, livelihoods, hopes and aspirations, of doing the right thing by others and by my family.

All I can do is try to refocus and keep my faith in the opportunity, in the business model that I am still genuinely excited about, in the team and in something within me that says: 'We'll do what it takes'.

In my presentations to investors, I set out plans for the big second fundraiser in the autumn to see us through to profit in Ireland and to fund our international expansion in France, Britain and later Australia. It was full of ambition, befitting a world of ample capital for an ambitious new business age. That plan has to be rewritten.

The obvious first conclusion is that we'll be sticking to Ireland for now. The second is that we'll struggle to survive without further funds by year-end. That's a scary prospect but one that I must face up to. The business will have to prove itself and fast.

In the meantime, I've got to hope that the business environment improves. We'll fund our launch properly, give it every chance, get our revenues going and stretch the cash as best we can beyond that.

A huge chunk of the money raised is already spent or committed to technology, brand development and other set-up costs. These suppliers have shown remarkable faith and trust in us getting off the ground. Our staff commitments are also beginning to mount. For the team, too, it's a leap of faith.

It's now May, and the dot-com crash has continued pretty much unabated. Press headlines worldwide are full of dot-com gloom, and being an internet entrepreneur is suddenly and seriously out of fashion. Our sector is damaged and scarred. We're one of those 'dot-coms', now a pejorative term, implying bust and shame.

Prominent Irish and international dot-coms are already failing all around us. Press articles are being written about the foolish waste of investors' money: the lavish offices and parties they blew their investment funds on. There's a prevailing sense that all things Internet, including the investments, are doomed. It's like the Emperor's New Clothes. I can only imagine the thoughts and jibes:

'Michael left his big job … for this!'

'What was I thinking when I invested in that?'

I'm feeling a vibe of regret from certain shareholders. It's mostly subtle, in the silence, but it's there, and I'm trying not to let it in. For weeks now, my message in any contact with shareholders, staff and potential clients is resolute and as positive as I can make it: "Sure, there was a foolhardy dot-com frenzy, but that wasn't us, and it's over now. What's not over is the march of the internet. It will continue to transform our lives through how we communicate and how we buy. It is not a matter of whether but when and by how much. We will do our utmost to adapt and be part of that. We are different: our venture is founded on a real need in the corporate world; we have a clear revenue and profit model. Finally, our team brings a track record of professionalism and honesty, not opportunism."

I am calm and confident on the outside but daunted too at times. I hope we have enough to prevail. I believe we have, but it's going to be a different type of marathon. Thankfully, those who really matter to me, those around me at work and at home, my good friends, believe too.

The team is all over the early feedback from consumer testing and from clients, which is very positive. It's a strange combination of fear and foreboding when I think of the business environment and the additional funds I will somehow need to raise, and then excitement and satisfaction at the little wins with customers and in our daily work on marketing plans, site development and sales.

Sadly, the wins are never too long-lived against the backdrop of stress and fear for the future and how it could play out for the venture, my team and our investors.

Nothing trains you for this.

———◆———

On the branding front, my initial concept name, I'llTryThat.com, has long given way to HelloPoints. This is the name Karen came up with after I added reward points as a central part of the proposition. That decision was partly inspired by MyPoints.com, a US business I came across in my research and a rising star until the dot-com crash.

HelloPoints was the name I used for our legally-incorporated entity and is the one shareholders are familiar with. However, to the younger generation in our team, it doesn't hack it and isn't cool enough for the internet world. Fair enough, I thought, but what's the alternative?

The marketing committee agreed to embark on a new naming process. We first got our team together to agree on and commit to a set of values that represent the brand and company we are trying to create. These must stand the test of time, but it turned out that they were relatively easy to establish.

We agreed that we need, first and foremost, to be **trustworthy.**

There needs to be **quality** in all of our offers and rewards to our members and in the campaigns we run for brands.

We must be **reliable**, always doing what we say we'll do.

We need to commit to **empathy** with each member, listening and responding to them as individuals who must sense that the service is 'for me'.

We need to keep our content and display **fresh** and **easy to use.**

Finally, it's important to have **fun** and convey that spirit of fun to members and clients alike.

Trust, quality, reliability, empathy, freshness, ease of use, and fun.

With the seven brand values agreed upon, we moved on to the positioning statement, which summaries what we want to mean to people, and, therefore, becomes a navigational aid in our marketing and communications: "a trusted service that offers me personalised and targeted offers and rewards from my favourite brands, in a fun environment." It's a mouthful, but it's only for internal use; more pithy brand and advertising straplines will follow.

We then put the various design and marketing agencies we were working with in competition with one another to crack the naming brief. Surprise, surprise: none had named a dot-com before.

Bríd Deely, a member of the young team at Octagon, came up with the name *pigs's back*, drawn from the phrase *"on the pig's back"*, a direct translation of the Irish phrase *"ar muin na muice"*, meaning to be onto a good thing or ahead of the game. It evokes advantage but also a certain cuteness and fun. Importantly, it cut it with the younger crew, and Pigsback.com was waiting for us as an unregistered .com domain name. I reached into my pocket straight away for a credit card to secure the domain. Getting the .com and not just the .ie is important with our international agenda, which I hope we'll get back to in the not-too-distant future.

I revealed the proposed new brand name to the marketing committee with some trepidation. Would they consider it trivial or in some way unserious? They didn't. It got an emphatic thumbs-up. But we weren't finished yet.

———◆———

It was the late Superquinn founder Feargal Quinn, a renowned retail entrepreneur and a consumer marketer way ahead of his time, who I first heard referring to 'empathy' in a marketing context. As a marketing student, I was very taken by Quinn, who set up his first grocery retail store in Dundalk in the 1960s. He became one of Ireland's most respected businesspeople and, in later years, a senator.

He was fond of quoting the old Irish proverb, *"éist le fuaim na habhann agus gheobhaidh tú breac"*, which roughly translates as "listen to the sound of the river, and you will catch a fish". Quinn organised regular customer workshops in his Superquinn stores, listening to the currents of his own business straight from the mouths of his customers.

Empathy is the elixir of marketing, the sweet spot of understanding that leads to the best insights and solutions. As I worked with my team on a set of principles and guidelines to govern how we propose to behave as the gatekeeper – managing our club of consumers and brands – it occurred to me that the term 'empathy marketing' would sum up our new marketing ethos perfectly. It's our take on- and, we hope, progression of Seth Godin's Permission Marketing.

This, in turn, led us to the name Empathy Marketing Limited as the formal name for the company. It sits above the Pigsback.com brand name and is really there for shareholders and clients to remind us what this business is all about. The marketing committee approved both Pigsback.com as our brand name and Empathy Marketing Limited as the new name for the company.

———◆———

Based on the initial reactions at consumer and trade levels, the name Pigsback is already working perfectly for us. It's distinctive, memorable and easily pronounced. Aiden Kenny, the brand designer at design agency BFK, is like a kid let loose with this brief, with pigs' tails, snouts and piggy puns throughout the first presentation. Wherever we end up, it will be striking – and there's going to be no getting away from pink! He has designed a logo with a little pig's tail for the 'g', and a pig mascot which Johnny Mc has already named *Curly*. It has caught on.

This quirky approach will give us much more bang for our buck in a cluttered advertising and PR world. What's more, it's appealing to our largely female target market, with its pink colours and its cuteness factor. It should be great for press coverage, giving the sub-editors a field day when putting headlines to their copy.

The marketing committee signed off on a large-scale outdoor advertising campaign in two stages: tease and reveal. It will be accompanied by some radio promotions, and we have 20,000 giveaways for our street promotions, catching commuters on the way to offices and colleges where they are most likely to have internet access.

There will be 10,000 stress pigs, a pink pig-shaped version of the squeezy stress ball. Given my experience at Jacob's, sourcing stress pigs for Pigsback will be James O'Connor's headache. He's up to it and I'm hoping the pig will go down half as well with our audience as the shamrocks did a decade or so ago.

We've also got 10,000 pocket booklets grandly titled *The Rough Guide to the Internet*, which have our pink branding all over them.

With such a layered and well-invested marketing campaign, we really are set to paint Ireland pink.

I have been asked if the name will cut through internationally. I think so. The Irish origin gives it character, whether or not people comprehend it, and it puts a smile on the face. That's powerful. Big internet brands like Yahoo, Google and the bank Egg stand out, and they don't worry about describing their product. So why should we?

We've already briefed a trademark attorney to register Pigsback and Empathy Marketing for Europe, North America and Australia. It's an investment and a leap of faith in the future, but a few ® and ™ symbols add a bit of gravitas to a business presentation too.

———◆———

In an early U-turn, we have realised that we need to get out there and meet and manage the brands ourselves. My initial hope that orders would flow to us through advertising agencies is looking naive already. Despite appearances and claims, Irish advertising and media buying agencies are very late to the internet game, and most are still ill-equipped to handle digital. And let's face it, digital is still very small.

So we have to sell to brands ourselves and manage the relationship subsequently. We're getting on with it. We have committed to growing a sales team under Gareth and Alan. It's an all-hands-on-deck effort. I am busily setting up meetings myself and sitting in on as many as I can, as are Valerie and Rory. We are nothing without revenue and content.

The first client presentation I made was to a lady from Chateau Online, a new London-based e-commerce business, who I met at their Dublin launch event. Presenting to a real potential client for the first time, I felt something of what an artist must feel putting their creation out there: how dare I? Have I been in a bubble with my small team for too long, all of us insulated from the real commercial world? Was it all a bit academic and off the mark? Thankfully, she didn't think so. To my immense relief, she nodded in agreement as I went through the presentation, slide by colourful slide: "Brands have new challenges in communicating with consumers in the internet era; consumers are spending less and less time watching TV and more time on computer screens or juggling their viewing between TV and internet; it's becoming more difficult to get consumers' attention with the clutter of information and messages directed at them; pop-up ads and unpersonalised banner advertising solutions are ineffective, even aggravating. Pigsback's new Empathy Marketing approach guarantees permission, relevance, benefits for consumers, carefully gauged frequency of communication and a targeted and personalised approach. As such, it will be welcomed and effective; this is a better approach and a new solution to fit the challenges. Every page features our *No Junk Mail Guarantee* graphic, a simplification for members of our approach to safeguarding their data."

She duly agreed to an initial campaign. It is hard to overstate the encouragement this and other early presentations since then have given us as a team.

We keep refining the master slides, and Valerie is ensuring that everyone is using the same ones. We're finding that most brands – but by no means all – understand that traditional media is no longer enough. But there's widespread frustration among brands with existing internet advertising techniques and broad agreement that alternatives are needed. That's a really useful consensus for us and fertile ground.

We've developed a suite of products to sell to companies designed to create interactivity or engagement between brands and consumers within the Pigsback environment. We know this engagement is something consumer brands are seeking but are failing miserably to create on their own. Our solutions are based on offers, competitions, coupons and surveys. Gareth is pushing the boundaries after a very positive meeting with UCI Cinemas. He's piecing together a special cinema section to include advance screenings exclusive to Pigsback members and occasional two-for-one tickets. This is the sort of softer content which will appeal to people and will be a counterbalance to the duller, more commercial offers, with due respect to banks and some FMCGs. Other examples are popular restaurants such as TGI Friday's, special offers on music CDs from DMGDirect and personal care and beauty brands such as Dove and Sunsilk. This content will help us win and keep consumers and, in the long run, will help us win a share of advertising budgets.

It's going to be a balancing act: the need for content and the need for revenue, but it makes sense to offer reduced fees to brands that have the power to draw in the public.

◆

We're aiming to launch in mid-July and are on track on most fronts from what we can tell. Between everyone, we've met with 50 companies and prepared 35 proposal documents. There's hardly a day goes by, weekends included, that I am not preparing a presentation, reviewing a proposal, or just sitting in on meetings alongside the sales guys.

It's a decent start, and we're set to beat the humble sales target of €25,000 for July. Although it's small, it's still an important target to beat. We are bullish about beating later targets too – we have no choice in the new funding environment – and have committed to recruiting extra salespeople. I'm getting my head around the economics of hiring salespeople fairly quickly.: a salesperson needs a couple of months to settle in and build a *pipeline*, as we call it: a list of prospects at various stages in their readiness to come on board. By month three, we expect the salesperson to be at least covering their own costs in the revenue they are bringing in. By the end of year one, they should be bringing in revenues equivalent to at least three times their costs to contribute to the running of the organisation and, hopefully, in time, profit. We can scale that formula until the market is saturated.

Our product list is also developing fast. Essentially, brands will pay to be included in the emails we send to our members and in the sections of the site or *categories*, as we call them, that are relevant to them. For an extra payment, they can get more profile as a 'Featured Offer' or placement on our 'Mega Bar', an area of the site with three or four brands featured that will always be present as members navigate into different categories.

As we develop more core email products for our members and special interest areas on-site, we will have more products to sell, including sponsorships. Our central email is 'The Sizzler', another porcine pun, bringing category-specific offers and competitions to members weekly.

We have a fortnightly Travel & Weekender Newsletter, which Rory has led the charge on, to get hotels on board, each paying us in the region of €1,000 per month. These packaged offers for short breaks to five-star and upper four-star hotels are getting a great reaction from the team.

Such is the interest among FMCG brands that we have decided to create a Shopping Savings newsletter dedicated to grocery brands with offers, competitions and coupons. It's hard to know how popular a grocery newsletter will be among our email subscribers, but we're giving it a go.

Finally, we've given our reward points a name: *PiggyPoints*. Our users see the full statement of how much they have earned and how they are spent in their *PiggyBank*. We may as well go the whole hog!

On the tech front, Johnny Mc has been working hard with NWC, who are reassuringly unfazed by our technical requirements. Every Pigsback member will have a number, and all of their details will be recorded and used to create a personalised experience.

The first thing I got to see was the database. Nothing too complicated, but I could see how the data is gathered, stored and structured. From that, it's easy to imagine its application in a personalised site. If a member ticks a particular interest box, they get the corresponding offer pages. If they don't, they won't.

Offer pages are pulled from another database. Even images on offer pages are drawn automatically from databases. Everything is data, as I'm learning, pieced together by programming rules.

Here's a working example:

Member Number: 0109

First Name: Maria

Surname: Murphy

Gender: Female

DOB: 1/1/75

Address: Templeogue, Co Dublin

County: Dublin South

Email Preferences:

Travel & Weekender N

Shopping Savings N

Sizzler Y

Selected Interest Categories:

Home & Gardening N

Eating Out Y

Cinema Y

Pampering Y

Travel Y

Music Y

Hotel Breaks Y

Technology and Gadgets N

Parents and Kids Y

Insurances N

Banks N

We will also be able to track what offers a member clicks on and credit PiggyPoints accordingly. The homepage will be personalised, with information drawn dynamically from the member's account in our database. For example:

Hi Michael,

You have 2000 PiggyPoints in your PiggyBank. Here are offers from your chosen categories *(click to change)*

It's a whole new world for us. I'm getting used to hearing about our SQL database, HTML and ASP.net. And we're all going around using words like cookies, browsers, navigation and database queries like we're used to them.

———◆———

June 2000

The last week or so was pivotal. Our launch is only weeks away, and everything hangs on the site working and bringing the personalised experience together. I'm very comfortable with the design element but the developers are making us wait to see the full functioning site.

I understand the complexity of a data-driven model but the waiting involves a lot of trust. Thankfully, NWC inspires confidence and our product is an adaptation of its existing platform, so it should be fine. If it's not, the whole Pigsback project could be scuppered and most of the precious investment funds lost before we even start.

2

This Pig could Fly

With less than a month to go to the Pigsback launch, Karen and I invited the staff to a party in our home in Naas. We're all ready to let off a bit of steam ahead of the final push to get the launch right. Johnny Mc excitedly took out a laptop to show us the first prototype. The design hadn't even been overlaid yet, so it was hard to visualise, but we could see boxes in outline on a screen that will hold offers and different placeholders for branding and navigation. It was dynamic, changing every time John clicked on a new category or refreshed the homepage. I let out a few loud cheers, relief more than anything. There was so little to look at, yet so much.

It made for a particularly good night, crowned by a few shots of Skittle Brew straight from the freezer, a colourful concoction inspired by Homer Simpson and prepared by another colourful character, Stephen Lennon, aka Ste.

John Rooney, marketing manager at Kellogg's, is the first executive from a large FMCG to nail his colours – and his budget – to the Pigsback mast. John gets the Empathy Marketing approach and professes to like the Pigsback brand. He wants to feature the Special K brand to start, conscious of our adult female target market. He has also agreed to look at sponsoring the weekly golf prediction competition with Nutri-Grain. What's more, John enthusiastically shared his support for Pigsback at a meeting with Mindshare, Kellogg's media-buying agency. Mindshare is part-owned by DDFH&B, who we are using as our creative agency at Pigsback. They are trying hard to recruit clients for us.

Alan has also secured a tidy initial campaign from coffee company Bewley's and another from our old employer Green Isle. We're advancing well in discussions with Unilever and Procter & Gamble too. It also looks like we'll have the First Active building society coming on board as the first major financial institution to feature on Pigsback.

Chateau Online, the wine company, is already on board, and I think we'll have a lot of content from DMGDirect by way of CD offers at a very good price. Denis Gannon, who set up DMGDirect as Ireland's first online CD store, is excited to be "piggybacking" on our launch activity.

Another pal, Ciaran Butler of Entertainment Enterprises, has been instrumental in securing cinema two-for-one promotions and preview screenings from UCI Cinemas, as well as offers such as free starters or desserts from TGI Friday's, and two-for-one offers from Leisureplex. This is crucial content for launch.

Ciaran has given me two notable pieces of advice, too: the first: "Do nothing for free"; the second: "Do not sign any personal guarantees for borrowings." Both tips are taken on board.

We've also done deals to use these brands in our rewards catalogue. Members earn PiggyPoints for registering, being active, clicking on certain offers, taking up offers or referring friends. Once members have accumulated enough PiggyPoints, they can go to their PiggyBank and redeem them on a 1 point = 1 cent basis.

We have made the rewards very accessible and real. Pigsback merchandise can be earned for as little as 200 PiggyPoints, while 1,000 PiggyPoints get you €10 in rewards, which can be used in exchange for vouchers for TGI Friday's or UCI Cinemas. There are CDs, rounds of golf and – the ultimate – a stay in the K Club, but also charitable donations, focussing initially on the National Children's Hospital in Crumlin. We're also busily negotiating phone credit with one of the mobile operators.

For the most part, the initial fees paid by brands are relatively small, but these brands give us credibility, and one leads to another. Early adopters are critical, as others will follow. These are the hard yards, the stepping stones we'll slowly build on.

I feel huge gratitude to these brands. They are the Pigsback pioneers and have no idea how much their support and encouragement matter. I've also never appreciated salespeople quite as much as I do now.

July 2000

We have taken a sublease on office space in the Citywest Business Campus on the outskirts of Dublin from a company set up to protect against the so-called Millennium Bug. The bug didn't bite in the end, so they had space to spare.

There's a good vibe around the campus with a few early-stage businesses – some in an incubation unit – mixing it with the established and sharing experiences in the cafés. Everyone is buoyed up by the move. We've had a beer fridge installed, our only indulgence, handy for Friday evenings and occasional late-night shifts.

The team of 12 has been yearning for a place to call home, particularly the guys managing the website and emails, who have been squatting in a corner of Octagon's offices. The rest of us are out a lot, moving from client meeting to client meeting, and are content to make the most of Dublin's coffee shops between times.

One of the best things about our new office is the green area nearby. When the heads get a bit fried, I know I can rely on the two creatives, Ste and Dave M, to grab the hurls and puck a sliotar around for 20 minutes. It tends to work its magic, and we go back refreshed.

I have been working full-time on Pigsback.com for three months now. Getting started is very exciting, even amid all the pressure. The stress compares to nothing else I have endured. There are so many imponderables and so much to do. It's a whole new business model, in a new sector, with new technology, a new brand, a new medium for clients and ultimately, a huge question: will the public take to it?

We're literally conjuring up products, features and prices from thin air. There are no precedents and few enough comparatives, but we take every pointer we can find and are piecing a rate card together. I think it's a blend of what the market will bear, on the one hand, and generating some campaign expectations to go with that, on the other. We can fine-tune it later based on performance.

So we're bundling one product with another for our clients; for example, an indicative number of email inclusions, a placement for an agreed time period in certain premium site positions (homepage, featured positions) and in certain interest categories. We then try to estimate the amount of engagement this will generate, which for now, we measure in click-throughs to an offer page, coupon prints and competition entries.

It will be hard to track sales in these early stages, so we can only encourage our partners to track it themselves as best they can and to share that data with us. Hotels are a prime example, where the practice is for consumers using a Pigsback offer to ring up the hotel directly and book. They will quote the Pigsback offer, but will we get that information and the credit?

In time, we should be able to track the revenue created in e-commerce campaigns and in hotel campaigns that are booked online. This will involve placing a cookie on the partner's check-out page, allowing us to claim the sale and associate it with a member number, so we can credit points to the appropriate member accounts. But we're a while off that yet.

———————◆———————

We are building a nice network, our "mafia", as I call it, a band of supporters who are helping the venture along in one way or another, whether as directors, staff, advisers, investors, friends, or anyone who might open a door or give us a bit of a leg-up. Every start-up needs its mafia.

I'm taking every assistance I can get. Every little building block helps. Every nod of encouragement is more energy for the team. I feel a bit like the friend you don't want to have: if I think you can help, I'll ask you nicely, but directly. If it's not for you, you'll tell me, and that's fine. When I think of what's at stake, I realise I don't have any choice.

The Pigsback business model is turning out to be extraordinarily flexible. We can find a relevant solution for any consumer brand or service by concocting a sponsorship opportunity or creating a special zone on the site around an interest area appropriate to the brand, like cinema, sport, music or pampering.

We've developed several sports prediction competitions like our weekly PGA and Euro tour competition, Premiership football scores, and on big horse races like the Grand National. Special interest zones, categories and competitions provide ample room for premium partnerships for brands.

Every contribution to our content helps as we frantically try to fill out the site. We need enough offers, coupons, rewards, opinion polls and competitions to grab and hold a visitor's attention and to encourage them to come back repeatedly.

We have been making progress on the travel front with Sunway Travel and Club Travel, so there are going to be a lot of inviting pictures of sunny destinations on our launch site. Both brands are keen to get in front of the Irish online audience. I have even recruited my local bicycle store to fill out that category.

Bit by bit, the push to fill out the site seems to be working. I've called it our 'Loaves and Fishes' challenge: we'll stretch what limited content we have across multiple categories by changing the headlines, descriptions, pictures and graphics. For example, a hotel offer can be placed in Short Breaks, but if it has the facilities, it could also be given a Beauty or Golf or Dining focus. The sales team is pushing hard, and the creative and production teams are responding.

But it is full-on. I haven't stopped working; weekends or weekdays; it makes little difference. There's always something to be done: an offer to be improved, a member email to write or edit, customer meetings to be prepared, a new zone to be specd out, competitors to be researched, shareholders to update, a legal agreement to review and sign... the list goes on and on.

Rory, John, Gareth, Alan and Valerie are all going above and beyond, and they're doing it without complaint. But I know we can't and won't try to sustain this pace over the long term.

In between, there's family time, of course. When it comes to the kids, it's immediate and equally full-on, with complete focus and energy required. There is nothing quite like it to clear the head, but business has its way of drifting back into the mind, the stress clouds looming again, but I'm always better for the break.

———◆———

Valerie did agree to go on that blind date with Gary Keating. She was to accompany Gary to a wedding reception at Sutton Castle Hotel in Dublin, but the festivities were in full swing by the time she arrived. A familiar face approached. It was Keith Duffy from Boyzone, the world-famous boy band.

"Are you alright, love?"

"I'm here to meet Gary… Gary Keating."

Keith was on it, and with a cheeky smile, he called across the room to Gary for all to hear:

"Gar, your bird's here!"

It broke the ice for everyone, and Valerie and Gary got on famously, exactly as Karen foretold. Now, even Gary is doing his bit for Pigsback, securing VIP tickets to Boyzone's upcoming concert as competition prizes – easy when his brother Ronan is the band's lead singer.

———————◆———————

I fear Ireland isn't quite ready for us. I guess I knew that. But that was when I foresaw us launching in other markets quickly, and we could let the Irish business tick away. Only one in every six homes in Ireland has internet, and it is poor quality hissy dial-up at that. Fortunately, many people have access through workplaces where the internet speed and quality are better.

I have forecasted that household internet penetration will rise to 60% by 2003. I guess I have to believe it, but not everyone is buying it. Alan gives us all a good laugh mimicking the laggards: "Sure, it'll never catch on". It's a ridiculously myopic view to our minds but worryingly prevalent. And if that's their attitude to internet uptake, I don't fancy them getting their heads around Pigsback.

E-commerce is only starting, and people are afraid to use their credit cards, freaked out by the frequent media headlines of financial and personal data being stolen. Because of that, we've positioned ourselves as offering communications solutions for brands rather than e-commerce solutions, but that will hopefully come in time.

We know brands need to communicate more effectively online and that they'll pay for the right solutions. So engagement with brands it is, through offer clicks, competition entries, polls, and coupon prints, as opposed to buying online.

On the spend side of the equation, the team has grown, and the annualised cost of our people at all levels is heading to €500,000. We're also preparing to invest close to €1 million on marketing in a few waves over the first 12 months. I know that the level of marketing spend is high relative to the funds we've raised and might even seem foolhardy, but it's a kind of land grab: we need to go first and own the market, ready or not, proving and improving the concept and trusting that we can raise more money on the back of it. The worst possible outcome would be to drip the investment away on salaries and overheads without really giving it a go and, therefore, never really knowing. It's my turn to walk the walk of branding and marketing investment. We won't win the market position and consumer franchise we want by accident. It's not for the faint-hearted, but what worthwhile prize is?

I originally targeted revenues of €500,000 from Ireland in our first full year in business, but that was at a time when we expected to raise a second round of funds with ease. We have to aim a good deal higher now, given the marketing, tech and staff commitments. We'll have spent the funds we have raised within months unless sales deliver. They must.

———————•———————

Pink was the colour of the day at our official launch event on July 10th at the Ocean Bar in Dublin. Pink cocktails were ready on arrival for all our clients, press, investors, and, of course, friends and family, many decked out in pink shirts and dresses for the occasion.

It was an ideal venue with its dot-com vibe and a view out over the waters of the Grand Canal Dock, with Harry Crosbie's old brick boathouse standing in splendid isolation to one side. Across the water, hoardings mark out a site earmarked for urban regeneration with offices, a theatre and apartments planned, giving a sense of the past meeting the future.

It was a hands-on day all around. My sister Geraldine recruited two pals from The Town for on-street promotions. They wore pig suits which were quite heavy for a warm July day. When one of them, Brian, took off the pig head for a breather and put it down on a wall beside him, it was snatched by a local kid on his bike. Brian must have felt that the very success of Pigsback was in his hands when, in full pig regalia, he gave chase. The cyclist eventually jettisoned the pig head as Brian got close. Now that's commitment.

In the same vein, Gareth spent much of his day working out how to get our huge inflatable pig tethered to a floating platform on the dock in front of us without falling in. Meanwhile, I was posing for photos, which included one with two piglets. Their owner was on standby in case of emergency, as was my spare shirt, but the piglets were on their best behaviour. Welcome to the start-up world!

The evening went off well overall. I was nervous, which showed as I struggled with the more formal speech I had prepared. It was only when I cast it aside and ad-libbed that I relaxed and connected with the audience. My father-in-law Gerry, with customary frankness, remarked: "I was wondering if the plane would get off the runway."

I went on to meet journalists, and we're already getting good brand exposure from the day. Our guests and clients seemed to have a great time.

My message was clear: the importance of permission-based access to consumers through their email inbox, the power of the new communications media, and how the marketing and advertising worlds would never be the same again. Pigsback will be leading the way in Ireland, I said.

When my mother declared that she now had a good feeling about Pigsback, I felt the tide was indeed turning our way.

For a full week in advance, our giant 48-sheet posters with images of Curly in different guises – representing categories such as Travel, Beauty and Books – had been posted around the cities and towns of Ireland with no brand name, just a teaser: *whatever you're into, you'll want to be on it!*

Yesterday evening, in tandem with the launch, the brand name was revealed to a by now very curious Ireland: *Pigsback.com, Get on it!*

It's simple, colourful, and fun. Of course, it doesn't explain everything, but we don't expect it to. Instead, we're planning to take double-page ads in the *Sunday Independent*, the country's best-selling paper, displaying our offers to show readers exactly what's on offer. We also have a partnership with eBid.ie (a kind of eBay curated for Ireland), promoting each other's businesses and sharing some goodwill and encouragement.

The stress pig is proving very popular too, and we seem to be making our mark while putting a few smiles on faces. There's no turning back now. We are off and running.

I met the well-known hotelier Julie Gilhooly in the Nuremore Hotel in Carrickmacross, not far from The Town, hoping she might support the Pigsback launch with a campaign. In the end, we agreed to do a swap: we got to bring the team for a night away, and the Nuremore would become one of the first hotels to trust its name to Pigsback.com.

What a time we had! Everyone was ready to let off some steam after a lot of intensity before and after the launch. We started with a workshop. Then I challenged the sales team to pay for our extras at the Nuremore by finding a sponsor for the weekend's sports competitions. Alan had it sorted in jig time, thereby bringing a positive end to formal proceedings.

Some went for walks, and others played a few holes of golf, but everyone was assembled in the bar by late afternoon. It was a very good one. There was plenty of competition for the guitar, and the songs kept coming. As I headed for bed, I left Johnny Mc impersonating Laurence of Arabia, with a tablecloth around his head, held in place by an improvised tiara; he was leading a sing-song with a wedding party he had just met, the bridesmaids belting out the chorus of American Pie.

Meanwhile, life at Pigsback has been progressing at pace. I'm sitting at home with a screen open, watching new entries flow into the Pigsback database. I can see each new entry pop up. It's exciting and concrete, and it's giving me great confidence and belief.

This is my new world. Our assets, mainly our brand and our membership, are defined by the accountants as "intangible", but they are no less valuable.

In my days in the food industry, I would happily stand by the conveyor belt mesmerised as thousands of Goodfella's pizzas or Jacob's Fig Rolls moved along the production line. Now, I'm watching new data entries stream in at pace as new members sign up to Pigsback.com faster than I can read. It's good to see the evidence.

Our report generator can tell us who clicked on any part of the site. It aggregates this data for every client. We know who visited, who entered competitions, printed coupons, entered quizzes and polls, etc. We also know the gender, age and geographic profile – nothing personal, of course, but it's all of value to brands.

Competitions are the greatest surprise, with entries going through the roof, literally several thousand entries per competition. All that's left is to understand offer take-up, and we're working on the cooperation of the brands for this.

There have been a few small technical glitches, no more than expected and no showstoppers. The site works as it should, and people are engaging in bigger numbers than we expected. We are already getting hundreds of orders every day for our rewards and are trying hard to fulfil them within a couple of working days.

We've heard that a whole floor of Bank of Ireland is competing to earn the most PiggyPoints. That's early adoption!

As a bit of distraction, a few of us don the pig suits and do our own early morning promotions. Most recently, Gareth and I led by example but had to make a quick exit as one distracted motorist rear-ended another. Gareth later told me that he spotted the HR director of Irish Distillers approaching in his car and that he just didn't feel like revealing his identity. He had left the big corporate set-up and career for this! I completely got it.

CDs are selling by the hundreds every day, and our CineClub, now sponsored by Coca-Cola, is proving a real winner. It's a great fit, and another great brand is on board. We are filling hundreds of places at cinema preview screenings, taking only minutes, as people compete with each other to get the limited places. Our members are also availing of any amount of two-for-one midweek cinema vouchers.

Restaurant deals and vouchers are very popular, too, led by TGI Friday's. In great news for revenue, grocery coupons for the FMCG brands are being printed by the thousands, and early indications are of very high usage – or redemption – based on a survey of those printing the coupons.

A high proportion of people who printed coupons don't use them, most likely forgetting them, but they claim in research to buy the associated product anyway. Such is the power of engagement with the coupon in the first place. Sadly for my local bicycle shop in Naas, he got inquiries but no sales. It's hard to win them all.

Of course, as we gain insights, we make the most of them through our sales presentations. More and more brands are coming on board as a result.

———◆———

I rather liked the headline chosen by the tech journalist Adrian Weckler in his article in the *Sunday Business Post*: 'spam, bam, no thank you ma'am'

He and other journalists picked up on our concept of empathy marketing too. A three-page feature by Paul O'Kane in the autumn 2000 issue of *Cara* magazine has been the pinnacle. *Cara* is the Aer Lingus in-flight magazine, read by countless passengers, which of course, include many Irish businesspeople and opinion leaders.

It has given the Pigsback brand great profile and much-needed credibility. It was a light-hearted business interview which O'Kane finished on a fun note: "if Michael Dwyer has his way [he'll be] on the pig's back. This pig could well fly."

The *Sunday World*, too, covered the launch in its series entitled 'The Internet for absolute beginners'. The editor had a field day with piggy puns, headlining us with: 'whole Hog Approach to Online Marketing'. It went on: "we're not telling porkies here, but there's a new website called Pigsback.com, which is going the whole hog to bring special offers to Irish consumers. And its backers are hoping it will really bring home the bacon."

I open any publication where we're expecting a mention for Pigsback.com with unsteady hands. Which way will it go? Positive or negative? Did I say anything stupid? Did the journalist get the model and brand?

It comes with the territory. Ours is a consumer-oriented branded business, so we need all the publicity we can get to amplify our media spend and give us extra bang for our buck. So far, the coverage has been good and is helping build the profile and awareness. The brand and colour stand out and we've had some amount of colour photographs in newspapers and magazines.

Not everyone believes the internet is so compelling, however, with one recent *Daily Mail* headline declaring, 'Internet may just be a passing fad as millions give up'. The article claimed that millions of people are abandoning the internet due to high costs and low connection speeds.

For that matter, not everyone believes in our Empathy Marketing commitment to "never sell or rent your data to anyone ever". One businessman attendee at a conference I spoke at admitted to putting our promise to the test. He set up a special email address to register for Pigsback.com so he could keep tabs on us. If any other correspondence arrived at this address, he would only have us to blame.

After all his trouble, nothing arrived.

December 2000

According to data from AC Nielsen, Pigsback members are spending 13 minutes per visit on our site, more than on any other Irish site. That makes Pigsback 'Ireland's stickiest website'. Evidently, the content is working with all of our offers and competitions and polls, keeping people interested and clicking.

We're set to hit a remarkable 1.1 million page impressions per month in December, just six months after launch and nearly double the initial 600,000 forecasted. All of this traffic is to Pigsback pages with brands at their heart. That's exactly what we hoped for: so it's working for the people who are paying us. Travel and Hotels is the most popular category, with other hospitality categories like Eating Out, Wines, Beers and Spirits and Going Out not far behind.

The number of offers from brands has grown from just 45 in July as we launched to over 150 now. Our revenues too have grown month-on-month across the first six months and are now projected to reach a total of €200,000 for that period. Again, it's ahead of target, and it's encouraging. Our search engine traffic is small and driven mainly by Yahoo!, with the newer Google search engine a long way back in second place. We have registered 54,000 members, well ahead of target, and have sent out 400,000 emails, sticking to our rules on frequency and relevance.

Patterns indicate people are mainly surfing the internet at work, where they can get free and better-quality access. We're not complaining, but our site is being blocked by some more nitty employers. Our biggest hours are between midday and 2 pm, broadly reflecting our members' lunchtime breaks. They are a responsible lot, after all.

We closed 2000 with a survey of our members. It paints a picture of a very young and urban Irish internet user. Our members are mainly single, female, and are either in offices or colleges. Those working have excellent household income, evidence of Ireland's digital divide. We are doing something right: 95% are satisfied with the Pigsback service.

We've managed to squeeze out a few extra months' runway from our cash thanks to good cost and working capital management, and higher revenues, of course. Indications now are that we're good until the end of May 2001.

March 2001

We require funding - and soon. We are doing our best to attract more money, but it's still a very arid environment for dot-com investment. A sector that once had cash pouring into it is now deserted by investors. Our high marketing costs at launch, coupled with the tech development costs, have consumed most of the initial funds raised. The ongoing cost levels are now much lower, but for all our progress, we're still a long way off breakeven. In December, our monthly cash burn rate was down to €70,000, and we're making further progress in the first quarter. With marketing expenditure shelved for now, we just have to live off the considerable profile and awareness we have already built, for a while at least.

Unfortunately, there is no appetite among the existing investor group to support us. Like many, they are nursing their own wounds from other investments or simply running scared of dot-com after the negative headlines. When I bump into any of them, some hold their ground and wish me continued progress, but others glance over the subject like they don't want to broach it or, worse again, fear that I'll ask them for money. The message from existing investors is clear: *if it's down to us, the answer is No.* For all my positivity, I am in a tricky and pressurised position, peering over the cliff edge of early insolvency. But I believe we'll get there, somehow!

———◆———

The team perceives and lives Pigsback very differently from the investors, thankfully. They inhabit their own bubble, one of passion for the brand and the Empathy Marketing approach. They savour the sales wins, beating targets and the clear evidence that Irish consumers are engaging in big numbers. They tell me they feel lucky to be part of our dot-com venture. That belief is abundantly evident in what they bring to client meetings, in the offers that go on-site, in our marketing, in how the team represents the brand generally, in the good humour in the office, at our team drinks or at the occasional away-night.

Our COO, Rory and I have a foot in both worlds: the internal world of Pigsback and the external financial world, currently ill-disposed to anything not backed by a property deed. We are obsessively examining all fundraising angles. There are regular meetings with corporate finance houses and known investors. Our script to new investors says: "Fund Ireland to profitability first, and only then start to consider a regional UK launch as a stepping stone to open up the international opportunity". I've offered the view that a successful pilot in the UK could be enough to secure an attractive exit. I don't know whether it will or not, but it seems reasonable to put it out there.

———◆———

In some welcome recognition, we have just won Best New Irish Company at the grocery sector's Checkout Awards, which Rory accepted from Denis Brosnan, the well-known chairman of Kerry Group, which he grew from a local creamery to a global food and ingredients business. There is a copy of Checkout magazine in every FMCG company in Ireland, so the profile and positivity are helpful indeed.

It comes on top of a Zeddy Award, which Dave Foody accepted for us, recognising our quality as a website. I commented on the rough edges on the wooden trophy the next day in admiration, only to learn that this wasn't part of the design. The lads had used the trophy as a ball in a game of tip rugby on Leeson Street after the ceremony.

Light relief is welcome, but the clock is ticking louder and louder in my ears. I've been working so hard to maintain a confident face to the outside world, but there's no avoiding the growing pressure within.

August 2001

Kevin Watson is an Englishman with a soft spot for Ireland. Kevin qualified as a chartered accountant with PricewaterhouseCoopers (PwC) in London, alongside my brother John, known to his friends simply as *JD*. They've been good friends ever since, and Kevin and I are friends too. In his early and mid-twenties. Kevin was a regular and popular visitor to Dublin for weekends, to the Galway Races or to New Year's celebrations in the west of Ireland.

Kevin is now CFO of the private equity-backed Thomson Directories, a UK Yellow Pages equivalent. JD advised the company through its funding and recent very successful exit. Kevin called me in May to say that the departing Thomson Directories management team are looking to make digital investments with international potential. They think Pigsback.com fits the bill.

There have been several discussions with Kevin as lead, and they have gone very well. We are on the point of agreeing on an initial investment of €600,000. I won't get a better offer than this, and they've agreed to sign a binding legal commitment.

It's huge progress, but there is an important caveat - it requires us to raise matching funds in an agreed timeframe. We're opening conversations with anyone we think can help, but as good as our early market and brand traction are, as much as our brand is being hailed as impactful and engaging, and as credible as the Thomson guys are, it's still an exceptionally barren fundraising environment.

Banks, of course, have no interest. Like most private investors, they have turned to Ireland's new gold rush, property. I've written to our shareholders and asked for their support with the funding round, to no avail.

More positively, however, it looks like Enterprise Ireland (EI) is going to support us with a first investment and grant package totalling over €100,000. The state agency, too, requires us to complete the full funding round. It still leaves a large gap.

It's frustrating. We are so close and yet so far away, and the agreed time frame looks like it will be over-shot. The press is beginning to write about the online survivors, the brands who made it through the storm. We were happy to make their lists, but we're not safe yet.

Just as I was beginning to fear the worst, one of our non-executive directors called me. Pat Shine is a former PwC Ireland partner turned property developer. He's a colourful character, very supportive and very well-networked. He suggested that we meet with the directors of Xtra-vision, a subsidiary of the American company Blockbuster. He teed up the "mutually interesting" meeting.

If our imperative is cash, Xtra-vision's imperative is a new business model for the digital era. The internet presents a huge looming threat to their film rental business model, and a stake in Pigsback might get them rolling in a new direction.

Xtra-vision's culture is rooted in its store base, so it is conflicted in its development of digital channels, which could cannibalise that base. Yet its CEO, Martin Higgins, is determined to learn about digital and to explore online models for his brand, all with the blessing of its US parent.

After weeks of negotiations, we agreed on a deal. There's an upfront €500,000 in cash investment by Xtra-vision and a big commitment to spend with us in coming years, which will mean revenue, profit and further cash into the future. Additionally, we placed a substantial equity value on the joint TV and marketing campaigns promised as part of the deal. This has the effect of increasing the headline investment (albeit it must be charged to the Profit & Loss account as it is released as a 'non-cash' charge). The deal gives us cash, revenue, and a much higher profile, which in turn will mean more members down the line. For all of this, Xtra-vision will get a 20% stake in the company over time, in an investment headlined at €2 million. Critically, there'll be enough cash to secure the Thomson and EI investments. It's a path to an altogether more secure place.

There are some reasonable rights and controls attached: the new investors are each entitled to a seat on the board, and certain key decisions will require board approval. All very reasonable. The board is happy, and so too are Kevin Watson and EI.

All going well, this deal will remove any further funding requirements for Ireland and will propel us to profitability much more quickly. As soon as that point is in sight, I will be planning the next chapters of the business.

As part of the deal, I agreed to give up shares valued at €81,000, to honour a penalty clause with the Thomson group after over-shooting the funding deadline. The agreement stipulated that the amount would be spread across all investors, but I hadn't the heart to go there. Furthermore, Karen and I agreed to write a cheque for €60,000 "to show our commitment" again! It helped get the funding over the line, but we're now stretched beyond our comfort zone, having just moved house and had our third child, Ella. Apart from a cheque for a further €18,000 from JD, the original investors supported the round to a total of €4,000. In this instance, existing investors are lucky, as not only have we managed to find new sources of investment to survive, but we've struck a robust valuation in the environment, improving the per-share valuation since launch and minimising dilution.

In Xtra-vision, the Kevin Watson group, and EI, I believe I have secured investors with stronger hands and deeper pockets, capable of – and intent on – supporting the later stages of our journey.

In one of the cheekiest moves we could have contrived, we brought the whole Pigsback team of 14 people to Disneyland Paris a few weeks before we closed the funding round. Rory and I were comfortable enough that the investment was secure to go with it. There was no doubt that the team deserved the lift.

We did it on a shoestring but had a blast. We flew Ryanair to Beauvais, hired a minibus, and got a great hotel deal for two nights. The daytime rides and spills were followed by line-dancing in the American barn-styles bars before Johnny Mc led the sing-song into the early hours. The team had looked forward to it for weeks, had a ball and will live off it for months to come.

A start-up's got to do what a start-up's got to do.

———————◆———————

I was in my office around lunchtime on September 11th. I knew something very serious had happened from the commotion in the open plan area. The news was spreading online, and we moved to the boardroom to watch in horror as one of Manhattan's iconic Twin Towers was burning.

A freak accident, we thought, until, in front of our eyes, a plane flew straight into the second tower. Smoke was billowing from both towers now. Everyone was stunned. There were no words. What was next? Shortly afterwards, one of the towers collapsed. The other followed not long later.

There was talk of further aircraft having been hijacked and heading for other prominent buildings. Human life was being taken in the most violent circumstances right before our eyes.

Everyone was in shock, and I told the team to go home. The world would remain glued to the news from New York for hours: parts of Manhattan covered in debris and dust; broken firemen exhausted from their heroic efforts, aware that many of their colleagues had paid the ultimate price to save others in the Twin Towers; later, swathes of shocked and emotional commuters making their way home on foot.

It emerged later that members of Al-Qaeda, an extremist Islamic group, had hijacked four planes and carried out suicide attacks. The third plane hit the Pentagon in Washington, and a fourth crash-landed in a field in Pennsylvania, the passengers (it later emerged) having overwhelmed the hijackers. Tragically, over 3,000 people lost their lives that day.

In the weeks since we've had time to consider events. That our world is wounded and has changed profoundly is the only conclusion we can draw. It's more uncertain, less trusting, and less confident. We're all worried that 9/11 may be the beginning of a wave of terror attacks by Al-Qaeda and others. Certainly, for the foreseeable future, it marks the end of the carefree air travel we've all come to enjoy.

Thoughts eventually turned to what it all means for the business. It's impossible to know, but like Dot Bomb before it, 9/11 is another major shock to the broad economy in which we operate.

———◆———

Our empathy marketing approach and implicit expertise in understanding and managing relationships with large groups of consumers have been recognised by a number of key clients. There is a realisation that we have the experience and required technologies to manage these groups well. This is opening up opportunities in the customer loyalty space, in particular. This year we won a contract to operate a loyalty programme for the mobile company O2. We do something very similar for Xtra-vision too. I have advised AIB on its customer loyalty agenda, which has, in turn, led to a deal with AIB to assist with its student recruitment programme. We've called this area of our business Empathy Communications. It's not quite a separate unit yet; I hope we can soon justify recruiting a leader for this area.

These are big contributors to the cost of running the company and will help us reach profitability sooner, but they come at a price. For now, I find myself leading the charge and my time is often sold out as part of these deals. Interesting as these contracts are, selling my time like that is not sustainable personally and not good for the business in the medium term. It has left me overstretched, which culminated in a wave of panic coming over me while driving home from the office recently. I thought I was on the verge of a serious medical incident and pulled into the car park at the Poitín Stil pub on the Naas Road on my way home. I recovered my composure fairly quickly, got a glass of water and made my way home.

I don't know what it was but went on to get myself checked. Nothing has shown up. I've put it down to stress. Either way, I've been trying to mind myself a bit more.

———◆———

Necessity is indeed the mother of invention, and we've just decided that if the internet is slow to reach the people, we'll take it to them. The idea is to showcase the best of Pigsback in a booklet of special offers and coupons from a range of hotels, FMCG brands and entertainment outlets, including our new partner Xtra-vision.

It will be delivered to all 1.4m households in Ireland by post, so it's a valuable marketing campaign for participating brands and for us. Brands will pay for their slots, so it's another new revenue source.

We've called it Curly's Coupons. The first one has just hit Irish homes, and it looks great. We've already had a flood of new members.

The irony is far from lost on me: a dot-com has just created its own new marketing channel using the most traditional of delivery methods, the postal service.

January 2002

I'm a lot happier entering this new year. With money in the bank, I'm back focused solely on growing the business. But even with a much more solid base, trading remains very challenging. The biggest problem is the pace of digital adoption: household internet penetration levels are way too low, and there's no sign of higher-speed connections coming to Irish homes any time soon. This is reflected in the attitude among many businesses that there's no urgency to look to digital and that our type of solution can wait. It means that the take-up of services is still a harder slog than I expected.

On the plus side, we've definitely benefited from the extra profile generated by the Xtra-vision campaigns on TV and in-store, as well as Curly's Coupons. Pigsback membership has topped the 100,000 mark, and our site is reaching over 2 million page impressions per month consistently, which has doubled in the past year.

We're issuing about four million PiggyPoints per month to members for completing certain surveys, taking up offers, spending with e-commerce partners, winning prizes, and clicking on selected offers. This number and its associated cost tend to broadly track our revenue growth; four million points every month are worth €40,000 at face value, although the net cost is about half of that (allowing for unused points and discounts we secure on reward vouchers). It's all good for now, but we're going to need to watch the cost and possibly box more cleverly in the future.

We've been active on the new product development front too. We've been gradually building an SMS or mobile messaging database with nearly 30,000 members. We have also added a chat or 'forums' facility, intended initially as a discussion area for a book club. Once our members got talking to each other, there has been no stopping them, so we've broadened the Pigsback Forums into multiple categories. Our members are moderating themselves and helping with each other's issues on the site. Finally, for the first time, we've added our own e-commerce facility, some two years into the launch of our dot-com.

•

About six months ago, we started a project to bring our technology in-house. This will mean managing it on our own but will address the very considerable annual fees we are currently paying. It will obviously require us to skill up to take control, manage and develop the database and codebase on our own.

In the way of big business projects, we decided to give this pretty momentous one a name, *Project Arthur*. It's a reference to the "ourselves alone" mantra promoted by the politician Arthur Griffith in the early days of the new Irish state. I had second thoughts, reluctant to bring anything political into Pigsback, but the name stuck. I explain it away by referring to the few pints of Arthur Guinness's best that we'll have earned when the job is completed.

Johnny Mc is overseeing the project, which includes hiring a developer versed in the new codebase. Looking back, we certainly paid a high price to get started as we did with the ASP solution. We had little choice back then and could have no quibbles. The technology has worked, and we've had enough time to gain an understanding of our needs and how to deliver them. Our development house, NWC, is developing the product for us for a considerable but fair fee. With their existing knowledge of the Pigsback system, they are the most obvious and surest route to success.

We'll focus in-house on managing the database and the code base, which together form the brain of the Pigsback platform. We'll happily subcontract hosting of our website for another while anyway, meaning that the powering, maintenance and security of our servers will remain under the management of a third party.

Payback on the €250,000 investment in Project Arthur will be about a year. That will justify the price of a few pints of Guinness for the tech team when they complete it.

March 2002

Through the closing months of 2001, Rory and I worked hard to progress discussions to a very advanced stage with Australia Post, the national postal service in Australia. We were contacted by intermediaries in Melbourne, including an old Irish friend, planning a brand and technology transfer to launch Pigsback there through a licensing agreement.

We successfully went through several stages of evaluation and fine-tuning of the business plan with the advisers and the Australia Post team. My old employers, Green Isle, were kind enough to allow us to use their video conferencing facilities at their head office for the early morning calls to Aus.

Encouraged, I was mentally dusting off my passport and boarding the flight to Melbourne for the launch. Unfortunately, we've just fallen at the final fence. Australia Post's MD has vetoed the project. A bummer. It's a sign of the continued nervousness among decision-makers about any dot-com investments. It's a big disappointment for all involved, in Melbourne and in Dublin. Thankfully our investment has been in time only. If there's a lesson, it's that we should have insisted on a sponsor at the very top of the chain of command or at least have *socialised* it directly with the MD earlier.

A licensing deal would have been very appealing. A large partner like Australia Post would have brought huge resources and credibility too. I don't see us funding an Australian launch on a go-it-alone basis any time soon. Not to be. Citywest it remains for now.

April 2002

Thanks to another edition of Curly's Coupons and the benefit of lower technology costs, we registered our first profit in March, less than two years after launch. It's only one month, but it's a milestone that we're all rightly proud of. A long way to go before we get a full year's profit, but it's an essential first step.

That progress has given us the confidence to create the new senior role of strategic development manager under Jo Malvern. Jo's profile and experience using data and market research look like a particularly good match. She and her partner, Mark, recently moved to Dublin from England. I see Jo helping in areas such as Empathy Communications, professionalising the organisation in how we think of and use our data, but particularly in consumer research.

We've been deploying consumer research extensively for our own ends all along, and it is invaluable. We get great insights, and so do our clients. It's easily accessed from a digital platform too. With so many willing respondents in the Pigsback community, it seemed an obvious idea from the early months to run a weekly member poll, tackling the issues of the day. That has been a huge success for content, but this is a commercial opportunity we must go after and Jo can lead that charge.

———◆———

As we watched the dot-com bubble burst in 2000, we had to freeze our international ambitions. I hoped we were down but not out. Australia held great promise for a brief period and might have been the first chapter in our international development. Instead, we've decided to move in baby steps with a launch in Northern Ireland.

It has required a separate installation of the Pigsback site for local brands, offers, coupons and rewards, all denominated in pounds sterling. We've undertaken a full communications programme with UK supermarkets, both at local and head office levels, to ensure our coupons are accepted. That has been a big job in itself – and it's ongoing – but it's good preparation for a full UK launch down the road.

As far as the marketing plan is concerned, we've been sticking to the winning formula of mixing outdoor and radio advertising with street promotions and PR. It's early days, but it seems to be working here too. We had a buzzy and well-attended launch night in the centre of Belfast and good subsequent press coverage.

There are very encouraging signs of early consumer traction and engagement. We hope to recruit 40,000 members in the first year, quite a chunk of the digitally engaged in Northern Ireland. In September, we'll run a separate Curly's Coupons booklet for Northern Ireland. That will get the name into every home.

Today's Belfast is a far cry from what I experienced in my meat factory days with Agra Trading 17 years ago. My free spirit found it difficult to adapt to the strictures and fears of such a constrained life in Belfast in 1985. At that time, Northern Ireland was still in the grip of the Troubles and dangerous if you found yourself in the wrong place; 'don't go to this area, to these pubs, don't speak up with your Southern accent and don't even jest about the national question'.

I was recently reminded by an old pal from Dundalk rugby club of an incident while driving to a friendly match in Armagh, north of the border, in the early 1990s. My car was full of Dundalk rugby players, and the boot was full of tins of Chocolate Kimberley with gear bags on top.

I overtook a slow-moving car on Armagh's main street and, on hearing the siren, realised I had passed an unmarked police car. The officers didn't appreciate my manoeuvre and were suspicious of the heavily-laden Southern-registered vehicle.

We had already been stopped by a routine army patrol at the border, so I was feeling nervous and worked hard to present a composed front.

"We're running late for a rugby match against Armagh," I volunteered to the RUC man in a conciliatory tone.

"Can I see what's in the boot, please?" He insisted.

I opened the boot.

"Just our gear bags and a few of these new biscuits. I work for Jacob's."

He seemed to be relaxing at the mention of rugby, and Jacob's too.

"Sure, here's a tin for yourself and your colleagues. They're hard to come by!"

"Very kind of you, sir, thank you. And good luck in your match."

He smiled, and we went our separate ways. I put the biscuits down to sampling and the manoeuvre down to experience.

I am glad to be back in Belfast doing business in peaceful times. I'm more self-conscious about my accent than I need to be and more prone to a nervous look over my shoulder than the younger team members.

The truth is, we're having lots of fun in Belfast with a small local team of three people, ably assisted by Ste, who is overseeing our site and communications management processes in the North. Ste is our knowledge transfer man, and his Skittle Brew recipe is now acclaimed North and South. He knows how to win hearts.

Our new address is The Stormont Gate Lodge, which is literally at one of the entrances to the famous Northern Ireland government buildings on the outskirts of Belfast. We have sub-leased an office from Open Fairways, one of our earliest clients. It puts a smile on my face every time: Pigsback.com, The Stormont Gate Lodge, Belfast.

We expect the experience in Northern Ireland to inform our launch plan for Britain. We're currently thinking of a regional English launch, maybe in the Greater Manchester area, following Green Isle's example when it launched the Goodfella's brand there. We are also considering Scotland and have been speaking to two Scottish media groups about a potential alliance, one of which is the owner of Willie O'Reilly's Today FM radio station. It's all very early stage, and for now, our focus is on Belfast.

———◆———

August 2002

According to industry data from the newly-formed Interactive Advertising Bureau (IAB), Pigsback is a clear market leader in revenue among Irish websites and publishers. No other site is coming close to us in revenues, which doubled in the first half of 2002 over 2001. I should pause and celebrate, but there's so much more to be done.

We've reached over four million page impressions monthly too. Considering that the impressions are all to pages led by brands - whether that's offers, coupons or competitions - that's an awful lot of click activity to brands. It's exactly what was lacking and what we hoped to achieve.

Gareth is now leading the client charge as director of sales and marketing. He is a natural leader and represents our business particularly well. He's getting plenty of scope to make his mark.

With the addition of more salespeople and content managers, the Pigsback team has now reached 24 people. The sales organisation now has several sales or business units reporting to Gareth. New managers are now emerging in the business, notably the young and ambitious Jenny Taaffe, who has joined the sales team from that particularly strong training ground - the Irish hotel trade.

We are making great strides in the FMCG sector and with many other key clients too. We're starting to see some six-figure annual deals from the bigger companies, a sign that we can scale our revenues. Our key partners now include financial brands such as MBNA and AIB, lifestyle brands such as O2, Nokia and Dublin Airport, and, of course, many FMCG brands such as Kellogg's, Unilever, Barry's Tea and John West. We're trying to match each brand to an aspect of the site that fits their brand positioning, so Pepsi and the Music Zone, Nokia and the Youth Zone, Danone Actimel and the Healthy Living Zone, and so on.

January 2003

Jo Malvern has been busy, and we are ready to formally launch a consumer research division which we're calling Empathy Research. We are using an internal survey tool and some external software to help us create surveys and gather responses. Our own data analysis tools aggregate socio-economic and demographic data from survey respondents to give a non-personal profile to our clients and to us. It's a hugely efficient process and very robust from a sampling perspective. We can bring large numbers to any survey, and we have the ability to filter these to create nationally representative panels.

One of our first commissions was to evaluate a very innovative new car insurance project to be called XS Direct. It was founded by Chris McCann, my co-promoter of the Dundalk tennis club sweetshop many moons ago. He and his management team have a massive appetite for data, and in Jo, they've met their match. She is busy cutting the aggregate respondent data every which way, from age groups to geography to household income to current insurers. We're optimistic about Empathy Research, and in time, it will recruit its own separate panel of respondents from the Pigsback membership for more regular research.

We have been winning a few more awards, which is nice and gives us all a lift each time. I was caught off guard recently when I was called out as the winner of the Marketer of the Year Award by the president of the Marketing Institute of Ireland (MII), JP Donnelly. I was delighted to win the MII award, and JP is a figure I hold in high regard. We were present as part of a shortlist for another corporate award, so my award truly was a surprise.

That was followed by a Net Visionary Award from the Irish Internet Association, also unexpected. It comes from a group who showed commitment to the development of the internet in Ireland long before most. Coincidentally (I was assured), it is now run by an old classmate, Colm Reilly, also from the CBS in Dundalk.

There seems to be a bit of 'credit to the survivors' in the air.

3

Up for the Punt

July 2003

Business has been strong, and we're now profitable! It's finely balanced, and no one is getting complacent but, for the 12 months to June 2003, we're showing a €200,000 profit in the Republic of Ireland on turnover of €2.5 million.

Now that's a proper achievement, a small miracle perhaps. It's a massive credit to the inventiveness and dedication of the team, especially faced with such an immature Irish internet market.

My first I'llTryThat.com concept was based on special offers or deals, envisaging that members would purchase the offers. We adapted and innovated on the hoof, developing our suite of consumer engagement products and, later, ancillary marketing services via Empathy Communications and Empathy Research.

That ability to listen and respond to the market gives me optimism for the future. I don't see us pausing any time soon. If anything, home market success is poking our international ambition again. We've been patient and survived, and I feel we've earned a shot at something bigger.

The opportunity in Northern Ireland, however, turns out to be just too limited, even for the small team and overhead we put in place. While we have had excellent consumer traction and have recruited 40,000 members, we are behind on revenue targets.

We've decided to manage the Northern Ireland market using just one market manager, Paul Dalzell, working from his home in Belfast and supported by the Dublin office. We are pulling back most of our Northern Ireland spending before it can hurt financially. No significant harm done.

The key issue is that many of the big media decisions for the region are taken either in London, as part of a national UK campaign, or (to a lesser extent) in Dublin. Rarely are specific measures undertaken for Northern Ireland. It is nigh-on impossible to get the attention of a London-based marketer – let alone get a budget commitment – to invest in this fraction of the UK population, which they are hardly aware of, let alone profess to understand.

Finally, the revenues we are likely to achieve from local brands in Northern Ireland are way too small on their own to sustain our investment. We will take certain advances and valuable conclusions with us: we have shown we can create and manage a separate local instance of our model, with local content and, in this case, PiggyPoints and coupons denominated in pounds sterling; we have shown that the local audience took to it too, and we've drawn the big conclusion that winning in the UK with a digital marketing model requires us to crack London where the big brands and agencies are located.

The good news is that the economic climate has picked up, and dot-coms are beginning to enjoy a new day in the sun. Amazon is already well known, but other relatively new global dot-coms are emerging, like Google, the search engine.

Many other names have come and gone, which regrettably include some of our own partners and suppliers, victims of the investment climate or of their own business models. But even the sceptics and laggards now see that the internet is here to stay.

Pigsback has achieved exceptional levels of engagement for all sorts of consumer brands in Ireland. I have every reason to believe that we can achieve similar member recruitment and engagement in the UK. I think we have earned a shot at the big prize.

———————◆———————

We convened a special meeting of shareholders to debate the next phase. As the environment improves, some shareholders are showing interest; we're friends again.

We had a turn-out of about ten shareholders at our Citywest office, a decent crowd by the standards of previous years. The mood in the room was buoyant, up for the UK launch. The general view was that their initial investment in Pigsback was always a punt on an international play, not just a local launch.

There was only one dissenting voice, that of David Madigan, a Dublin businessman and publican. He questioned the risk, wondering if we might jeopardise the value created in Ireland and the hard-won survival and success.

It was a very fair question, but the room was up for the punt.

———◆———

We now have this very large, loyal and engaged audience, plus the additional reach of Curly's Coupons. So it makes obvious sense for us to add relevant offerings.

Rory has led the latest charge with the launch of Pigsback Connect, a virtual ISP offering dial-up internet services. We have no wires in the ground – or indeed any ISP infrastructure at all – but have secured these services on the wholesale market via UTV Internet. The launch got a few more press headlines than we expected, all good. There isn't a lot of news or progress on internet offerings in Ireland.

We're offering people the choice of a pay-as-you-go internet service, charged on a per-minute basis, mainly replacing their existing service; or a fixed rate offering with 27 hours' access for €9.99 per month. Customers earn points to sign up and for usage.

We've had some good early traction, with over 2,000 members signed up in the first weeks and our sights on 10,000 subscribers in year one. Ultimately, the challenge is to secure a high-speed broadband offering from the incumbent, Eircom, as UTV Internet can't provide it. So far, our efforts to engage Eircom have fallen on deaf ears.

Valerie organised a launch party for Pigsback Connect, held in the trendy Pod venue, a former railway station on Dublin's Harcourt St. There was a great buzz before and afterwards. I wore a bright yellow Pigsback Connect t-shirt, as did our staff and many guests, and mingled with our invited members before the formalities. One member seemed reticent to engage in chat with me, but I thought nothing of it. He later told me that it wasn't until I got up to welcome people and say a few words about Pigsback Connect that he realised he was at the launch of a new ISP and not a dating service, and that I was the CEO, and not some guy trying to *connect* with him.

After our recent shareholder meeting to discuss the UK opportunity, we didn't waste time in getting a UK task force in place. It is led by Jo Malvern, who is likely to return to England in time, and Cillian Barry, a relatively new but already accomplished account director. I recruited Cillian after meeting him at a *Sunday Business Post* conference in Dublin on the future of media. I was impressed by his quietly confident and calm demeanour and felt that our clients would be too. Cillian has moved to London for personal reasons but has agreed to stay on in a dual-market capacity initially.

Plans are afoot to begin recruiting a small team in London. Jo and Cillian continue to monitor the competitive and market landscape and have completed an initial consumer test. So far, it has all been positive. At the trade level, they've been talking to prospective clients too and, there too, we're getting very positive feedback.

A couple of weeks into Cillian's UK tenure, we went for a walk in Hyde Park. It was a decent walk from Kensington Gardens to Marble Arch. We passed the great bronze statue of horse and horseman called *Physical Energy*, which the artist George Watts described as "a symbol of that restless physical impulse to seek the still unachieved". Whether we had fallen under its spell or whether it was just the endorphins and oxygen of exercise, we both departed bullish about our UK prospects. I left buoyed up to go raising money, and Cillian went off to find us new clients.

I am relying on Cillian on the sales front for now but need to find a replacement as he has made it clear that – for personal reasons – he is not in London for the long haul.

October 2003

I flew into London the day before our UK field marketing test at Liverpool Street train station, which kicked off at 7 am. The idea was simply to learn if and how consumers would respond to our marketing techniques and to our brand. It was quiet at first, but by 7.30 am, a steady stream of commuters started to emerge from the exits.

Little did they expect to be accosted by branded promotional teams in pink, eager to give them a stress pig and invite them to visit Pigsback.com. There was soon something festive in the air: taxi drivers were pulling up, honking their horns for a pig for themselves and their passengers, and even the local police enjoyed it, too, posing for photos with our staff.

We will use the data to extrapolate the costs of a full-blown London launch and then a UK national roll-out of Pigsback. We believe that the scale of this test is adequate to trust the conclusions, and Liverpool Street was chosen by Jo as representative of wider London. We measured how many sign-ups we got and listened carefully to the feedback from the promotional staff.

24/10/03 Email to Board (extracts)

Subject: UK Field Test - Liverpool St Station, London on 22/10/03

The Test

3000 pigs were distributed by hired promotional staff at Liverpool St from 7 am to 9 am, observed by our staff. There was a subsequent review meeting with the promotional team.

The Results

Very successful trial in terms of on-the-day reaction and subsequent sign-ups. [The report went into more detail] Team's reaction was excellent "one of the best, fun, women love it." Very strong female recruitment bias (4 times more likely to register than men).

The Learnings

A very clear picture emerges of what we can achieve through field marketing. Our 1m distribution target can be achieved in about 40 promotions, and we'll create excellent brand theatre and impact. We should recruit 100k members in the week of the promotions and, we estimate, double that through subsequent word-of-mouth. Given our budgets, we could possibly achieve up to 500k members in year one, making the 1 million member mark achievable certainly within 3 years.

January 2004

I am under no illusions that this is a big challenge, but it's an irresistible one, and I believe it's a risk we must take. Everything about Pigsback since its inception has been risky, so why stop now?

The team is enthusiastic about getting to the next step quickly. Cillian and Jo are now based in a small short-term serviced office off the Edgware Road, which is handy for Paddington Station and Heathrow. They are getting ready to expand the team as soon as they get the nod.

They continue to consult with brands, and the Irish team is helping to open doors too. The soundings are positive, and we're already getting some advance commitments. Jo has overseen further qualitative consumer research. Again the feedback is very positive.

Right now, the plan is for a pilot launch in London as soon as we can fund it, to be followed by a bigger UK roll-out depending on early market results and on further funding. We need €2 million to fund stage one, and I estimate we'll need a further €3 million to roll out nationally.

If the market response to the pilot is good, we should have every chance of securing a new investor or partner for the second stage. I'm hoping our existing investors, particularly Kevin Watson's group, Xtra-vision and Enterprise Ireland, will make a big dent in our target.

June 2004

A lovely plan on paper is proving much more challenging in practice. There were a couple of major early setbacks.

Firstly, Blockbuster, Xtra-vision's parent company – which has a big UK subsidiary – has made it clear that it won't be diverting any of its scarce cash to support our plans. Unfortunately, Blockbuster is struggling financially with a weak balance sheet and a business model with obvious challenges.

The Irish managing director and Pigsback board member, Martin Higgins, has battled hard for us, but to no avail. This is very disappointing from our biggest external shareholder, which I hoped would pay its share and lend the weight of its big British subsidiary to our launch efforts.

Secondly, one major player in Kevin Watson's group, a very experienced investor, has also said 'no'. He's of the view that this type of geographical expansion is highly risky, adding his opinion that we need much more money to fund a UK launch properly.

I countered that we ran the field test to get a clear and real measure of what it will take to achieve our objectives in member recruitment, the major investment area. I'm not sure who's right, but I don't realistically see us upping the ante any further at this juncture.

These were two big setbacks, but it looks like there have been enough other positives since. Kevin himself is committed to the idea of the UK launch and is supporting us financially. Enterprise Ireland, too, is stepping up support with grants, equity investment and preference shares, otherwise known as 'Prefs'. The agency's support also means tax relief for qualifying private investors on any investment made at this point, allowing them to recover approximately half of the investment. That's a very attractive incentive for private investors.

I have promises from family members and other individual investors, existing and new, and Karen and I will have to be seen to follow. It looks like this combination will get us close enough to go forward. We need it, as our investments in extra staff, the new server infrastructure required to host the UK site and marketing merchandise for the planned launch will soon be necessary if we are to hit our summer launch target.

Karen and I have been considering a move to London, the ultimate commitment to the UK. I'm hesitating, acutely aware that we mustn't neglect the bedrock that is the Irish business. But mostly, I'm conscious of the huge family upheaval. We're all-in financially already; do I really need to add this to the mix? I'm biding my time and looking for a strong UK MD.

August 2004

Our Irish revenue and profit have continued to progress in 2004, with turnover forecasted to be up 24% at €3.2 million, which should yield a healthy profit of €500,000 for the calendar year. That's very satisfying, given the sheer turmoil we faced in the first two years in particular. This profit is absorbed very quickly to fund the UK business, but it's very helpful.

There has been progress in our product offering in Ireland too. We've continued to add to our services and to execute well at a sales level. We've launched a new Pigsback Travel section, hoping to get a share of our members' spending on foreign travel. It features partnerships with Irish travel providers as well as the Gulliver international travel search engine. We've also launched Pigsback Tickets, a very promising concert ticket section launched in conjunction with Aiken Promotions.

The ancillary services are all delivering well for us: Empathy Research continues to progress well, and we won a new Empathy Communications contract with Nokia, already a top-tier client, full of enthusiasm for what we offer in Pigsback too.

In total, we're up to 34 people, a very sizable monthly salary bill, but in a new challenge, we're having to fight to retain our staff. We're one of the very few businesses recruiting and training in the digital space, but with more internet businesses coming on stream, there are moves to target our people. It's an easy strategy for a recruiter and an employer: we've done the hard work and have a justifiable reputation for the quality of our people.

I believe this year will go down as a year where dot-com confirmed its return in a big way. Six years after it was founded by Larry Page and Sergey Brin at Stanford University, Google completed a successful IPO in August. It has become the world's largest search engine, strolling past Yahoo! Having found a way to monetise its search activity through sponsored results linked to search terms or keywords, it is becoming a money-making powerhouse.

The e-commerce giant Amazon has expanded its product range well away from the books, which were at the core of its original mission. There's a lot of talk about TheFacebook.com, a new and in-vogue online community for friends. It's being called a "social network" and, in that sense, is not dissimilar to the very popular UK site, Friends Reunited, which has over 10 million members.

In 2000, the bursting of the dot-com bubble led investors worldwide to scarper. There were high-profile failures at the time. Boo.com was the high-end fashion website which ran out of runway in May 2000 after burning through $135 million of venture capital; Value America hit the heady heights of a $2.4 billion valuation post-IPO in April 1999 only to fail in August 2000; the search engine eXcite, sold for $7 billion in 1999, was off the radar by 2001; Pets.com, the portal for all things pet-related, lost its bite by the time the dot-com crash finished and its $300m in cash was spent; the grocery delivery service Webvan was a huge play, raising over $1.6 billion before crashing. On a smaller scale, MyPoints.com – one of the first comparable sites I researched and took some inspiration from – is now a faded light. Funding was the major issue, but some businesses grew too quickly, weren't market-ready or had the wrong business model.

If dot-com was precarious over those years, it still is, with more and more competition coming on stream. We did well to survive and become profitable. That's hugely satisfying, and it's down to some mix of dogged belief and inventiveness on the part of all involved. Now, with dot-com back in vogue, we have a chance to realise our full ambitions.

———◆———

December 2004

It has taken much longer than I hoped, but we're set to raise another €1.7 million, which, together with our positive cash flow from Ireland, will fund the initial London pilot. I am nervous about these funding promises landing, having just signed off cheques which will bring our cash to below €100,000. I guess it's the nature of these funding rounds: we have to trust in the promises.

Jo and Cillian are capable, calm and focused. They have a small but growing team which will do whatever needs to be done. Several of the Irish team have already moved or will soon move to London in various sales, communications and design roles. They are very excited to be part of the project and transfer the know-how and practices that have served us so well in Ireland.

There's an incredible buzz and the best of Anglo-Irish camaraderie in the office. They are a sociable lot, and the neighbouring Wargrave Arms does very well from a young team that is seemingly incapable of going directly home from work.

For me, it's like the Irish launch all over again, only this one's bigger – and this time around, we have a few more reasons to feel confident. We know the website works for a start; we have defined and tested the marketing formula, and the early feedback from brands is positive. That's a few more boxes ticked than we had in Ireland when we started out. In addition, I know we have Ireland as our fall-back, though I am trying not to think that way.

As well as driving revenue, the UK commercial team has the same secondary objective of generating enough 'soft content' for launch as we had in Ireland: the likes of the cinema two-for-one offers, the family restaurant promotions like a free starter or dessert at TGI Friday's and CD offers. We thought this would be easier, but for now, at least, some of those national brands who are enthusiastic supporters in Ireland are far less amenable and accessible in the UK. It would seem in some cases that they are trying to avoid any form of discounted promotion.

We will soon be up to 50 people on the payroll as we fill out the structure in both markets. It's a huge financial commitment, so there's no room for slippage on the funding front. We're very bullish in our revenue and profit forecasting at home in Ireland, where a very nice business is emerging. Thankfully, the sales pipeline in Ireland suggests that 2005 will kick off strongly too.

January 2005

I met a very senior player in Viacom, a huge player in media and entertainment in the UK, with a massive network of outdoor and commuter advertising sites.

Viacom owns Blockbuster. Blockbuster owns Xtra-vision. Xtra-vision owns 20% of Pigsback. So I was hoping for a bit of collaboration, at least some kind of preferred access to spare advertising space. It turned out that my host had no interest in our common shareholding ties and, worse still, he wasn't buying this "internet craze" (his words), even questioning the credibility of internet advertising spending figures published by the IAB – the Interactive Advertising Bureau – in the UK. It was a particularly negative encounter.

To cap a bad week, advanced contract negotiations with Match.com, the dating company, were abruptly stalled when their bosses realised that we have a separate ticket-selling partnership in Ireland. Match.com and Ticketmaster.com are both parts of Interactive Corp, the huge internet conglomerate, which is obviously paranoid about any competition affecting their companies.

One bad date followed another, it seemed. It took most of the weekend, but once again, I dusted myself down.

April 2005

Yesterday, the board formally approved our London launch. Pat Shine quipped philosophically that "it will be any plan but this one", alluding to the unpredictable and volatile journey ahead.

The UK is a huge and happening market for digital, with broadband in 50% of homes and online marketing growing by 60% in 2004, according to the IAB. All of the directors were excited about our plans.

Again, Karen and I have led by example, borrowing for the first time to fund our follow-up investment of €100,000. Enterprise Ireland stepped up in a big way. They did ask for a guarantee of completion from us before releasing some funds, which JD and Kevin agreed to underwrite.

Kevin has played a very important part in the funding round, backing his belief in the UK expansion. The balance was made up of family, as well as some existing and some new private investors.

24/4/05 Investor email {Extracts}

Hi All,

Funding and UK Launch

We have confirmed the UK launch ...the summer period will be relatively "soft" with a ramp-up in marketing activity from September.

Ireland Q1 2005

A very strong performance by the Irish team in Q1, in particular in revenue and margin generation. Profits before grants are up 63% to €182,000. Pigsback and Empathy Research were the key positives, with Empathy Communications on track for the year. We have also successfully sold the Spring edition of Curly's Coupons which will be recognised in May. Site activity was encouraging throughout the quarter. Our marketing activity for the remainder of the year will focus strongly on recruitment ...The outlook for the year is positive. We expect our revenues to exceed our budget at €3.85m and a profit of €740k is budgeted.

Michael

Getting everything ready for launch in London has been a lot of hard work all-round. The team deserved a lift and the mood certainly picked up when we announced a team outing to London in a few weeks.

The teams in Dublin and London have been working together but many haven't actually met so it serves a couple of objectives. The prospect of Johnny Mc leading from the front, guitar over the shoulder and revelry on his mind, is a welcome one right now.

Johnny has had a lot on his plate recently, suffering from a procession of kidney stones, gallstones and sleepless nights. His work can be a haven for him, but he needs to mind himself. My father-in-law Gerry is fond of Johnny too and seems to have a heightened sense of his vulnerabilities. He understands how important our double act is and reminds me to be there for him. He is 100% right.

Gareth is also a bit tired, but for very different reasons. He's into his sixth year of new sets of challenging targets and now I'm asking him to put his shoulder to the UK wheel too. Many of our Irish clients are part of international companies and can facilitate introductions and meetings. Some are active themselves in the UK market. We need every help we can get.

May 2005

A day in the life:

– I was pleased to get confirmation from Gary that Ronan Keating has agreed to MC the official launch night of Pigsback in the UK in the autumn. The fee is fair enough. He's ideal for our UK female target audience.

– We confirmed a couple of new recruits, one in the communications area to assist with the copywriting of emails, offers and competitions; and another who will oversee the entertainment category for us.

– I had a very difficult phone call with my correspondent in Tesco, who completely missed the point and wasn't interested in hearing more: "we don't want another loyalty scheme". Bummer.

– I managed to squeeze in a 40-minute jog in Hyde Park, a different perspective on things. It was a sunny day, and the park was at its best. I love these London park runs.

– We confirmed a new and bigger office in the same serviced building in Winchester House, just off the Edgware Road – should be good for a year anyway.

We are making progress. We need more. I am working on my calm.

Press Release, June 6th, 2005 {Extracts}

Subject: Pigsback launching in the UK

Pigsback.com brings its successful club of consumers and brands to the UK in June .... The company has already secured UK partnerships with Blockbuster, UGC cinemas, eBay, CD WOW!, Figleaves, lastminute.com and Virgin Wines among others. The company plans to spend over €6m launching its model in the UK with an initial focus on the Greater London area and a gradual expansion to other major urban areas, with a field marketing strategy.

Michael Dwyer, CEO, added: "Pigsback.com is a clear market leader among Irish online media .... We aim to take this new [Empathy Marketing] sector to the UK, where a niche position in the €650m online marketing market, presents ample opportunity for us."

The announcement came from Johnny Mc late last night: *'Curly was born in the UK at 10.22 pm on 13/06/05. His little legs are a bit shaky, but he is taking his first steps.'*

There was little time to spare, as today we completed a final field test with the distribution of 7,000 stress pigs by a team of four promoters, each wearing Pigsback t-shirts, fleeces, caps and shoulder bags laden with pink pigs. They were accompanied by an actor in a pig suit. It made for great theatre and hardly a commuter left without a stress pig in hand and a broad smile on their face.

Registrations were in the hundreds, a slightly lower conversion rate than the 2003 test, but satisfactory nonetheless. The plan now is to launch in early July, with a view to a full ramp-up in September.

In addition to the stress pig distributions, we have joint activity ready to go with very large brands like Lastminute.com, CD WOW! - who have a 1.4 million member list - and Handbag.com. We also have plans for a five-day advertising campaign in the Metro newspaper (the free commuter paper with readership estimated at one million readers).

The full-page colour ads are very striking, and good fun, featuring our stress pigs in various guises:

o   Notorious P.I.G. (complete with earphones and heavy jewellery)

o   Pigs can fly (strapped into his seat on an aeroplane)

o   Hambo (a Sylvester Stallone take)

o   Pig out (a fine-dining take)

o   Happy as a pig in shoes (Curly upside down in bliss, surrounded by designer shoes)

As we recruit members through street promotions and advertising, we'll run 'Refer A Friend' campaigns to make the most of our new membership.

We've commissioned some pre-launch trade PR activity and got a good response. We're trying to get the brand and concept into the trade magazines and business pages, read by our clients. There was a feature piece in the *Sunday Times*, no less, profiling the business and the planned launch.

———◆———

My day started at home in Naas with very tired eyes as the alarm rang at 6.15 am. It picked up with a good mid-morning session on content and communications plans with Jo and her team in the London office. They feel our product is close and their excitement is growing about what Curly has to offer in London.

Our sales pipeline is encouraging with strong indications and commitments from brands totalling nearly €350,000, ahead of the launch. My main concern remains the recruitment of an experienced and networked commercial director, but the recruitment agencies have come up short on a replacement. With Cillian about to move on, this is getting beyond urgent now.

In a very welcome distraction, I accepted an invitation from my brother JD to lunch at Richard Corrigan's Lindsay House with Richard himself and Brough Scott of horse racing fame. JD has been in London for well over 20 years and has built a strong business and friends network around London, including in the Irish business community, and horse racing circles, of course.

Brough was charming and generously shared his own story as an amateur jockey as well as his exploits in marathons. Richard can be a larger-than-life character but he's also a very serious, ambitious and committed businessman. It was a treat and very welcome.

———◆———

July 2005

Last week, on July 7th, four Islamist extremists set off four bombs in London. Tragically, 52 people were killed and hundreds injured in the '7/7' terror attacks.

One bomb was ignited close to our local Edgware Road tube station. Fortunately, none of our team was injured although one of our staff members was among the commuters who made their way by foot through the tunnels of the London Tube to safety.

The bombings have profoundly affected life in London, throughout the UK and in many parts of the world. We were scheduled to run our first full-on stress pig promotions at Tube stations in London in the coming days but have pushed back our field activity until it feels safe again. The mood in the office has inevitably taken a dip.

Like the 9/11 attacks on the US in 2001, the bombings have made the world feel less safe and less optimistic. I can only admire the resilience of Londoners, determined to get on with their daily life and not give the terrorists the slightest victory.

We waited for a couple of weeks after the attacks, then hit the streets. The cheerful teams and stress pigs were welcomed by commuters. Footfall was down after the bombings, and our access was understandably more restricted by anxious station staff.

We plan to distribute 350,000 stress pigs across July and August, and a further 650,000 in the autumn roll-out. We're ploughing on but we don't quite know yet how this delay and the new environment will impact the distribution of our stress pigs and recruitment of new Pigsback members.

We decided to send a promotional team to the larger cities of Manchester, Liverpool and Birmingham to spread the word and test reaction further north. The team visited train stations and office blocks, including the council offices in the strongly Muslim suburb of Dudley in Birmingham. One staff member took offence, complaining that distributing our stress pigs was inappropriate during Ramadan. At no point did we ever consider the question of the sensitivities of the Muslim community to our squeezy pigs. It simply didn't arise during testing. We consulted where we could and, anecdotally, concluded that the vast majority of Muslims were unlikely to take offence.

I got a call from one tabloid journalist looking for a comment. On the advice of our PR company, I sidestepped it, deciding that it was better not to get embroiled in the controversy. We are, after all, seeking to do business with quite conservative brands and companies who would mostly consider discretion to be the better form of valour when it comes to such issues. This won't stop us from giving out our pigs, but we'll be more sensitive about where we do it.

Halifax and NatWest banks have banned the centuries-old piggy bank in response to sensitivities. That feels like an overreaction to me.

September 2005 Board Report {Extracts}

The company has made huge progress in its launch in the UK.

Our membership target of 200k is in sight. After a delayed launch, revenue booked or committed is already over €400k with a further €300k in the pipeline (target €700,000 in 2005, and €1.8m in 2006). The best sectors are e-commerce, entertainment and travel. September and October advertising and promotions will bring further progress.

The biggest issues we are encountering are:

o   *Attracting senior commercial talent quickly enough*

o   *Slowness and conservatism in FMCG brand decision-making.*

It is a fair summary and wouldn't be bad for just six months in the UK market. Membership and site activity are very encouraging. The big brands and FMCG, in particular, are slower to reel in but we are at various stages of advancement with good brands like L'Oréal, Goodfella's, Britvic, Danone water and dairy divisions, Kerry Foods, Innocent, Pernod Ricard, Kellogg's and Weetabix. Not surprisingly, I've found myself in the middle of many of these conversations. That's fair enough but I fear that I am doing neither the UK commercial role nor the group CEO role particularly well.

———————•———————

Our official UK launch event in Café de Paris in Leicester Square went off well, with Ronan Keating as host. Denis Taylor, the snooker player, was an invited guest and did an impromptu and excellent comedy sketch.

We had a great attendance from clients, some shareholders and various friends of the business. My parents, Alf and Elma, attended too, and there were a few celebrities. The coverage wasn't anything to write home about, with the exception of a Ronan Keating-led piece in OK! magazine.

It's a proud moment to get to this point. I enjoyed it and put in a better performance from the stage than at our Irish launch. With so much at stake, I am not the most relaxed just now but I don't think anyone could have told that on the night.

Meanwhile, in Ireland, our 200 or so Pigsback.com clients are incredibly 'sticky', meaning they are loyal and we lose very few from one year to the next. We are expecting more good growth for this year, which will be our fifth consecutive year of growth since launch, and there's more to come in 2006.

Empathy Research and Empathy Communications will both have done well in 2005 and we will have successfully completed two editions of Curly's Coupons. In another effort to leverage the Pigsback.com brand into new areas, we have launched a Pigsback credit card as an affiliate of MBNA.

I love producing the black card with a big pink pig on the front at restaurants or shops. It never fails to put a smile on the face of a shop assistant or waiter. It somehow brings Pigsback into the real world too. Members earn 1 PiggyPoint for every €1 they spend as well as a big sign-on bonus, so they've been quick to sign up. We should hit 5,000 new cards in the first 12 months.

The biggest threat I can see for the business is the churn of our senior salespeople. They get tired of the same challenge year after year, and there is a lot of opportunity in the broader digital market for well-trained commercial people.

After that, we need to improve our traction with advertising agencies, which are now beginning to play a bigger role in the digital advertising market. We have sporadic success with agencies, often client-driven, but our revenue models and our view of what is effective for clients in the digital world are both poorly aligned with the agency approach for now. That's not easily fixed.

Blockbuster's lawyers have been giving me a big headache. We agreed with Enterprise Ireland to put a new shareholder agreement in place before they release the final part of their funding, the €500,000 in preference shares. These are critical to complete this round.

This requires the signature of a new shareholder agreement by 70% of shareholders, including Xtra-vision via its Blockbuster parent. But their lawyers put the brakes on wherever they can, showing zero sensitivity to us and to the urgency of these funds.

It has been a bit of a nightmare but eventually, Xtra-vision's CEO intervened strongly to secure their signature and get the new shareholder agreement over the line. They've dragged this one out for months, far too long, with a careless disregard for the consequences. It has left a very bad aftertaste.

Enterprise Ireland has since released the funds, which is a huge relief. That means the vast bulk of the funds raised for London is now in, albeit most of it spent or committed.

Despite the new funding, AIB, our main bank, wants to limit its exposure to us and has cut our overdraft facility. They're seeking a personal guarantee (PG) from me for the remainder, which is a new request from them and one I am resisting ferociously. PGs now seem to be the order of the day with banks. I abruptly closed a recent meeting with Anglo Irish Bank when they insisted on one. "Standard terms of business," the man said.

Karen and I have invested at every stage of the development of Pigsback and have enough on the line. What's the point in having the protection of a limited liability company if banks insist on PGs? It's a complete contradiction in terms.

And, of course, the bank looks to me and to me alone, on behalf of all shareholders, to offer them this soft landing. I'm already the most exposed shareholder, so they won't be getting their greasy hands on whatever we might have left by way of value in our home should things go wrong.

December 2005

We will record another year of progress in Ireland in 2005, with revenues of €3.6 million and operating profits of €700,000. It might have been even better but sales weakened unexpectedly in November and December, costing us about €200,000 in profit.

We continue to get much-appreciated recognition for our efforts. We won two awards at the prestigious Golden Spiders Awards – Ireland's Internet Oscars – earlier in the year, including the Internet Hero award, which I was honoured to accept. The trophy is by far my favourite; a large leggy bronze spider. Awards have a role; they give the team a lift every time.

How are we doing? It depends on the day or who's answering the question. I know my glass is always more half-full than half-empty.

In the last six months or so, the UK team has achieved about €500,000 in sales from about 100 brands and has recruited 150,000 new members. They're all significant numbers by any objective measure and very good traction, but they are behind target by about 25%.

It hasn't been an easy introduction with the shadow cast by 7/7, a weak commercial structure in the UK, and the bigger brands with the bigger budgets proving so tough to reel in. We've applied the brakes to spending, pending clarity on further funding. But the UK has already cost us €2 million, and we know there's a lot more ahead of us.

We're forecasting €1.8 million in UK sales in 2006, and we have visibility of about 20% of that right now. It hasn't been plain-sailing – and the UK was never going to be – but it feels like there is enough traction, enough positives and enough belief all-round to keep going.

When I zoom out and look at the broader communications environment, it augurs well for our sector. Internet access and quality, notably broadband, have come a long way since we started the business, although still very underdeveloped in Ireland.

There are question marks over the effectiveness of TV advertising, with so much channel hopping, recording and digital distractions. In this new online world, brands need new channels of communication and new channels to market.

I'm meeting people every week in positions of influence in media and marketing, getting our message out and listening to the market. We're in the right space. We just need one or two key people, time, money for the roll-out, and focus.

———◆———

January 2006

In Richard Corrigan's new London restaurant, Bentley's Oyster Bar & Grill, it was fairly quickly ordained that Hazel Hutchinson would be our UK corporate finance adviser. I had just met Hazel at an Irish Women's Network event at the Irish Embassy in London. JD and I were among the few males present, along with Hazel's husband, Jim O'Hara.

Hazel runs her own boutique corporate finance business in Richmond. She's been in the English 'system' for many years now, is very polished, good fun, and clearly commands a lot of respect. Jim lectures in Irish history at a university in London. He is president of the Irish Cultural Centre in Hammersmith, which does really important work for the Irish community and for promoting Irish cultural connections in London.

I told Hazel all about our business, its progress, challenges and plans. She seemed to warm to it straight away, with the Irish affinity helping.

In the intervening weeks, she has already secured an invoice discounting facility for Pigsback from a UK lender I'll refer to as ID Bank, solving one part of our funding challenge. She is now engaged in raising the equity funding we need to take the UK to this next stage. That would be some relief.

In further progress at the corporate level, we've just announced the appointment of Kevin as chairman of our company, a role I have been covering up to now. I am happy to cede it to Kevin, whose reputation, experience and commitment to us speak for themselves.

Since he first invested in the business in 2001, he has been an active director, and he is a key supporter of our UK market entry. Kevin knows more than I do about funding, growing and realising investments. All in all, two very positive developments.

First quarter UK revenue feels like it will be at about 80% of target – again, good numbers - that's important - but still a bit shy of plan. The business is mainly with the mid- and lower-tier brands and many of the campaigns are performance-based, where we are being paid by the activity, be that bookings, sign-ups or traffic generated for the brands. Campaigns are delivering well against their expectations, which is a good sign.

Ireland is still strong, but there's a new concern on the horizon: the German supermarket chains Aldi and Lidl are starting to eat into the grocery market. One of our own Empathy Research surveys shows that 60% of Irish consumers are shopping in discounter stores at least once a month. Many of our FMCG clients are justifiably nervous about the future, and beginning to budget accordingly.

———◆———

Meanwhile, my own personal investments in the business, combined with a relatively modest salary, are putting an increasing toll on our personal finances. We're moving to consolidate loans into a single bigger mortgage. My brother Harry runs a mortgage and investment brokerage called Moneycare in Monaghan town. He has had to work hard for this one, the business casting a shadow over the exercise as company accounts were requested to show that my income was reliable.

It's all about property in Ireland right now, and digital ventures such as ours with our intangible assets are not doing it for Irish banks. We secured the funds in the end, but I'm now mortgaged up to my official retirement date, which is not something I had anticipated at this stage of my life.

The weekly commute to London can be a bit stressful too, but I've got no choice in the matter until I get the UK sorted and one or two more senior people in place. It's not ideal, but two or three nights a week are manageable. In some ways, these few days away help me to ring-fence the business stresses from the family. It needs a strong firewall, however that is achieved. A bit of London can be energising too. I have decided to upgrade my hotel choice; the Marylebone Hotel has lifted my mood. Some savings are just not worth it.

———◆———

My heart sank as I read the sub-heading on the front cover of a well-known Irish business magazine, which is out there selling on newsstands nationwide: 'The Dotcom Entrepreneur who has blown €5m,' it read, beside my mug shot.

I did an interview around the New Year period, and it has just been published. It hurt, deeply. I said as much to Brian Skelly, the journalist who wrote the article. But the article itself was fair and balanced - the headline was the problem. Brian was sympathetic, and clearly, he didn't write or approve the headline.

It played to the old dot-com crash narrative: 'look at the eejit in the dot-com world,' kind of thing. The magazine and its editors owe me nothing, but I felt it was particularly insensitive, bordering on reckless. Our business is relying on new funding from investors – some of whom may read this article – to keep an ambitious show on the road, with 50 employees, many suppliers and a bunch of shareholders.

I suppose I've sensed that there could be a price to pay at some point in playing the PR game. Why should I expect an easy ride, whether fair or unfair?

In the article, Brian referred to the speech I made at the Golden Spiders in December as "a typically stubborn performance", which was kind. I had misread the room of revellers with a long speech that addressed matters relating to policy on entrepreneurship and broadband investment. Why should I bother?

But Brian knows the business and me, saying:

"Pigsback has been a hard graft all the way....The business has got no support from banks or VCs and that it exists at all is testimony to Dwyer's refusal to lie down and his own outstanding ability to persuade literally scores of private investors to part with their cash.....In many ways, Dwyer is an old-style boss. He's got a strong work ethic [and] prefers to spend his weekends with his wife and three children in his Kildare home and expects his staff to have a life outside work too. He's not into the trappings of business either, such as flash cars."

He then quoted me striking a realistic note in relation to the UK, saying: *"England is a very difficult market and you need to be on top of your game and have staying power. But I suppose if there's one thing we have in spades, it's staying power."*

The pressure on me was evident too when I said: *"I proved my commitment in no uncertain terms by emptying my pockets."*

It's true, I couldn't be more committed - financially and emotionally. I feel I'm at the mercy of the deck. I wouldn't recommend it. No wonder I'm sensitive.

———•———

March 2006

It does feel like we are on the verge of a significant breakthrough in the UK with real progress from the bigger brands. We have secured campaigns from Garnier, part of L'Oréal, Green Isle, Carpe Diem, Punch's, Rustlers and Grolsch, all of which are on the site in the first quarter of the year. It's enough to give the UK members their very own Food & Grocery Newsletter, something we think will help win over new brands.

We're also at various stages of advancement for Q2 with Danone's dairy and water brands, Carling, Fox's biscuits, Unilever, Bacardi, Jacob's Creek, Lucozade, Kellogg's, RHM, United Biscuits, and Nestle. We're not there yet – it's a hard slog getting a decision through these companies – but these are signs of progress.

In another breakthrough, we got news that the Daily Mail Group has agreed to a pilot partnership. Both the *Evening Standard* and *Metro* websites will carry a link to a co-branded Pigsback website with all of our offers and content.

Both papers will email their members monthly with co-branded Pigsback content including offers, competitions and rewards. This is probably the best endorsement we've got to date, elevating us in the eyes of the British public and among the agencies and brands. It's also a very useful one in our sales and investor presentations.

———————◆———————

May 8th, 2006

I boxed up my worries for a day out with Karen and my mum and dad. It felt like a kind of consolation from the Gods. We were attending DCU's inaugural Alumni Awards ceremony, and I was among the recipients, as the nominee of the Business School. 'I hope I don't let them down,' I thought privately but gratefully accepted the invitation.

I looked forward to the day out and wasn't one bit disappointed. President Mary McAleese was presenting, and she delivered some well-chosen words and thoughts on education. She quoted from Seamus Heaney on the Ireland that was and referred to her own experiences meeting the beneficiaries of DCU's Access programme, which gives grants and assistance to students from disadvantaged backgrounds to prepare for and attend DCU.

We have seen the Access students and graduates in action first-hand in Pigsback, in summer placements, and in one particularly successful recruit. These are lifetime impacts made by the Access programme. It was quite inspiring, and even Karen, a graduate of rival University College Dublin, warmed to DCU that day.

My Dad met Seán Óg Ó hAilpín, another award winner and one of Ireland's – and certainly Cork's – most talented and best-known hurlers of the recent generation. He was most friendly and affable and seemed to enjoy Dad's stories about Cork, the North Mon (the well-known former Christian Brothers school they both attended) and the Blarney Road, where Dad grew up.

I met Gay Byrne too, a proud Northside Dublin resident and supporter of the Northside DCU. He has recently been appointed chairman of the Road Safety Authority. It seems like a brave move for a man of his age to pin his reputation to such a challenge. But it's typical of the energy and attitude of Ireland's greatest broadcaster. Of course, I slipped him my business card and ten days later we had a meeting with the CEO of the Road Safety Authority, thanks to Uncle Gaybo.

It was a welcome break and welcome recognition from my alma mater but in the background, I couldn't help but contemplate the insecurity of my venture and my fortunes. Part of me felt like a fraud: here I was accepting an award knowing that my business's fortunes and reputation could cave in at any time.

Rory Duggan, my right-hand man for six years, has given me his notice. It wasn't a big surprise but it certainly wasn't a vote of confidence. With no exit in sight, the opportunity cost for someone of Rory's calibre gets higher with each passing year. He's heading off to a big role in a hotel group, which includes the Morgan and Beacon hotels in Dublin. Rory is a top-class operator and served us very well indeed. I wish him well.

We have appointed a very capable financial controller, Paul Baily. His first job will be to manage a tight cash situation.

There's a lot going on and the team has been showing signs of stress. Johnny Mc was unwell for a while, but he's back in operation. I need him to come through strongly as he's taking over responsibility for the operations side of Rory's old role, adding to his technology portfolio.

Gareth too is weary of the same grind. He has been leading the charge on the Irish business for a few years now, with constant pressure to make the numbers. He has a good team around him, which continues to deliver, but I can't ignore the signals.

If I can get the UK commercial leadership sorted, that will ease the pressure on me and on Gareth too. Fortunately, that process may, at last, be about to bear fruit.

To lift the spirits, we took the team to Bunratty Castle and Folk Park in Co Clare, a gesture of support to our new regional tourism clients in the Shannon region. It was a pretty efficient exercise, as usual, renting cottages and flying the UK team to Shannon Airport on a Ryanair special. It was a classic Pigsback session – a bit of leisure activity, dinner and drinks, guitars out as Johnny Mc took on his rock star persona. There was plenty of singing and dancing, Skittle Brew, and, of course, a few dalliances (which I cast a blind eye to) and sore heads the next day. Nothing like it to clear the air.

The board recently signed off a new funding document seeking a minimum of €3 million to see the UK through. Hazel's investor feedback is most encouraging, positioning Pigsback as 'a relatively developed opportunity with a profitable and strong Irish base and some decent green shoots in the UK'. She has been meeting London VCs and private equity groups. The reaction has been very positive, which is timely encouragement. I suppose I've been in the trenches and inclined to focus on the negatives in my own head, taking all we have achieved in Ireland for granted and tending to discount what, more objectively, is good early traction in the UK.

Despite my self-flagellation for missing UK sales targets, for a start-up and completely new brand and service, we've actually achieved very decent levels of revenue, consumer awareness, sign-ups and of site engagement. Our client numbers are very high too and we're making progress, slowly and steadily, with the larger brands.

Jo summed it up well with this email:

To: London Office

Subject: Happy Birthday UK {Extracts}

In the last 12 months, thanks to a great deal of hard work from everyone involved, we've brought in more than £850k in revenue, recruited more than 270,000 members, issued more than 82 million PiggyPoints and sunk goodness knows how many pints of beer at the Wargrave!

The next 12 months will, I'm sure, be equally challenging/frustrating/exciting, but we'll be well-positioned to make the most of it and will no doubt be celebrating further milestones in the years to come. The first pint is on me at the Wargrave after work, Jo

If we could crack the senior recruitment challenge, get a few more top brands over the line in the UK, and bag the funding, we'd be in a very different place. What a relief it would be to proceed with that greater certainty. We would be able to recruit with confidence and invest again in marketing and in our people. We have overdue salary reviews to address and need to do a better job pre-empting staff departures in Ireland. I may even feel comfortable drawing down €60,000 in accrued pension funds that I have been reluctant to withdraw from the company for the past couple of years. These things can't be put off forever.

Another AGM has come and gone with a handful of shareholders present and no exchanges of any note to report.

———◆———

My weeks can get a bit cramped these days; it is stressful at times but fulfilling for the most part. Here's one such week:

Week commencing June 7th, 2006

Monday

Morning meeting with the CEO and COO of Independent News and Media (INM)

Full afternoon of meetings.

Leave the office at 7.30 pm.

Tuesday

Up at 5.20 am for my 7.20 am flight to London.

A full day of internal meetings and conference calls.

Return that same evening.

Wednesday

Get to Dundalk from my Kildare home for 8.30 am.

Speak at a conference alongside Frank Ryan, the head of Enterprise Ireland, who also hails from The Town.

Depart for Leopardstown Races for an evening meeting, a bit of fun and networking, at the invitation of Pat Shine.

Home late.

Thursday

Up at 6.30 am for an 8 am breakfast with Nokia in Foxrock.

11.20 am flight to London. Two funding meetings until 7 pm.

Play a poker tournament with JD.

Ring Kerry for her birthday.

Friday

Two senior interviews in London.

Lunch with a client.

Office briefly.

Get to Heathrow for a 4.50 pm flight.

Home for 8 pm.

Enjoy the weekend.

That was a busy one but there's not much let-up. I book the window seat on the Aer Lingus flight home, knowing I'll be asleep within minutes. So many times, I've woken up and the refreshments trolley has just passed me by when all I want on earth at that moment is a cup of Barry's tea and a KitKat. I mostly pluck up the courage and ask anyway. It's the simple pleasures.

July 2006

Mad, mad, mad!

That's the only way to describe the breakthroughs of the last couple of weeks. We've signed an outline agreement with Hotbed, a kind of high-end London investment club, which is expecting to invest between €2-€3 million in our business. That's Hazel's work.

We've done a deal with Blockbuster to buy out its shareholding in Pigsback! That will simplify life. Hotbed has already agreed to take up its share of the Blockbuster stake and the rest has been offered to existing shareholders, tied to further investment in this round.

Last, but not least, I've found and appointed a very commercial UK managing director, Brian Harrison. Brian, coincidentally, is ex-Thomson Directories and was endorsed by Kevin Watson, our chairman, without hesitation, which is very reassuring. And Brian is bringing a strong commercial director with him in Gavin Hughes.

That was enough by way of positive developments for us to book a family holiday in France for the first two weeks in August. I'm hoping to come home rested and free at last to do a better job, playing the role I should be playing, of group CEO.

In my absence, Brian hit the ground running and his arrival has given a lift to the UK team. What a positive it is to see a senior UK executive with an excellent track record put his faith in Pigsback's UK future and fill the leadership role.

There's still not much room for error but at last, we have the right man. Brian has already impressed the board with straight talk and determined plans. He's clearly excited too. Gavin's role as commercial director was another key missing link in the UK. That's progress, indeed.

I've also got a message from Hotbed that they have already secured commitments of upwards of €2.5 million from their investors. That's big news and an even bigger relief. The valuation of around €20 million is encouraging too. How did that suddenly happen?

Having marketed the buy-back of the Blockbuster shares to investors in a way that was linked to the sale of new shares, we'll take in a further €680,000 in new share subscriptions. Some employees took up these shares too, showing both serious commitment and belief in the future. Kevin has been able to buy into a bigger stake in the company, which is good for everyone.

Taking Blockbuster out eliminates an unaligned shareholder. The local Xtra-vision management team did its best, but Blockbuster's UK arm and US head office were of no support. Quite the contrary. We can all move on now.

That's quite the turnaround in a few short weeks.

———————◆———————

Meanwhile, I've had some interesting distractions, meeting a couple of London entrepreneurs through Hazel. The first was Sinclair Beecham, founder of the fast-growing sandwich chain Prêt A Manger and more recently the man behind the new Hoxton Hotel. The Hoxton is purpose-built and high quality, with a vibrant comfortable lobby, bar and restaurant area, and free Wi-Fi. The rooms are comfortable, well-equipped, not too big, but functional. This type of hotel is so lacking in London. He lets the product and service do the talking, but sadly for Pigsback, he has no need for a marketing budget. He's a very impressive and driven entrepreneur. If I was to take something from the encounter, it would be to focus on product excellence and simplicity.

Then there was a meeting with Simon Woodroffe, who warmly welcomed us onto his boat on the Thames near Chelsea. Simon founded the Yo Sushi! chain and has appeared as a start-up investor on the Dragon's Den television show. Like Sinclair, Simon was genuinely interested in my entrepreneurial story and very encouraging too. His barge-like boat was *interesting*, and I didn't ask, but I hoped he had a house somewhere too.

———————•———————

We cleared the final UK investment hurdle with written confirmation of Enterprise Investment Scheme approval from HMRC (the UK Revenue Commissioners), securing tax benefits for UK investors. Hotbed were instantly on to transfer some €3.5 million.

I could feel myself palpably relax. It's a massive relief, even if the stakes have got much higher. We have now raised over €10 million in investment since the foundation of the company, about €8 million of it in cash.

———————•———————

Jo has been doing a great job on the marketing and communications brief since the UK launch. Our membership and site activity numbers are improving all the time. We're currently recruiting members at the rate of about 5,000 per week, having peaked at about 8,000 sign-ups when we were spending most heavily on marketing. We're back giving out our pigs again and have brought over our giant inflatable pig from Ireland and used it in Canary Wharf and Leicester Square.

We've just completed a brand upgrade, Project Curly, a large and ambitious project to study our Brand Proposition (or what we offer members, mainly, but clients, too) and our Brand Positioning (or how people perceive us). Jo directed the project, galvanising the strategic and creative energies of the UK and Irish teams and managing the consumer research through every stage.

I'm not a believer in frequent brand redesigns, which sometimes pander only to the ego of the marketer and enrich the design agencies, but research-based upgrades are a different matter. I wasn't an easy boss for Jo on this one but, to her credit, she navigated the different demands and got us there.

I felt it was my job to defend the Irish market with its fun positioning. In Ireland, we are big enough, relatively speaking, and have spent enough to just be what we want to be and to express it emotionally. For most of our journey, that has been expressed using the strapline *Pigsback.com – Get on it!*

Gary Joyce has said that our brand positioning is simply: "You're on the Pigsback". That is certainly true for Ireland, but the large UK market, where we are a mere minnow, seems to demand that we nail our colours to the mast in a more functional way. We are a marketing service that gives members personalised offers and rewards in return for their custom with our partners, and they have a lot of fun along the way. So we give back, economically and emotionally. We have just unveiled a new strapline, which I think expresses the evolving spirit of Pigsback and will work in all markets: *You get more back with Pigsback.com*. We haven't touched the Pigsback logo typescript itself (and won't), but we knew that we needed a contemporary expression of our brand that would work internationally.

Our members are responding well to the new version of our character, Curly. He is the introducer of brands, the trusted guide and a bit of welcome relief in their day – though some felt he was a bit sinister in his original guise! Many iterations later, we have finally unveiled the new character, and consumer research certainly says we've cracked it.

Jo and the teams in both markets have already implemented a programme of activities to launch the new strapline and character. One initiative allows members to dress up the new Curly online by dragging and dropping hats, facial features, clothes and other guises. Their personalised Curly will greet them from the homepage every time they visit.

We have a 'Curly around the World' competition up and running too. This encourages members to book their holidays via Pigsback and bring their squeezy pig with them. We've had hundreds of members in Britain and Ireland sending us brilliantly posed photos of Curly from the Great Barrier Reef to the Great Wall of China, most world capitals and from boats, beaches and hotels all around the globe.

The latest addition is 'Pimp My Pig', asking members to dress up their stress pigs and to send us photos. The reaction in number and quality of entries has been phenomenal and very amusing.

For all that the rebranding project was complex and painstaking, it gives Pigsback the essential brand foundations for the future, wherever that takes us. If recent levels of brand engagement are anything to go by, that future is bright.

4

For Whom the Bell Tolls

Palpably relax? That didn't last too long.

Activity is picking up under our new UK MD Brian Harrison and commercial director Gavin Hughes, but the sales team is reporting that the business environment in the UK has got more challenging as 2006 has progressed. The UK has had a stop-start year, with some good months and some poor months. Companies are now even slower to commit spending across the board.

In Ireland, revenues stuttered again in October, as they had in September. We are facing a year of 5% or less in revenue growth at home, with profits static. Any further revenue shortfall is sure to directly hit the profit line at this late stage of the year.

Gareth, now our Ireland MD, puts it down to a few factors: the trickier environment for grocery brands or FMCGs, with the growth of Aldi and Lidl; the growing role of agencies in the digital space where we are not adequately represented; and the flight of ad budgets to Google and Facebook, both of which are on the radar of most brands now. We're trying to address what is in our control.

An immediate concern was dropping the news of weakness in Ireland to our new investor, Hotbed. I contacted their main man without delay and – with Brian in tow – we agreed to meet for a pint after work near their offices in London.

In fairness to our Hotbed counterparts, there was no pressure. Brian's line was welcomed: "at least the UK is coming together." We had a couple of pints of ale. They listened but claimed to be unconcerned, suggesting that we'd have time to get it all together by April. That will be their first communication to their investors on the performance of Pigsback.

———◆———

November 2006

I got an email out of the blue, followed by a phone call: "Hey Michael, my name is Sean O'Leary, and I'm ringing from Bell in Canada."

It turns out that Sean O'Leary is a senior vice president of Bell's New Ventures division in Canada. As I gathered myself through the initial formalities and heard enough to satisfy me that this was for real, O'Leary told me about Bell, one of the world's largest telecoms and media companies.

"My relatives are from Ireland. The name's a bit of a giveaway."

We laughed. He's selling himself, I thought. This is interesting. As calmly as I could, I talked about Pigsback.

"We've been around since 2000, light years ago in the dot-com world! What differentiates us is our empathy marketing approach. We're very pleased with the progress we are making in the UK, and it's nice for us to have an established position here in Ireland – it gives us the test bed and a solid platform. May I ask what you have in mind, Sean?"

It was like I took these calls every day. O'Leary spoke clearly in a mild North American accent: "my colleagues and I see your empathy marketing approach as the future of smart advertising for the consumer packaged goods sector, and we want to take it to North America."

Holy Moly, I thought. Consumer packaged goods, CPG, is the North American equivalent of FMCG, so that's a big vision.

He continued: "we're familiar with joint ventures in Bell. In fact, Canada's biggest ISP is a joint venture between Bell and a US company. We're interested in companies that are innovative, but we want a long-term relationship where our partners provide, develop and support the business model and intellectual property."

"Okay, Sean, I think we'd be interested in looking at this with you, alright."

"Let's advance this reasonably quickly, Michael. My boss, Ron Close, is keen to pop over in January with me to meet you and your team. Ron is the President of Bell New Ventures."

"Sounds good. Goodbye so, Sean."

I knocked on the wall beside me, a mutual signal between myself and Johnny Mc that either a crisis needed attention or, more frequently these days, that something good had happened. He could sense something in the air. I was fit to burst.

"Where will I start? Is your passport up-to-date? North America, here we come."

I was half-expecting John to be sceptical, his counterbalancing reflex. Not today.

"Wow! That is some phone call." A beaming smile broke across his face.

"Trust me, John: this could be the game-changer."

There are echoes of our ill-fated negotiations with Australia Post in 2001, a partnership deal that fell at the final hurdle in the wake of the dot-com crash. But there's a big difference here: this project's sponsor Sean and his boss Ron are the top dogs at Bell New Ventures. They make the decisions.

Johnny Mc and I resolved to keep a lid on this one. There is no deal yet, but it is exciting. This is potentially the kind of licensing model that could fulfil our international ambitions, at last.

———◆———

December 2006

Our home was burgled and ransacked last Friday afternoon, which put a premature end to my travels for 2006. I was in London but did the quickest turnaround imaginable to get back home within hours. Our neighbours had offered their support, and the Gardaí had come and gone, but Karen was understandably bothered and in fear of a repeat.

It forced me to take a good break. It was welcome, as I was beginning to crumble under the fatigue of a challenging year.

I penned an email to the team to mark the year's milestones and to maintain an upbeat note:

To: all@pigsback.com

Subject: 2006 Milestones {Extracts}

– A new chairman in Kevin Watson

– A new UK MD and Commercial Director in Brian Harrison and Gavin Hughes

– Many other great arrivals, incl a new Account Director in Ireland and a new Accounting Team in Dublin headed by Paul Baily

– Huge growth in personnel to leave us just shy of 70 employees as the New Year approaches

– A very successful €5m funding round incl the buy-out of Xtra-vision

– The arrival of Hotbed as our single biggest external shareholder

– A strong new non-executive director in Douglas McArthur OBE, representing the Hotbed interests

– A brand overhaul

– Over 400k members recruited in Britain

– 20% national brand awareness among British females

– Great new Zones developed from Entertainment to Parents & Kids to Mini Breaks and more to come

– Some very healthy competition between Ireland and Britain for weekly users and weekly Clicks (Ireland continues to lead, just about)

– The repositioning of Empathy Research with the products to be a serious direct-to-client player

– A potentially interesting international development (too early to comment)

My 20+ years working tell me that all of us are very fortunate to be part of an international pioneering venture in a fast-growing and fast-changing space. I think this can only get more rewarding for everyone as time goes on. We've also made sure that everyone has a piece of the action in their share options, which, if everything goes to and beyond plan, could have a nice bit of value in them. Michael

It wasn't plain sailing but, looking back, we actually achieved quite a lot. I may have made it sound a little too easy, choosing not to dwell on another year of heavy investment in the UK. Kevin and I also sent a fairly positive note to shareholders in December but we chose to hold back on the Canadian development until the news was more solid. As chairman, Kevin focused on the investment news:

Our biggest challenge entering the year was to secure additional investment to finance our UK development, and we are delighted to welcome the Hotbed group as new shareholders. We were encouraged by the strong interest in the business from potential investors and the many positive comments on our business model, management and future prospects received during this fundraising process. We were successful in raising more money than initially sought and delighted that the fundraising supported our business valuation....... We now have the resources, team and structure in place for what I am sure will be a very successful 2007.

For my part, I focused on the challenges and a little hint of what might be coming down the line:

2006 was a challenging year in many ways, but it was one in which we have laid a much more solid platform for our very ambitious growth plans for 2007 and beyond....turnover will have more than doubled in the UK in 2006, but is still relatively low at c.€1.1m..... [the] team is now recruited and in place and is expected to hit the ground running from the beginning of the year.

In Ireland, the many distractions of the year, and some recruitment difficulties, will have left us shy of our customary growth. We will have progressed both in revenues and operating profit by about 5% and will have maintained a 19% EBITDA margin [earnings before interest, tax, depreciation and amortisation]. The team and focus is in place to restore strong growth in Ireland in 2007.

With much still to be achieved in the UK and Ireland seeking strong growth in 2007, we are loath to dilute our focus too much. However, with a deeper and more settled structure in place across the company, I will turn some of my attention to other markets in 2007.

January 2007

Glass half full: 2006 might have been my best year's work so far. The numbers aren't pretty, but we secured the funds we need for now, recruited Brian and Gavin in the UK, and have Canada teed up nicely. North America could be the game changer. Canada is a great opportunity with a great partner. And what a business model: Bell bears all the costs, adds enormous credentials, and paves the way in all regards. It beats the brave but thankless UK strategy of going it alone. You'd think I could relax a bit now, but no.

Glass half empty: Gavin and the UK sales team are continuing to encounter a negative shift in business sentiment and, with it, a squeeze on marketing budgets. The talk is of a recession looming, which is making brand commitments even harder to extract. The Hotbed team is aware of it but would prefer us to spend the money on marketing as intended. I guess we won't die wondering.

Marketing investment works at consumer level and has tended to work well for us in winning clients over too. We have very little choice, but where do we draw the line? Ireland has its challenges too, but we have a strong and established position, which I expect will deliver again in 2007.

It's not for the faint-hearted. We're closing off 2006 accounts showing another year of over €2 million in losses, more than we planned. It's all down to the slower-than-planned progress in the UK business. We've already put quite a dent in the cash raised last year, much of which was spent back-filling earlier commitments and funding a ramp-up in marketing in the autumn.

Our cumulative investment to date – or losses, to be more blunt – stands at a pretty massive €9 million since the company was formed (about €7 million in cash). The investment thesis is that Pigsback will be worth a multiple of that amount should we succeed. If we succeed.

I met Hazel, our corporate finance advisor, today. We talked about the slower-than-planned UK market progress, the increasingly challenging business environment and the cash burn before going on to talk about the North American opportunity.

She ventured that if we come out on the right side of these opportunities, the business could have a value in excess of €100 million, confirming a previous view she offered. Her positivity was welcome indeed, but I'm more hopeful than confident. We need to get out of the blocks quickly in 2007. I am back on the road again.

———◆———

When asked by Hotbed for a few words for a newsletter aimed at budding entrepreneurs entitled 'Advice for Entrepreneurs from Entrepreneurs.' I didn't seek to dress it up. I planted a message of a long, hard battle ahead for Hotbed and its investors, as well as the potential audience of entrepreneurs.

"Be ready for nothing less than the Grand National: one challenging obstacle after another on a very long course. When you're feeling the pressure, and you will, focus as much as possible on the next obstacle. Try to enjoy the thrill of the ride, and remember, in the enterprise race, if you're still running, you're winning."

———◆———

I had a couple of trips to Canada before Christmas, and Sean and Ron made a reciprocal visit to our London office in January. I brought Kevin and Johnny Mc with me on the second trip to Montreal, where we were negotiating the key points of our consultancy and licensing agreements. Our hosts were welcoming and very straight-talking negotiators. Kevin and Johnny Mc both enjoyed the trip, with Johnny Mc striking up a friendship with one of Bell's lawyers, Gordon, as only he can. Turns out they both have an affinity for Irish whiskey – and both had their best brave faces on the next day.

We have already registered our first North American revenues, part of the consultancy agreement, which takes immediate effect. The licensing agreement with Bell is pretty much there too, and I certainly don't anticipate any issues.

Bell will launch Pigsback in Canada using our trademarks Empathy Marketing, Pigsback, PiggyPoints and PiggyBank and, of course, our tech and know-how. We have agreed to a revenue share, giving Empathy Marketing Ltd 6% of gross sales generated by the Pigsback Canada site in perpetuity, as well as consultancy fees, to ensure we are not out of pocket at any stage.

The agreement covers the US market too with a similar structure, requiring Bell to launch Pigsback there by 2008 or lose its rights. Bell has the right to buy out two-thirds of our royalties within five years for CA\$ 9 million in Canada and CA\$ 35 million in the USA.

A pilot launch planned for September is critical. We're getting ahead by planning and preparing as much as possible. The Canadians are very positive, expecting what they call a 'presumption of success' to confidently lead brands and agencies to come on board early. It stands in contrast to our UK experience, where, going it on our own, we were greeted by agencies and many big brands with something more akin to a 'presumption of failure'.

Bell is one of Canada's largest companies. We've seen the brand in the marketplace and its tower blocks of offices. They don't enter into agreements like this lightly. They are serious people, and it's a serious plan. We'll give it our all, and maybe that presumption of success will be well-placed.

Perhaps this is the true dividend from our expansion into the UK: we've invested heavily in time and money in our tech development, brand development and our team. All of those are paying off already in our planning and execution in Canada.

What a pleasure it is to work with a partner of this scale too, and with the Bell team. Straightaway, our management costs and overhead are now spread across three markets, thanks to the consultancy agreement. If success looks anything like what's anticipated, the future in North America is very bright indeed.

———————◆———————

April 2007

We are well into 2007, and it's a mixed bag. Gareth and the team in Ireland did well in the first quarter of the year, recording strong operating profits, which is a relief. Canada is moving along nicely, and we anticipate a significant contribution to group overhead soon. Britain is still tainting the overall picture, however.

UK sales started very poorly in January, a particularly painful month, though February was better and March was good. After investing heavily in UK marketing, we are set to book net losses of nearly

€500,000 for the quarter. We'll have to moderate the marketing spend from here on in, but I will need Hotbed's agreement on that.

Despite the increasingly cautious climate, we've made some good progress with the big brands. Unilever is upping its investment with us after "exceptional results" (their agency's words) for a Dove campaign, Tetley has agreed to a campaign, and new big brands like Diageo, Robinsons, Cussons and Sara Lee are all close to sign-off for the second half. Another very big name, P & G, is in discussions too. So it's happening, just very slowly, and for relatively small budgets every time.

———•———

We got a great response at all levels to an email looking for four secondees to go to Canada. That the young and single would want to embark on this adventure is no surprise.

Much more significantly, Gareth has put his hand up for the international leadership role based in North America. That's ballsy from the man who has risen right through the ranks to the position of MD Ireland since joining Pigsback, and whose wife is expecting their second child in a matter of weeks. With a decent salary and leading a relatively strong business at home, he might not have bothered. Then again, the young marketing executive I recruited in 2000 wasn't looking for a cushy life. He had worked in New York for the Irish Export Board and internationally as a brand manager for Jameson, a relatively safe haven he was prepared to leave for the Pigsback adventure. It makes sense that he would be drawn by the international and by the big corporate partner on the other side of the table, Bell. *Director of international development* it is for Gareth and an initial six-month secondment to Toronto.

The plan is that he'll return after bedding in the Canada business and then seek out other opportunities in new markets, possibly using the licensing model we're deploying in Canada. If Bell opts for the USA, as is its declared plan, I hope he'll go there too for a couple of years to get that one up and running.

With one move comes others. Jenny Taaffe, a senior and proven account director and team manager is chuffed with the opportunity of becoming MD Ireland. It's a big promotion for Jenny and has got a ringing endorsement all round.

Jenny has been a remarkably reliable and progressive contributor to the business over the past few years. She is a strong, determined manager, and clients respond very well to her. She is in the Gareth mode of commercial marketer and consultative seller and is more than capable of moving up the ranks. Jenny's senior managers move up a notch too, so everyone is happy.

Unfortunately, it's not all upbeat. Johnny Mc's mother passed away quite suddenly and he is once again under the weather in a continued pattern of health worries that have besieged him for a couple of years now. He's taking an extra couple of weeks off and needs adjustments in his lifestyle and work patterns. The most obvious example is his commute. He just can't keep spending three hours in his car most days completing the round-trip from Thomastown in Co Kilkenny to our Citywest offices in Dublin.

———————●———————

Londoners have taken to the Pigsback brand in big numbers: we have over 500,000 UK members now. Our squeezy pigs are highly visible on office desks throughout London.

Our new Pigsback UK offices are at 100 Dean Street in Soho, just off Oxford Street. It's as buzzy as London gets, lined with pubs and restaurants, with the Groucho Club just a few hundred yards from our front door.

Soho and the neighbouring Charlotte Street area of Fitzrovia are at the heart of London's media district. There are loads of theatres and restaurants nearby too, in Piccadilly, Chinatown, Leicester Square and Covent Garden. Soho is particularly cheeky and fun. I think we fit in and the team loves it, spoiled for choice by the bars and venues around them. It is still a handy hop to Paddington by Tube from Oxford Circus; I have the timing down to the minute.

Curly's Towers, as the team have named our new office, is a big improvement on the tired serviced offices off Edgware Road. I wanted to put a pig dispenser at the front door, where you could insert a coin, do a quick twist and release a squeezy pig. Then I learned that the team had found its own way of dispensing pigs, lobbing them from the office window to the crowd below on Friday evenings. Some rules are there to be broken.

———————●———————

We had a full turnout of directors for our first board meeting in our new offices, including our new board member Douglas, the OBE, appointed by Hotbed.

The pattern hasn't changed much: Ireland is managing to deliver quite well but progress in the UK is too slow. The UK site is now looking more and more as we envisaged, with a great mix of brands. The problem is that they're all paying smaller fees than we hoped for and contracts are coming through much slower than we need.

Losses are already higher than forecasted. We invested heavily in marketing in the first quarter of the year, but the levels are more prudent now, which all parties have agreed to.

Product development efforts continue too. Stephen Rappaport, one of the UK account directors, mobilised his team to recruit offers from local businesses. It was an effort to improve content and traffic to the site. It created a lot of excitement among the businesses and the team, but there's no revenue of any note in it yet.

We've launched a new 'Live' area on the site called Curly's Lounge, featuring impromptu competitions, quizzes and the latest and most popular offers. Webcasting, or live video, is all the rage and video is certainly set to play a much bigger role in the future as broadband becomes universal. Innovations like Curly's Lounge will give us an avenue to develop and test new applications.

Bell is planning to spend CA\$3 million on a pilot launch in Calgary and a subsequent CA\$46 million on a national launch. Not to mention the USA, an outline plan for which is clearly spelt out in the contract.

In Gareth, I have one of my most trusted and capable lieutenants on the job. In addition, we have so far appointed four secondees, who will spend six weeks each in Canada as 'advisors' supporting and training the new local team, overseen by Gareth. They are chuffed and every one of them will do a great job.

The advisers are already working under Jo on our knowledge transfer system, a kind of A-to-Z of operating the Pigsback.com model, which we are simply calling 'Passport'. It's an easily accessed and read repository of all the key business tools, processes, sales documentation, case studies, etc, that we use at Pigsback.

The partnership with Bell and the North American growth opportunity could be transformational for us. These kinds of developments are few and far between. It's good for the spirit.

———◆———

June 2007

This week we had a launch event for some Toronto-based brands and agencies. There was a good turnout and lots of positivity. What a difference the big partner makes. When I declared to the room that a new business needs "lots of graft and lots of craic", the place erupted. Graft, I discovered, means a bribe to your average Canadian. And of course, there's Irish craic and there's crack… that speaks for itself.

Gareth and I got to a baseball game at Rogers Centre in Toronto last night, a first for me. The Toronto Blue Jays beat the Los Angeles Dodgers 12 – 1 in front of a crowd of about 24,000 people. It was a very relaxed affair with beer and hot dogs. We're learning the culture and we're certainly making friends.

Sean told us about a recent baseball game he attended, where he was caught on the big screen working on his Blackberry, oblivious to both the game and the attention of the camera. Only when the crowd started to boo him did he realise what was happening and put the Blackberry away.

Earlier today, President McAleese addressed a large assembly of Irish Canadian businesses and associations, which Sean and I attended. She had already unveiled the Famine memorial in Ireland Park, where immigrants once alighted on the Toronto quays from the horrendous journeys fleeing famine at home. She literally brought tears to the eyes of all assembled, recalling the almost 40,000 such immigrants who arrived in Toronto in 1847, when the Canadian city's own population was just 20,000 people. They would disperse across the country but the massive generosity of the locals in assisting with their plight was striking. It stands in contrast to the ambivalence in many quarters of modern Ireland to the plight of immigrants and refugees.

The president also referred to the economic ties between Ireland and Canada and went on to talk about the Northern Ireland peace process, as well as the confluence of factors that have moulded Ireland and the Irish worldwide. Quite a tour de force.

Later, Sean took me aside. Ominous, I thought. He wanted to give me the heads-up that Bell and Telus, another huge Canadian telco, have announced merger talks in competition with three private equity bids that are being prepared for Bell. Sean is taking the attitude that it is business as usual. I'm not convinced and don't believe Sean is either.

I don't know what to make of it. It could amount to nothing or it could change everything. It is impossible to know but I have a bad feeling in my gut.

Our team has just moved in and we have only just announced the deal with Bell, attracting a lot of media interest. I brought Gareth into the loop on the news before leaving Toronto. As my Air Canada flight taxis towards the runway, I'm left thinking that Canada may not take off for us after all.

Only time will tell. For now, all we can do is take the lead from Sean and Ron, who want to get on with the launch as planned.

————•————

We have just completed the migration to a new technology platform, V3. It was a challenging and delayed migration but we're there now and it's a huge leap forward; V4, V5 and maybe V6 will be written on V3, such is the advance. We got there and I kept the message to the team positive.

To: all@pigsback.com

Subject: V3, a platform for the future

Hi All,

As you know, V3 is the tech platform for a new chapter for Pigsback including Canada and hopefully other international markets. It is an entire overhaul and upgrade of our platform into the latest computer code (asp.net) to cope with greater scale, give us more flexibility and meet the potential demands of multiple markets. It incorporates a new design we can be proud of, all just in time for a big communications and marketing push.

In time, we will realise the full extent of the design and technical challenge posed by V3. It has been an outstanding effort by everyone involved and I hope you are suitably proud of what you have achieved with a relatively small team in a relatively short period of time. Most importantly, the quality of the end product is right up there with the best of the web.

Thanks to everyone

Michael

I'm off for a family holiday to the sun.

———◆———

I came back from holidays to learn that the Bell crew is visiting Ireland and the UK in the coming days, a welcome sign of the continued commitment of their senior people to our plan. They are here to learn from our teams on their home turf. All other priorities were put on hold for a few days, as we set about building relationships.

We played golf at the luxury K Club in Kildare, followed by dinner, when we were joined by Jenny. Tuesday was Ireland early and London by evening time, where Bentley's served up its top-class fare and a warm welcome from Richard Corrigan. Wednesday was spent with Brian, Gavin and Jo in the London office. I'm feeling a bit bloated and missing my normal jogging and exercise.

And guess what? Tomorrow night, it's more of the same.

———◆———

September 2007

Right now, I'm a living battleground between optimism and pessimism. Pigsback's Irish business is still doing well and we started TV advertising last night. However, the UK business remains stop-start in an increasingly tough environment. It is patently at a crucial juncture and any further slippage will require a serious reappraisal.

The outlook hasn't been helped by a 'run' on Northern Rock, a UK high street bank, as customers queued to withdraw their money amid rumours that it is facing liquidity problems. The Bank of England had to step in to support the bank.

Canada is exciting and – listening to our very bullish Bell team – the USA could well be on the cards. But the corporate skirmishing at Bell has not abated. So here I am thinking, on the one hand, we could be looking at a huge opportunity and valuation in a few years; but on the other hand, we could have two out of three duds on our hands.

———————●———————

October 2007

It's our 13th wedding anniversary today, October 14th, and I have just opened a beautiful card from Karen. I'm 34,000 feet high in the air on my way to Toronto. I've just watched the movie *Once*, which I happened upon in the in-flight offering. What beautiful music and a touching story set in Dublin. I was feeling pretty emotional before it, reminded of how lucky I am in so many ways. Now I feel proud to be Irish and somehow more determined to face whatever is ahead of me.

I'm off to Toronto and Calgary to witness, support and review our progress there. The launch in Canada has been a very positive story to date. Our guys have excelled in supporting the venture, with excellent early results. We have a great Canadian site and content, and very good buy-in from consumers and clients, including a few FMCGs, banks, mobile phone operators and leisure brands. Compared to the UK, it's been a cakewalk. What a difference a partner makes.

———————●———————

Our Canadian marketing team, led by Kristina Hayes, is having a ball with the new Curly and with Bell's budget! They are bringing Pigsback advertising to a whole new level with the very striking and amusing use of a few real pigs. We had the pigs at the cinema, in the restaurant and at the gym. We have brought them in their massive pen to the streets of Calgary with Canada's own new giant inflatable pig in the background. I acquired a Stetson and was interviewed for Calgary TV, the local TV station, on October 15th. They made the most of every piggy pun, while I was happy to thank this dynamic, happening city for its welcome. Kristina explained the working of the model for the local Canadians and brought plenty of local brands into her commentary. The clip made its way to YouTube, where it can be found by searching 'Pigsback Calgary'. We're already making waves in Canada and recruiting members beyond expectations.

I wasn't long back in Ireland when I got a call from Sean. Bell is set to be taken over by a private equity consortium for about $50 billion. It will be the world's biggest buyout. The deal has been approved by Bell's board and is ready to proceed to the formalities of due diligence and regulatory approval. The private equity guys are already calling the shots. Bell New Ventures, along with all of its fledgling companies, is to close as soon as practicable. Pigsback Canada will be funded only as the agreement between the companies prescribes - for another three months. It must be wound down or taken over by us or by another party.

 So much for the excellent launch results, my journey across Canada, Calgary TV, our licensing agreement, Project Passport, Gareth and Deirdre Lambe's relocation and the enormous collective efforts of an extraordinary group of Canadians, Irish and English. It's a very sad day all round. Sean and his boss Ron and their colleagues will lose their jobs. The end of Bell's funding, in all likelihood, means the end of our North American dream.

There is a brief window of three and a half months, including the Christmas break, to secure funding to take the Canadian business on ourselves through a new partner or venture backer. Sale to another party is unlikely due to the dependencies and franchising arrangement between Pigsback and Bell.

I rang Gareth in Toronto to prepare him for the news and to get him to put his arms around the Pigsback Canada team, clients and business until we worked it through a little more. We would at least explore going it alone.

After an initial shock, Gareth left to let the news distil overnight and to prepare for the staff briefing the next day. He called me back around midday, 7 am for him, and typical of his mettle, he had digested the situation and was up for the day ahead.

The following evening, I got a call from Brian, our UK MD of just 14 months. "I know the timing could be better MD, and I don't want to do this over the phone ..."

But he did.

He couldn't refuse the role of head of new media at *The Telegraph* newspaper group. A big job and, no doubt, a very big package. His recent appointment to our board, his share options package, and his many words on being 'up for it' and tough enough, counted for little in the face of a big number at the Telegraph. A rolling stone, I thought, but I couldn't blame him. I was helpless to respond.

As this forgettable day drew to a close, my doctor called me with results of a recent blood test and ECG. My cholesterol, at 6.4, isn't responding to my lifestyle changes and the ECG results confirmed an irregular heartbeat. For good measure, one of the liver indicators is rising a bit too consistently. No wonder. I need to pay a visit, he says.

I have suspected my heartbeat is irregular for the past few years, but it hasn't bothered me. I am quite fit and running makes me feel alive and well. I will try to get to the bottom of the problem, with a clear diagnosis and plan. That might take the worry away. I do need to watch out for myself.

Thankfully, Johnny Mc seems to be back to his best. Small mercies! And Jenny is doing a very good job in Ireland too and the quality of her team is very impressive. She's a winner when one is needed.

The news of Brian's departure from the helm in the UK was a blow. Our future there is looking less and less auspicious. For now, I'll support the UK commercial director Gavin and marketing director Jo as best I can. Gavin is stepping up to the challenge. Jo has been a stalwart, a mature and steady manager and influence. Gareth takes over the UK business in the second quarter of next year, which is the current likely outcome.

I am battling with all the hope and will I can muster. I do need to keep the board and team onside. I need to watch out for my health too.

———◆———

Bell funded the Canada launch, lent its market knowledge, constructed an organisation, teed up the clients and agencies using its brand's power, spent amply, and now will walk away, writing off its investment, oblivious to the opportunity lost. This is pretty typical of big corporations. Even the tiny minority of Bell's employees who are aware of the venture will soon have forgotten. We are mere minnows in this game.

I try to tell myself that Canada could yet be a business-transforming opportunity – if we can find the funds. On that front, we're getting some encouragement from Hazel and from Ron, the outgoing Bell New Ventures boss, who's showing an interest in a personal capacity. We're trying hard, but it feels like a long shot.

———————◆———————

January 2008

I've been easily ruffled over the Christmas period. There is stress just under the skin. I feel anxious, a little dizzy, with a nervy feeling on my left side. I have to stall sometimes before the end of a sentence, in case I black out before I get there. I haven't yet, thankfully, but I'm sure some people have noticed.

It could be the irregular heartbeat, perhaps a trapped nerve. I don't know, and I try not to go there. Most likely, I tell myself, it's psychosomatic, a bit of panic induced by stress.

For the new year, I have given up caffeine, and I am determined to give myself more time to rest and repair. On this note, it has been a great Christmas and New Year break so far, and we're on a Ryanair flight to Faro in Portugal for a week's holiday *en famille*. Just what the doctor ordered.

———————◆———————

After the initial shock to the system, I have settled energetically into 2008. There's a big funding challenge facing us if we are to salvage anything out of Canada and cover our requirements in the UK and Ireland. I'm working with Hazel and another potential corporate finance partner in Dublin. February and March will bring meetings and, hopefully, progress.

We have challenging plans for Pigsback this year in Ireland and the UK, across product development, member activation, sales and people. We're up to nearly 80 staff, excluding Canada, so we need everyone focused. I'm trying to mind our cash and I know we'll need more funding to see the job through.

Meanwhile, there are early positives in the UK, outlined here by Jo:

To: all@pigsback.com

Subject: Record-breaking week in the UK [Extracts]

Last week we broke 3 records in the UK – more than 1.5 million Brand Engagements with nearly 37k unique site visitors and more than 68k unique members actively engaged across email and the site.

This is down to the combination of the relaunch of our marketing programme, netting us more than 8k new members last week, the new email delivery and some innovative site initiatives around some great commercial content.

Nice work, everyone!

May 2008

The UK had a very strong first quarter (up 133% year-on-year), before a dip in April. There were new campaigns from Comfort, John Frieda, Typhoo, Simple, Yoplait, Kalo, Aquafresh and others. The FMCG sector is now showing its potential and accounting for 41% of revenues. It's the culmination of a lot of good work last year – but it feels like too little too late. We have been feeling a nervousness among clients for at least a year, first in the UK, now in Ireland. Sales teams in both markets are facing major cutbacks, frozen budgets, and redundancies in marketing departments. Recession it is, officially. The finance departments have literally taken charge. Overall, our net losses reached €950,000 in the first four months of the year, €300,000 worse than budget, driven by a shortfall in sales, mainly in Ireland. We have had no choice but to very actively reduce costs in both markets to adjust to the new reality and to protect our cash.

We know we won't achieve revenue growth in the poor economic climate, so UK headcount has been the inevitable first target, but Ireland will be hit too. We're cutting salaries, starting with mine, and pushing out any discretionary expenditure. We know we need to raise funds in double-quick time to shore up our cash. Our costs are already coming down significantly – and will drop sharply in the second quarter as a whole – but not quickly enough. Our very latest estimates, integrating all cost savings achieved and planned, indicate we need about €1.2 million in additional funding to see us through in the UK and Ireland. That's now my focus, and I've started to address it with our shareholders and with Enterprise Ireland.

In the middle of it all, we have got an offer of $3 million to fund Pigsback Canada. It sounds great, but the new funder is insisting on a senior convertible loan note at the top company level: Empathy Marketing Ltd. This would give the funder seniority over all other equity and shareholder debt, with a juicy interest rate on top. In addition, they would have an option to convert the loan note to equity at a later stage, should they choose.

It just feels like they are asking for jam on all sides. It would be a huge gamble to accept such an offer just as the world economy seems to be going into meltdown. I don't think we'd get through due diligence right now anyway and have gracefully declined the offer. We just can't be distracted any further by Canada, given the difficult circumstances closer to home.

That's the end of the American Dream, for now, anyway. We made a valiant effort to fund it, but it wasn't to be, with so much other background turmoil to preoccupy us.

The closure of Pigsback Canada was sad for all of the team there and for all of us on this side of the ocean too. The Bell folk were decent to staff in Canada and honoured all of their commitments to Empathy Marketing. A venture for which we justifiably held out so much hope has come to this abrupt and ignominious end. I could cry – and probably should – but that's not going to serve anyone too well right now.

Gareth assumes the position of UK MD from June 3rd. We are still showing progress and are so close to the new budget figures, with just over €100,000 in revenue per month on average in the UK this year. That's not bad in its own right, but it will take us some more time to reduce costs to match those levels, and that's hard to do without damaging sales further. A classic Catch-22. It will be a relief to let Gareth take it on and to hear what he makes of it all.

In Ireland, there are more client budget cuts, and we continue to lose staff to what they perceive are better opportunities with larger digital companies and agencies. It all contributes to lost sales at a difficult time.

Our Empathy Research business in Ireland, though relatively small, is the one bright light so far this year. It is Ireland's biggest online research panel, and the mix of a robust service combined with good value to clients is attractive in the climate.

July 2008

I had to report to the board that "we got a predictably poor response in the current environment to our interim funding, reflecting the mood among private investors in this climate". In a throwback to our 2001 funding, the vast majority didn't respond.

Inspired by our Canadian experience, we are exploring a senior convertible loan note of our own to fill the remaining funding gap in Ireland and the UK. It will give the providers of these new loan funds seniority, a coupon or interest, and a right to convert the loan to equity at a later point. It seems to fit the times and is a way to incentivise and reward investors who are prepared to stick their necks out for us in this climate.

Early indications are that we have enough commitments from those close to me to trigger the drawdown of a first tranche of grants from Enterprise Ireland worth €180,000. It's a useful start, but we need another €500,000.

Board Report, July 31st, 2008 [Extracts]

...the digital advertising market in Ireland was down 15% ... we expect worse in May and June ...trading is particularly difficult ... outlook very uncertain ... large deals are difficult to achieve... significantly cut our forecasts to year-end... British revenues, too, have experienced severe budget cuts over the past few months ... As a relative newcomer and a small player, this kind of environment is more difficult for us ... Another round of redundancies in the UK last week ... Cost cuts in other areas continue in both markets .... as much as possible without counter-productively impacting revenues and member experience.

The recession and complete loss of momentum are buckling. Marketing and advertising budgets have been chopped mercilessly by small and very big names alike, with a more severe sub-crisis in our biggest area, FMCG. On top of the advances of Lidl and Aldi, Irish FMCGs have borne the brunt of Tesco's centralisation to the UK, as well as the consumer move to private label products and deals. We still have a great client list, but there's a lot less money going around.

I hate redundancy announcements and the individual discussions, but sadly I'm getting more used to them. We are as generous as we can be and try very hard to safeguard people's confidence: we apologise, and take all the blame, but emphasise what they've learned and how this has readied them for the emerging digital world. Despite the economic backdrop, our leavers are finding jobs very quickly in the emerging digital world with the help of a few years in Pigsback on their CV.

The remaining team could not be fighting harder, but I know the cutbacks and redundancies are energy-sapping at every level. The lack of resources to create some 'go-forward-ball' is very dispiriting. Surely, this is as gruelling as it gets.

———————•———————

We've just had one of our better board meetings. There was a good balance struck between the short-term figures and discussions of our customers, products and teams.

I have learned over time that it is better to address the preoccupying financial matters upfront. When I don't do it in this way, I see it in the body language of the accountants pretty quickly, shifting around like there is itching powder in their drawers.

We shared our new forecasts for this financial year and next with a big dip in revenue. It is the same in both markets, Ireland and the UK, and the new numbers are appropriate to the prevailing economic and market conditions. We are planning another level of cost-cutting involving staff in London, support staff in Dublin and another dip into the marketing and rewards budgets.

This will leave us with no above-the-line marketing and rewards only for those members who are transacting through Pigsback. It is like driving on empty, but we need to do it for a while. Gareth is getting stuck in and putting a brave face on it, targeting UK profitability in 2009.

It has been a time for resourcefulness too. We are planning to relaunch the Curly's Coupons booklet in Ireland. It brings in some extra revenue and profit but a lot of extra profile, too, at a time when we can't spend on marketing.

We are also hoping to pilot-launch Pigsback Local, an advertising service for small businesses like hotels and restaurants, and we are looking at a very recession-appropriate community concept under the working title MoneySavingIdeas.ie.

For all of the turmoil, my belief is still very strong in our company's core empathy marketing ethos, in the strong and loyal following that the Pigsback brand has built, in the innovations that lie ahead of us, and in the Pigsback.com business model itself.

On the upside, Karen and I are blessed to live in a fabulous old farmhouse-style home on about four acres in County Kildare. It has got a naturally beautiful garden with large beech trees and a weeping willow leaning over a stream which runs idyllically through the garden and adjacent to the house.

There's great colour at times, with a prominent cherry blossom whose brief bloom is worth the wait every year. There are swathes of snowdrops at the base of the old beech trees from mid-winter, clumps of daffodils in the early spring and pockets of bluebells from late spring. It can be balmy in summertime and wild in winter storms.

We love the respite it gives and the lifestyle that comes with it. The girls have ponies in our wooden stables, bought and borrowed. There won't be any more purchases. They appreciate fully what they have and willingly put in hours of stable work and ride out every day. Karen and I do our share of the feeding and mucking out too. There's nothing like it as a counterbalance to the pressures of Pigsback.

I'm a novice on a horse and a danger to myself, but I'm enjoying a bit of hacking on the roads and have done a small bit of cross-country. Mucking out a few stables is a decent workout, and being close to horses is therapy in itself. There can be a deep connection between humans and horses that has to be experienced, an empathy of its own kind. I have sometimes dwelt mindfully, patting a pony or leaning my forehead against its neck in a few moments of deep calm. I'd swear the horse knows he's giving back, drawing my anguish and stresses.

When I was much younger, I dreamed of retiring to a stud farm with thoroughbreds in the fields beside me, studying bloodlines in my spare time, and maybe racing a few. That dream is well and truly on ice, but hope springs eternal.

The more immediate question is: can we keep what we have, including our home? We're under far greater pressure than I expected at this stage of my life. I put more at risk than I intended to or than I should have. I'm not getting any younger, and I certainly don't feel like I am edging any closer to my dreams right now. There's a lot of financial pressure accumulating all around me, personally and professionally. On the personal front, our very large mortgage is due to move out of the interest-only phase. My mortgage broker brother, Harry, is on the case, applying to delay the inevitable. We were so lucky to get a tracker mortgage; I know that, but I can't put off the day of reckoning forever.

Both of our cars are clapped out. Mine is a pretty worthless 1997 Land Rover, which I love, but I can't trust it to start. I am still getting over the sunroof leaking onto Kerry's Communion dress; it's a credit to her that she only told her Mum a few days later.

———————◆———————

September 2008

Days roll into weeks, then months, and we'll soon have put another year in, but there's no end in sight. At times I see the positive: well, we're still here. Soon it's a new year, a fresh start with a new budget. At other times, I'm more despondent: there's another year gone that I won't get back, lost to the struggle that is Pigsback. And I wonder, is this my lot? Is this what free enterprise amounts to for me?

Maybe this is the normal lot of most business founders. Years upon years of toil, but you only keep afloat; you just keep ahead of the banks, the creditors, and the liquidator. It would be a sick entrepreneur to wish this on themselves. We don't wish for it, but we get trapped in it. What twisted part of me still prefers these struggles over a return to corporate life? For all the stress and toil, I'm still in play and just about in control.

Is my belief fading? Of course, it is.

I was always so sure of success. Somehow. Ultimately.

I've taken a lot of humility on board with every passing year, particularly this one. I'm worn out from the bumps, the bruises, the darts and the jibes from those who have a say – correctly, of course – by virtue of the money they invest or the grants they control. At the last board meeting, there was a keenness among the non-executives to explore "exit opportunities". Straightaway! Surprise, surprise!

It was my turn to shift in my seat. I couldn't shut the conversation off. From the first moment I took on other people's money for Pigsback, there was going to have to be an exit – some kind of realisation event to give the investors their outcome, good or bad. But when it's just not happening for the business, and the subject of exit lingers around the boardroom table, it's an almighty pain in the arse.

Sure, I'd love a tidy exit more than anyone, the chance for another chapter, a rebirth. But it has no chance of happening before 2010, by which time, hopefully, we'll have come out the other side of this. A wormhole to that day would be handy. By then, I'll have served over a decade with the business - more than enough! Right now, we need to get our house in order before there's going to be any kind of exit.

But what if, someday, I just can't stem the tide anymore, and it all goes belly-up? It doesn't bear thinking about. I don't want to go there. It would be hard to contain the mess: staff, creditors, bank, investors, all let down, all left feeding off the scraps in a disorderly queue, and me and my name mired for life.

And then what? Get a job? I can't see it. I'd prefer to take a step back. I might be forced to - to recover my mind, walk the mountains, live in isolation for a while, write my book and poems, have some slow time with Karen – and then emerge calmer and wiser, make my sullen apologies to all I've let down, citing the extraordinary times we traded in. And maybe they'll accept. And maybe then, my head and conscience clear, the hard lessons embraced, I'll start again, stealthily this time.

We've been on this crazy conveyor belt for too long, and there's no end in sight.

In the meantime, the economic situation has gone from bad to worse. In mid-September, the US investment bank Lehman Brothers filed for Chapter 11 bankruptcy protection. It looks like another bubble has burst, this time property-related. In the USA, sub-prime property mortgages have got big banks into a lot of trouble.

Here in Ireland, the government has taken the unprecedented step of guaranteeing the liabilities of the country's six major banks to soothe market concerns about their stability. Anglo Irish Bank, a big lender to the property sector, seems most exposed, and there are some dire predictions about how bad things could get.

I don't know what's next, but I do know that marketing budgets are fast becoming a rare commodity. That means more cost reduction. We have already taken out over €2 million in annualised costs, a quarter of our operating costs, and there is a lot more on the way. Since we lost our contribution from Canada and then took the full brunt of the revenue slowdown in Ireland and the UK, we have been faced with a do-or-die scenario. And I am left doing a few jobs, none of them to my satisfaction.

I know we will be in a much leaner and hopefully stronger place going into 2009 in Ireland and the UK, where Gareth is now stuck in. He has already managed a lift in August and September, and I'm hoping his team can get to the big goal of breakeven in 2009 off the much lower UK cost base.

UK breakeven would give us welcome oxygen and a very different perspective. Ideally, we'd love to find a Bell equivalent in the UK, a partner who might lend their market weight and balance sheet to our venture in return for equity in the UK or at the top-company level. For now, we're drawing a blank on that front.

There is no choice but to continue navigating the very choppy waters we find ourselves in, rowing with one hand and bailing with the other.

November 2008

In response to a request from a journalist, I wrote a few thoughts on what the government should do to help businesses

I shouldn't have. What was I thinking?

Amid my lengthy contribution, I expressed the view that the cost of the public sector "has been allowed to run amok" and urged the government to cut costs rather than increase personal or business taxes. My comments were edited and skewed to come across in a way I didn't intend. I read back on my submission, which – as I suspected – was reasonably balanced. I did encourage Enterprise Ireland to loosen up on the red tape during these trying times. Of course, the shorter published comments had no such balance and came across quite critically.

How foolish of me. How sorry I am. A salutary lesson in media savviness.

How optimistic I was in my recent observations on the UK. October sales were very weak, and, more significantly, Gareth informed me that he is ready to look around for an alternative role. It is an unequivocal no-confidence vote in our UK future.

There are important personal factors too. Gareth's wife, Deirdre, is pregnant, and they would prefer to move back to Ireland now. Gareth is feeling a bit burnt out by the same challenges over eight years, but he is clear in his prognosis as far as Pigsback's future in the UK is concerned: there is none.

What a servant to Pigsback Gareth has been, taking leadership roles in Ireland, Canada and the UK. After years of battling together through thick and thin, we have become friends. I have no right to hold him back, and I want what is best for him.

I discussed pulling right back from our UK venture with Kevin, our chairman and biggest backer. He resolutely defended the need for a UK presence. He believes it shows real commitment to keep the dream alive, which he feels will represent value during exit discussions. I hope he is right.

At times like these, the perspective of a very committed chairman must count. I've already picked myself up and dusted myself off, and I have begun interviews to replace Gareth. Ireland is scrappy and challenging, too, but Jenny has restructured with a team of four capable women now in charge.

Meanwhile, the consultants we appointed to assist us to raise funds in Ireland have drawn a blank. That means stretching the financial headroom we have for as long as we can. It's very tricky. I am optimistic that there may be better times ahead. Of course, I am.

I'm trying hard to bring a calm attitude and body language home, conscious that the relentless bad news is very stressful for Karen too. It's coming from all angles: the economic environment, the fortunes of people close to us wiped out, her concerns about her own Christmas hamper business as the season approaches, and the huge worry about our personal financial situation should Pigsback fail.

We're still trying to complete the new senior loan note to release Enterprise Ireland's grants and preference share investment. Some of our more supportive investors have made verbal commitments, but the bulk of investors don't want to hear our appeals for cash. Somehow, we'll have to find a little bit more. I laid out the case again to investors:

Email to Shareholders {Extracts}

Dear Shareholder,

.... The most critical action we took was the achievement of over €2.8m of annualised operating savings from our business, or 38% of all operating costs budgeted in 2008 in Ireland and the UK ....

Seeing the job through will require an additional investment of €600k. We know that the external environment is not conducive to fundraising and have concluded that we must look internally for a solution. We know it is a difficult time to be seeking investment and that the instrument we choose must give both very strong security and an extra reward to the shareholders who participate. Non-participating shareholders will have to accept this dilution.

On that basis, we are proposing to offer all shareholders a Senior Convertible Loan with a 10% coupon and an option to convert to ordinary equity ...

This round will be supported by myself, Kevin Watson, our Chairman and other senior managers.

We have lean and highly focused teams in Ireland and the UK going into 2009, with strong underlying demand for the services we provide. I firmly believe that we will progress strongly in 2009 and trust we can count on your support.

Michael

Goodbye and good riddance to 2008. A shocker.

5

No Luck Left to Push

January 2009

Having raised our investment and followed our expansion strategy, a loss of €2 million was always on the cards for 2007, but repeating that result in 2008 – despite huge cost savings efforts – is a poor result. I don't know how we could have done better. We have had two rounds of redundancies in the UK office and one in Dublin, in addition to pay cuts all-round. Not a line of cost has gone unchallenged.

In this economic climate and given how hard we have been hit, our teams expected redundancies. That doesn't make it any easier. I am not comfortable either doing it or writing about it. However, we have a fiduciary duty to do the right thing by the business, which means acting quickly and fairly and somehow trying not to destabilise the future or lose all momentum. It's a tough balancing act.

The most protected people in these situations tend to be those directly or indirectly generating revenue - a sales role being the obvious example. The most vulnerable are those in back-end roles like accountants, member service personnel and content managers.

Trying to quickly reenergise the remaining smaller organisation is a challenge. Perhaps it's some human survival mechanism, but the remaining staff seem to react with relief and a keenness to embrace the future rather than any inclination to dwell on what just happened. It's easier to live with knowing we did our best to be fair, transparent and as generous as we could be to the leavers.

Our balance sheet is showing negative to the tune of about €2 million. That said, the shareholder loans and Enterprise Ireland Prefs make up most of that, and our working capital remains just about manageable. The cost measures and additional funding can still put it right. We can't do any more.

Budgeting in this volatile environment has to be dynamic. Budget 1 quickly gets superseded by Budget 2 and so on, as we continually react to a deteriorating market and results. In Britain, every time we try to move our costs closer to our revenue level, revenue drops. Of course, it does. It's very difficult to cut your way to profit - I'm learning – not to any great surprise.

———◆———

The new year is starting on a sad note: Jo Malvern is leaving Pigsback, an innocent victim of our need to cut costs. I am truly sad and sorry that the business has come to this and can't afford a place for someone who has done nothing wrong and so much right.

Since she started in 2002, Jo made some of the most important contributions across the business, from professionalising our sales processes to starting Empathy Research to overseeing marketing and communications in Britain, to implementing an exemplary knowledge transfer process through Project Passport in Canada.

She leaves with her head held high and with typical dignity in her departing note to the team, still brimming with pride and belief. In Jo's words:

There is something unique about Pigsback and the people here that you just don't get anywhere else, and I will really miss it. …. it's a phenomenal business with some amazing people who I have worked with over the last 7 years in all three countries. Collectively we've created something really special, and I feel proud to be able to say that I was a part of that and look forward to seeing and hearing about bigger and better things in the future.

———◆———

March 2009

I am on a midday flight to London after a few hours in the Dublin office. We are pretty much at breakeven for the first two months of 2009. That's progress. We have enough funding from the initial loan note commitments and Enterprise Ireland to take away the immediate extreme pressure, but we've left the loan note open.

Kevin has gone above and beyond; some Hotbed investors and some family members are in, too, as are several other Irish shareholders who supported the last funding round for the UK expansion. The majority of our shareholders, however, are lying low.

I don't think there is much more we could be doing. We are renegotiating with all of our suppliers; we have imposed a second level of pay cuts across the team, more modest this time; we are challenging our Dublin office lease agreement and have taken in subtenants in the UK; we are stretching payments; we have renegotiated arrangements with the Revenue Commissioners; we are nursing the banks along.

In short, we are sweating every asset, human and otherwise.

Britain is still our biggest challenge. The new year kicks off with a new UK MD who has come in with his eyes open, fully briefed on the precariousness of our situation. He is very commercial, so, hopefully, he can take the much smaller UK base to profitability soon.

My eyes were opened, meanwhile, at a dinner with a senior UK agency executive in Dublin recently. He will remain anonymous, but he explained to me the game that *some* agencies play to improve profit margins, squeezed excessively by client procurement teams (they say). Special status is awarded to media owners who meet certain criteria but who then agree to put financial kickbacks in place to the agency.

The degree of transparency on this matter between client and agency varies widely, no doubt, but it feels murky at best. Not all agencies engage in this by any means, but it is enough to have the nasty side effect of making market access difficult for new marketing and media propositions that are outside this loop.

In the meantime, Britain remains a tough grind, with the team doing ad hoc deals, one at a time, for small money. It's a business that has been walking the precipice between breakeven and closure for a good few months now. Unless our new man can work some magic soon, its days are numbered.

◆

Running a business in difficult times can feel like serving a sentence. Pigsback's woes are such that they are inevitably going to take some time to fix. I know I am tied to the business and won't be going anywhere fast, so I have taken to reading tomes from the classics section.

I am not a fast reader, but it suits me right now to pick up a big read and get immersed in it. In the time it takes me to finish it, all the chipping away at Pigsback's problems in that period will hopefully have amounted to a chunk of progress. It's a mind game, but I think it is working.

I have finished a few by Dostoyevsky, notably *Crime and Punishment* (dark but gripping) and *The Brothers Karamazov* (a marathon but a great tale of the contrasting lives and values of the Russian brothers). I am off on a whaling mission now with *Moby Dick*, which should take me into the winter. I'm relishing the prospect, drawn in from the narrator's famous opening line: "Call me Ishmael."

I wouldn't normally read the classics. I doubt I would have read any of these books in my normal mindset, but if this latest habit points to a damaged state of mind, I think the reading is helping to repair it. My normal fare is literary fiction with an Irish bias, with the likes of Sebastian Barry, Colm Toibin, Roddy Doyle and John Banville featuring strongly, with a bit of Sebastian Faulks, Ian McEwan and a few biographies interspersed.

I like reading the physical book, even if it makes for heavy hand luggage. As I go, I rip out the chunk of pages I've just finished reading – which tends to come off with the spine intact – and I leave that little teaser for the next passenger to discover on a plane or Tube. Hopefully, someone has been inspired. I'll never know.

———◆———

We let Empathy Communications go when we were in mid-expansion in the UK and Canada. As contracts lapsed, we didn't seek to replace them with new ones. In its heyday, Empathy Communications had contracts for bespoke loyalty, communications and tech platform services for clients including AIB, Nokia, O2, and Xtra-vision. It was a lifeline of revenue and contribution. We tended to get a run of two to three years from each new contract, so we didn't see it as scalable into a long-term business. But just when we need it, we're about to get another lifeline with two new contracts.

Valerie is still making an impact at Pigsback, albeit on a part-time basis in recent years. She organised a lunch with Rob Jordan of the dairy, food and nutrition group Glanbia, one of the most visionary and positive marketers we have met on our travels. We discussed the door-to-door milk delivery service operated by Glanbia through its network of milkmen, with a view to finding a new solution to managing the relationship with consumers online.

Between us, we drew out the concept on a napkin, literally. I found it very exciting, and it plays into our expertise in terms of platform development, consumer proposition development and branding. Rob has codenamed it *Project Doorstep* for now. It looks promising and could mean a good six-figure contract over the first 12 months, which would be welcome.

We've also started a very interesting project with the Cuisine de France team, some of whom I worked with in Green Isle Foods. It is mainly an Empathy Research project, but it could lead to some form of trade loyalty platform and programme for Empathy Communications. There's been a substantial chunk of additional work for me in both programmes initially, but Angela Healy and Johnny Mc are now taking over. It is good revenue and an important contribution to our overhead right now. Gratefully accepted.

———◆———

In a lighter moment, I met a rather posh lady at a client meeting during my last visit to London. At the mention of Co Kilkenny, she straight away brought the conversation to hunting trips in Ireland and asked in her high-brow English accent: "You don't by chance know Paddy? Paddy McDonald?"

It was, of course, Johnny Mc's father, Paddy, the former huntsman at the Mount Juliet estate. Well, his son got a good laugh out of that one.

Johnny Mc's back story is worth telling. John is the son of Paddy and Kate McDonald from Thomastown in Co Kilkenny. Paddy was the keeper of the hounds for Victor McCalmont, then owner of the Mount Juliet estate and stud farm. Paddy rode out at the head of the hunt alongside the Master and was renowned as a fearless adventurer, something that delivered him a few scrapes in his time.

Johnny's childhood was in some ways idyllic, with the freedom to roam Mount Juliet, helping his father and other men on the estate. The family was comfortable, living in a house on the estate and never worrying about electricity or heating bills.

McCalmont was one of the last of and, by all accounts, one of the most decent of the Anglo-Irish estate owners. Johnny recalls the huge hamper delivered every Christmas. He depicts home as sociable and unruly at times.

Johnny showed encouraging early signs with his school results, always in the top one or two in his class. He turned down the offer to succeed his father as keeper of the hounds, feeling there was more in store for him and his life. His mother had ambition for her son too and ensured he would complete his education by attending third-level in nearby Waterford, studying accountancy.

Johnny also played in a band, touring the local pubs and venues for cash and kind. Life in the band was "all out", and before long, the academic life suffered, and alcohol was threatening to take hold. It was then that he recalls "being rescued in a very sorry state" by a young woman, Tricia Woods.

They would marry some years later, but not before John opted for a self-imposed detox and exile in his home for several months with his guitar and computer for company. He was soon ready to take on the world of work again.

Little did Johnny or I know that our paths would soon cross and form a most resilient and enduring business relationship and friendship.

———————◆———————

In the midst of all of this, there is some really positive energy coming out of the Pigsback business in Ireland, where our membership, site activity and our brand loyalty all remain strong. Mindful of the challenging economic conditions, with government-imposed tax increases and rising unemployment (now over 12%), we have persisted with some new product development initiatives.

We are nearly ready to go to market with Pigsback Local, a service offering local deals in your area. These will mainly be low-ticket sales for businesses with smaller budgets, managed by dedicated local reps. We expect to have our first sales rep in a pilot programme very soon with, hopefully, several more to follow very quickly.

The team in London ran a similar initiative, but their focus was on member engagement, and they omitted the revenue model. We will be charging a small fee for all deals that are posted to our site. Some small wins here could create a lot of excitement, give morale a real boost and help our finances too.

———•———

June 2009

A young man by the name of Nick Coen started work with us recently. It is on a fairly flexible basis, initially anyway. Nick is providing reception and phone cover, as well as helping the team in packing and posting rewards to our members.

I met Nick's parents a few years ago when we were buying a pony from them. As I signed the cheque, his dad Patrick asked if I was anything to John Dwyer, originally from Dundalk. It turns out that my brother John and Patrick worked together for the accountancy firm O'Hare Barry in Dublin in the mid-1980s.

We kept in touch with the Coens and got to know Nick, with whom I share a keen interest in horse racing, golf and rugby – whether watching on TV, going along as a fan, or having a punt. Nick loves a punt. He is a regular at Irish race meetings and is very well-known among the jockeys, trainers and regular punters.

Nick brings a big smile to work with him every day, which is great for everyone. He is enjoying the job and the company of his Pigsback colleagues. He regularly wheels into my office to discuss our betting fund; we have had several funds at this stage, designed, of course, to beat the bookies. It's a good distraction.

Nick has a knack for reading my moods. He sometimes just pops in and hangs out as I work away on something. I'm very happy to have him there, and he is exceptionally discreet. No surprise that he has hit it off with Johnny Mc too.

———•———

Trading in the first half of the year finished very slowly in Ireland. We have pushed through another lower-cost plan. We avoided further redundancies this time, but there are leavers we won't replace and a series of other cost measures.

Each time we cut, we think we have done all we can. Once the new structure and processes settle, however, we reassess, only to find new ways of doing things and of doing without. The savings have added up to about 20% of our remaining cost base this time.

It's always painful to implement cuts, and we are surely at the bottom of the barrel. But I am beginning to feel more optimistic, eyeing up a breakeven year in 2009 and a return to profit in 2010.

In the middle of all of that, we hit our wobbliest point yet on cash flow. We were hit with an unexpected and random reduction in our invoice discounting facility from our UK provider, leaving us uncomfortably tight on salary day. We got there, but it was close.

The digital advertising world, meanwhile, continues to bring change and opportunity. Several of our team have left for Facebook, Google and other digital agencies.

Some months ago, Jenny asked to meet me. She outlined her plans to go out on her own with a new digital marketing agency in partnership with her husband, Alan McGovern. I can't blame her, and I appreciated the extended notice she gave me. There is a big market opportunity for entrepreneurs with good digital experience, which Jenny has in abundance – plus professionalism and commerciality too. Yet another Pigsback stalwart is moving on.

———•———

'Contra advertising' is where we do business with other owners of media by swapping services. It's like sharing audience access and eliminates the need for cash marketing budgets. It has served us well this year, really lifting Pigsback's profile again and bringing a buzz back to the office.

We have agreed to accept a Today FM radio campaign in return for promoting its programming on Pigsback.com. We also negotiated a fleet of four branded Fiat 500 cars in return for Fiat's sponsorship of the Motor Zone on our site. We have the right audience for Fiat, and the growing Pigsback Local team could certainly use the cars.

We have done some magazine contras too through the Harmonia group, and we are getting good ad space from the Dublin Airport Authority in return for getting our members to use Dublin Airport's car parks. It adds up to a big brand presence for minimal cash outlay. Like the earliest days of assembling the site, the *Loaves and Fishes* strategy is serving us well again.

Meanwhile, we have been through very difficult negotiations with Enterprise Ireland, who made it clear that they don't care for our UK operation. They won't be releasing any further funds if the money is used to subsidise UK losses. It's a hard message, but I get it. The UK is operating at a much smaller scale than we originally foresaw. We explained to Enterprise Ireland that it was no longer a material concern, and we'll be true to that. We need the funds to survive.

◆

It's a sign of the times that the inevitable day of reckoning has come at Jacob's, as the biscuit factory in Tallaght finally closed. Production has been contracted to overseas suppliers. It has been on the cards for some time, but it is nonetheless a sad day for a factory that once played such a big part – economically and socially – in Dublin and Ireland, and one that played a big part in my career and life too.

In an uncanny coincidence, I had a Pigsback client visit a few days after the closure with the majority owner and CEO of Jacob's, Michael Carey, who led the purchase of the business from Danone in 2004. We met in Jacob's offices, adjacent to the Belgard Road factory. I gave Michael a gift of my scrapbook containing mementoes like sales leaflets of the new products and promotions I was involved with during my time in Jacob's in the late 1980s and early 1990s, together with a commentary I had prepared at that time.

Michael was grateful, saying that such relatively recent history hadn't been recorded very thoroughly. He promised to forward it to Douglas Appleyard, the official safe keeper of Jacob's archive. Michael brought me down to visit the empty factory. It was obvious to me that, despite the brave face, he had been touched by the closure. I was sympathetic: the axe may have fallen under his watch, but the sentence had been passed long before.

The factory was eerie. As I walked around, I could still get the sweet smells of sugar and syrups that lingered in the air. In my day, I was fascinated by the mechanisation and giant conveyor belts in the factory. I could easily visualise old images: the neat blobs of red jam merging into a line between pillows of mallow on each Mikado; the scented waterfall of coconut shavings falling softly onto perfectly rounded Coconut Creams, layer upon layer of dough giving the world's best Cream Crackers their airiness and texture; the Kimberley lining up in imperfect synchronicity for their chocolate bath; the click-clack of the packaging machines which had sealed millions of biscuit packs in their time; the watchful eyes of a community of workers – some in blue, others in white – putting in their honourable day's work, trusting the bosses and union leaders to work out the future.

That was the Jacob's famed for its inventiveness and creativity. Mikado was designed and launched to celebrate the Gilbert and Sullivan opera of 1890. Kimberley, with its brown-white-brown layers and sugar crystals, was launched to commemorate the siege of the eponymous diamond mining town during the Boer Wars. Cream Crackers date all the way back to 1885. Thousands of families depended on Jacob's in its prime, and it looked after them for a century and a half.

In 2009, the void left by the closure of this great factory is all the more gaping as Ireland's property-based economy has just been found out.

———————◆———————

November 2009

It is ten years since I scribbled down the concept for what would become Pigsback.com on the back page of the *Irish Independent* on November 25th, 1999. We will have our tenth birthday celebrations next year, on the official anniversary of the launch, and celebrations they should be. For all the ups and downs, sleepless nights, drained faces and dodgy heartbeats, we're still here.

We have had over 200 people work with us at various points, and I'd like to think they're mostly better off for the learnings and experience they acquired at Pigsback. Our members have been loyal and supportive through thick and thin; our clients embraced us, and many for stuck with us for years; our staff have been committed and passionate and – in the main – of exceptional quality, talent and application.

There have been times when the case for throwing in the towel was strong. I couldn't, and I didn't. In increments, we have nearly got things sorted now. There is a relatively modest funding gap – if there is such a thing these days – and there's an outside chance we may even trade our way through that.

Ten years is a big statement of longevity for a dot-com company. I hope to use it to breed confidence and support among our clients and members. I hope we will reawaken the interest of lapsed members. I hope we will rise to the challenges and present a ten-year-old Pigsback that is compelling, attractive, multi-channel and as rewarding and fun as ever. I hope.

To: all@pigsback.com

Subject: Merry Christmas and Thanks

Hi Everyone,

It's been – to say the least – another very challenging year, but a challenge we all rose to together. Well done! Everyone dug in and excelled in one of the toughest years imaginable in business. We've learned lots of lessons, and provided we show the same stuff – the abundant work ethic and great spirit – we are looking at the likely prospect of much more positive times ahead from 2010. Michael

It was just days before Christmas, and our UK Invoice Discounting Bank chose to play Scrooge. Our invoice discounting facility was dramatically and unexpectedly frozen. There was no notice and only the most unprofessional and degrading of communications. They cited new "standards", new "reserves", and extra "prudence".

This move was in nobody's interest. It was callous and reckless in the extreme, a move they had to know could push us over the edge. That didn't seem to concern them.

We desperately sought an explanation and eventually secured an eleventh-hour conference call with our 'relationship manager' on December 23rd. We called at the allotted time and again and again. He didn't answer, preferring to disappear into the warm glow of his festive season.

The following day, I travelled to Valerie's house in Seapoint, County Louth, for the annual Dwyer family Christmas get-together. A group of us headed to the beach. The tide was out, leaving a rippled wet strand in its wake. There was a thin, motionless layer of cloud high overhead, so the light was dim and the air chilly.

All day I worked hard to stay in the moment, engaging in conversation as well as I could. I was happy to kick a ball and to indulge the kids in a few races and games of tag. But under the surface, I was extremely stressed. What should I do? What fallback had I got? Is this the end?

After a respectable period of play, I broke off on a tangent with my eldest brother, Harry. Fifteen years managing the vicissitudes of his very successful financial services practice in Monaghan made Harry a rock of practical sense. He also had a good insight into the kind of people I was now facing.

"What's up with ye?"

I told him.

"I knew you weren't yourself."

He thought for just a few seconds.

"They're treating you like dirt. What are your options?"

Harry was right. ID Bank had not honoured its agreement with us. There was simply no need for this degrading and callously-timed withdrawal of funds. We recently learned that this bank has no business left in Ireland and wants to cut and run from the Irish economy. But the cycle of dependency on invoice discounting turns nasty in a downturn; this is one lesson I'll never forget.

I talked through the options with Harry. Talking helped. Later that evening, I worked through the detail of a plan with Paul Baily, our financial controller. It's going to be exceptionally tight.

———◆———

Today is December 30th, and salaries are paid. It could have gone either way. I have no luck left to push. I now have no choice but to put a new and, I hope, final refinancing package around the business. We will have some scampering to do in January to restore order. I'll deal with that, then.

Behind it all, we have managed to affect quite a transformation in our business and will have achieved breakeven in 2009. Our costs are running at about 40% of what they were at their peak, and that's not to say there won't be more savings. It's not easy. The whole year was another dogfight: the constant onslaught of pressure from staff redundancies to pay cuts, to never-ending cashflow worries, to pressures from banks tightening credit lines, to insensitive and utterly unwelcome snipes from a shareholder here and a journalist there (easy for him to fill his column inches with cheap stories of corporate car crashes gleaned from the annual filings of Ireland's besieged small and medium enterprises).

On a national level, the picture is grimmer than ever. The government has just established the National Asset Management Agency, a 'bad bank' that will acquire all property-related loans – most of them distressed – from the Irish banks. Using government bonds, the state is paying €30 billion for loans that were originally worth some €68 billion (plus interest). No one knows how this experiment will pan out.

And the personal toll just grows; the successive sleepless nights wondering how to make the end-of-month payroll aggravating the cardiac arrhythmia, worries for my family, my income cut and under serious threat, our savings swallowed up by the enterprise, my pension funds a doomed accrual in a hopeless balance sheet, my debts rising, another looming demand that we move beyond interest-only payments on a mortgage bigger than we should ever have allowed, and our highly-leveraged home dwindling in value in this economic mire.

I may well need to start again, but involuntary reinvention at 45 years of age, after crashing to a halt, is a daunting prospect. It is certainly not something I foresaw.

The past couple of years has been painful, stressful in the extreme and eminently forgettable. I hope against hope that, through these struggles, we are laying a new and lasting foundation for better years ahead. That would make it all worthwhile.

January 2010

Thanks to a Ryanair flight to Faro in Portugal and an off-peak offer in the Country Club at the Quinta do Lago resort, we had a great break with our fellow entrepreneur friends, Pam and Gabriel. I put the best foot forward and jogged the beach most days before eating plenty of Piri Piri chicken in the family restaurants that the Portuguese do very well. It was a very good break.

No sooner had I landed home than I was off again to London. I got into the hotel early and didn't fancy the look of the walls. I went around the corner to a pub to watch a football match and sip at a pint. As you do, I got speaking to this guy whose mother and father were originally from Goa in India. His old man, he told me, didn't have much, but he had a great attitude to life: 'You've got a roof over your head and you've got food, you can go out tomorrow and try to make a go of it.' Now that's perspective.

———————•———————

Our meeting with ID Bank seems to have got us back on track but we know we can't count on that facility and that the working capital shortfall needs to be filled. The occasional but very useful bit of flexibility from the Revenue Commissioners is under threat too, after a High Court judge called the two brothers who owned several well-known Dublin hostelries "delinquent directors". They were, at best, far too loose in using tax monies for working capital and drawings. Justice Peter Kelly called it "a form of thieving" and said it was "systematic". The pair were rightly pursued, rebuked and punished for it. In doing so, they have threatened the bit of leniency which the practical folk at Revenue regularly show SMEs through late payment or agreed arrangements.

I suspect Revenue has always taken this approach, particularly in tough times or when the banking system is failing the small and medium-sized businesses which are the backbone of the economy. It's an important role when it's not being abused. Sure enough, a week or so after the headlines, our end-of-January request for some flexibility from the Revenue fell on deaf ears. Our contact in the Revenue pointed out, for the first time that we recall: "Part of what is due is your P30. This is money you collected from your employees".

We paid the Revenue on time, and thanks to debtor payments, we had enough leeway to pay salaries. For the first time, we held the three senior salaries back for a few days. Yet another end of month challenged our survival, but we got through it.

On the plus side, we have traded profitably in January, which augurs well. We have also recruited a few more Pigsback Local reps and a manager for this area. Hopefully, they hit the ground running!

———————◆———————

On a recent night out, after a few pints, I shared my challenges with a good friend, Michael Mc, laying out the experience of recent years in the raw. There is no pride left. This guy is experienced, and he too has serious challenges to manage in the current environment. His advice was blunt: "Wind it up and if there's something worth salvaging, then buy that back yourself or just start again. But don't continue as you are. You're wasting your most valuable years."

Winding up the company isn't a route I want to go down. An examinership or receivership could allow us to start again with a fresh balance sheet and fresh capital, but only after creditor and investor fall-out. It would wipe out existing shareholders. But I feel loyal to those who have repeatedly supported me. It is not in me to abandon them when there's hope that we can work our way back out of this.

The market has continued to change around us at pace, with Google and Facebook playing bigger and bigger roles, and with ad agencies continuing to take greater charge of client budgets. I can't be sure we won't be superseded. I hope not. I think not. But who the hell knows?

I really do think that we should be profitable and cash-generative this year. Perhaps I'm delusional, but I have unwavering faith in the brand, not to mention our membership, our team and our technology. The team has been through so much together. We will rally again. It's just very hard to do with a crippled balance sheet, worrying day-to-day about surviving. I simply have no choice but to address the cash deficit again.

———————◆———————

Finding a solution to our working capital and deeper funding crisis has become my priority. I flew to London in February to meet our chairman Kevin and my brother JD, two of my key supporters. JD booked us into the Groucho Club in Soho, and the guys were teed-up and in solutions mode. We know that contributions from other existing shareholders will be hard to secure, but I feel some will respond positively if they see the basis of a lasting solution. Kevin and JD carry credentials and clout as far as other shareholders are concerned, and their support will speak volumes to others.

I had a proposal ready for discussion. We need to remove the shareholder loans at 20 cents each, which will remove a €1 million liability from the balance sheet plus accruing interest) and to issue new shares for cash at 10 cents each. It was a far cry from the €3.30-per-share paid when we raised investment in 2006.

This is the Emergency Round, a leveller for everyone and for no one more than me. But the fundamentals are not good: we are struggling to break even, and our balance sheet will remain negative by over €1 million. Enterprise Ireland's preference shares weigh the balance sheet down, but they don't put a cash demand on us. If we can get this investment in, it would be an achievement of note given where the world is at and where we've come from.

Kevin reminded me that the holders of the loan notes, as secured creditors of the company, could choose to apply the letter of the law and take ownership of the company assets to the exclusion of normal shareholders. He is, of course, correct: having failed to keep up with interest payments, we are technically in default of the loan note agreement. This gives the loan note holders the right to claim the company's assets as their security.

Fortunately for me and for our passive shareholders, neither Kevin — who is by far the biggest holder — nor any of the other holders seem minded to go this route. Personal loyalties apart, I suspect none of them fancies the prospect of taking over the running of the business. But this is the point where a harder-nosed venture capital or private equity company would almost certainly turn the screw and wipe us all off the share register. It can be a blessing to keep the right company.

We agreed on a few revisions for a draft proposal to go to the board for consideration and approval, and then on to shareholders. It felt like good progress.

The board signed off on the final package of measures, and we sent it to our shareholders, accompanied by our 2009 financial results. They show a net loss of €300,000 after group and financing costs, but there is a bright spot between the lines of a tiny but very significant €4,000 operating profit. That compares well to the €2.1 million loss in 2008. I outlined our forecast for a small net profit in 2010.

I urged all our shareholders to follow their investment in the latest funding round and take a little more than just their strict allocation. I also emphasised how shareholders who did not reinvest would suffer major dilution of their existing stake.

———————◆———————

March 2010

Right now, it looks like we will have taken in about €400,000 in new funds. it doesn't solve everything, but it's a big help.

The different investor responses tell the full story: the majority of investors have been very inactive since their initial investment and are mostly incommunicado. Fair enough. They are down but not out, and we will continue to do our utmost for them.

One shareholder was particularly critical when I bumped into him at an event in Dublin. He asked:

"Why would we invest more money when you've lost what we've given you? What's to say you won't just lose it again this time round?"

The question was fair, and I said as much, but the tone gave it a personal edge. It is hard to listen to, having fought so hard for everyone, including my critic. This shareholder has a few others close to him on our shareholder register. I'm pretty sure they are talking to each other, and none of them is reinvesting, despite my entreaties to use the opportunity to rebalance the price they have paid for their shares, ultimately improving their prospects of getting their capital back.

Friendships change over time; new ones are made, some grow, others fade. These relationships had already begun to fade in the normal course of life, regardless of Pigsback. These are shrewd, experienced investors, so I can do no more. My card is well-marked, however, and as I move on, I've resolved to carefully record my communications with them.

Kevin and I have made ourselves widely available. I encouraged him to fly in for a particular meeting with a larger investor, hoping his efforts would be rewarded, only to be pushed down the chain. We secured the minimum investment, but I was disappointed for Kevin (and for the investor, too, if we succeed).

Kevin himself is knee-deep now with a total of €1.3 million invested in the company. He has made it clear to me – for the first time – that he is at his limit. He could not have done more, and his reward is to become the largest individual shareholder.

Our family supporters are up to their boots too. There has been good support from family, as well as from a few of our loyal friends. Some chipped in for the minimum, which is understandable, but a small few are taking a bigger gamble and reinvesting more than their share.

There was a very mixed reaction from our UK investors, which is no surprise. It reflects their understandably low opinion of our performance and prospects after years of matter-of-fact reporting by Hotbed. One of their members wanted out altogether at the 10-cent share price. I would have liked to oblige, but apart from having no spare cash, we needed everything available to go into the company rather than 'off the table'. There were no takers.

I am very grateful to all of our supporters, who are funding a second chance for everyone. And on we march, having hit the bottom. There was no dressing it up, but I have concocted a plan to survive. There's very little cushion, but there is just no way I can go back to shareholders again for more funding.

I have spent the last period telling myself that the only important thing is to 'do the right thing for the company.' I did what was required to get the funding over the line. But as it settles, it feels a little like I have protected everyone's interests but my own.

I have had to sacrifice all pension accruing to me for the past ten years, totalling about €160,000. I had to scrape up €25,000 to invest just to do *the right thing* and support this latest funding round. I have had two salary cuts in the past couple of years to lead by example. There is no prospect of a pension contribution, a health insurance contribution or any kind of bonus any time soon. And, after all of that, my personal holding has fallen significantly.

JD's support pre- and post- the funding round came with more warnings to me, not about his exposure but about the prudence of me committing much more time to this venture if it doesn't come good for me soon. He's consistent, to say the least, and I know his heart and head are in the right place.

I am more and more conscious of the ever-accumulating opportunity cost of this venture. Am I hanging on too long? Maybe, but it's my baby, and I can't just walk away. Gareth, Rory, and others can leave for better opportunities, but I feel like the captain who won't abandon his ship. There are many people relying on me to make this work. What if I started something similar again from scratch? I have learned so many lessons that I'd probably be a lot more backable. What if I got a job? Perish the thought.

For now, for the company's sake and for my own sanity, I have resolved to put any negative thoughts to one side and move on. The board has agreed to issue share options to improve my personal position and to increase the ownership participation of the management team. That will help. The team is motivated and with a bit of oxygen now from the improved balance sheet, I am in the mindset for reinvention.

———◆———

We have convened an extraordinary general meeting to ratify our funding and all that goes with it administratively. These shareholder gatherings can be occasions for very open and frank discussions, with an often small but supportive group in attendance.

I have prepared a table showing profitability and balance sheet movements in the past few years. 2007 was slated to be a year of investment but turned out to be a gargantuan challenge. Then 2008 was pure carnage; as fast as we pulled our costs, our revenues nosedived faster in a woeful economy and market. While 2009 was most encouraging at a profit and loss level, our working capital keeps on presenting us with new and unforeseen challenges. Over the past six months, a succession of events resulted in a squeeze of about €750,000 from reduced bank facilities, reduced creditors and reduced liabilities to the Revenue.

The Emergency Round has brought a lot of improvement, but it's not a panacea. We are still in a precarious position with our ID Bank facility and have known for some time that we need an alternative. With this in mind, we have reshuffled our non-executive directors, and Tom McCormick has joined our board, replacing Leo Kearns.

Leo has resigned his directorship after ten years of great service, as his own commitments to Ireland's health sector have grown, culminating in his appointment as CEO of the Royal College of Physicians in Ireland. He has shown his own ability to pivot and use his talents to the benefit of new sectors.

Tom was introduced by Leo and was one of our early investors, as a backer of Octagon. He recently sold out of a printing and office supplies business. He is clearly keen to get into play again quickly. He has offered us a facility to replace ID Bank, and he made a chunky ordinary share investment as part of the re-funding. His thinking is that I will be free to focus on customers, members and product development while he assists our financial controller Paul Baily and Johnny Mc on funding, financing and cash management.

The proposed facility is conditional on Tom having a chance to get in and assess the business more thoroughly. I think we can work together, and we do need the cash injection.

———◆———

April 2010

It's the centenary of Theodore Roosevelt's address to the Sorbonne in Paris on April 23rd, 1910, under the title 'Citizenship in a Republic'. I've found myself repeatedly and emotionally drawn to the famous extract from that address known as *The Man in the Arena*:

It is not the critic who counts, not the man who points out how the strong man stumbles, or where the doer of deeds could have done them better. The credit belongs to the man who is actually in the arena, whose face is marred by dust and sweat and blood; who strives valiantly; who errs, who comes short again and again, because there is no effort without error and shortcoming; but who does actually strive to do the deeds; who knows great enthusiasms, the great devotions; who spends himself in a worthy cause; who at the best knows in the end the triumph of high achievement, and who at the worst, if he fails, at least fails while daring greatly, so that his place shall never be with those cold and timid souls who neither know victory nor defeat.

It's during the hardest and most trying times when we are physically and emotionally challenged, somehow ploughing on because we must, that we find out most about ourselves. It's when we repeatedly face challenge, take the knocks, and look failure in the eye, that we truly understand resilience and test our reserves of optimism.

———————•———————

Pigsback has a new partnership with Guaranteed Irish and *Checkout* magazine, the grocery trade publication. The grandly-titled Pigsback Irish Enterprise Awards are focused on encouraging emerging independent companies, mainly in the grocery or FMCG arena. It's more of our Loaves and Fishes approach. The awards give us good profile in the trade through *Checkout*, and with minimal cash outlay, we have had a big response from small and medium-sized brands seeking to win campaigns on Pigsback.com.

The campaigns are sought after; the brands know Pigsback is a powerful medium for building brand profile and engagement. This year's winner, artisan food producer Cully & Sully, has got record levels of interaction from its prize, a Pigsback.com Brand Feature with coupons, quizzes, a poll to determine their next soup flavours and a competition with a chance to head to Ballymaloe, Cullen Allen's (aka Cully's) family business.

For my short address, I chose a theme based on an old Irish proverb or 'seanfhocal': *'mol an óige agus tiocfaidh sí,'* meaning - praise the young, and they will flourish. On the day, one of the winners described Pigsback advertising as "a big boost to a brand", recognising the very high levels of exposure through our email campaigns and website, bringing consumers to brand pages where the interactive content awaits. This is something we have always done particularly well, but for all of our virtues, competitive market forces (the magnetic draw of the giants, Facebook and Google), the ad agency dynamic and the continued poor state of the economy continue to conspire against us. Richard Corrigan happened to be in town and kindly agreed to present the awards.

———————•———————

After a row with Tom, our new director, ID Bank secured a freeze on our main AIB bank account. They just want out. It was a grossly disproportionate act, but they hold all the aces. What's more, banks dance to each other's tunes. AIB froze our bank account at the first sight of a legal document. They shouldn't have, but a lawyer covered his ass, despite the entreaties of our excellent – but, on this occasion, unempowered – relationship manager in the local AIB branch. Thankfully, sense quickly prevailed at AIB, and the freeze was lifted.

It fell to me to negotiate exit terms with ID Bank. Their group of bankers and lawyers didn't give one hoot for Empathy Marketing Ltd, Pigsback, Tom, or me, for that matter. They just want out of Ireland, which means out of Empathy Marketing Limited and fast.

Eventually, they agreed on terms, and within a week or two, we had a Deed of Reassignment freeing us from ID Bank for good. Tom then gave us the new working capital facility he had promised and, as agreed, assumed a more active advisory role in the finance area of the business.

Tom is quite a successful accountant and businessman and is used to being in charge. He is also now at a stage where he needs to fill his time. On the other hand, I am used to Kevin and non-executive directors like Leo Kearns, Pat Shine and Gary Joyce, who, over the years, have been content to observe and make occasional constructive suggestions but who largely limit their interventions to board meetings and special projects.

So I find myself sincerely grateful to Tom for his cash and, occasionally, for some well-intentioned advice, but tetchy when I feel the boundaries of his role being crossed.

Meanwhile, we have battled on. Trading is solid, if slow, in both our markets. In the UK, the team is justifiably encouraged by new campaigns from P & G, Walkers and McCain. They are low-budget campaigns but might lead somewhere better. Our redesigned homepage got a three-to-one ringing endorsement from members in research.

In Ireland, Pigsback Local is showing more promise, albeit early, and we now have a small team of local reps and a manager. It is already self-financing. We are making good progress with our integration of Facebook and with our plans for getting Pigsback in good shape for mobile smartphones.

I took this tone into an in-depth interview with Gavin Daly in the *Sunday Business Post* in March. I didn't sugarcoat the difficult times, but Gavin was very fair in his coverage. Britain, I conceded, has been an expensive experience, but we are still hoping to enjoy new growth from a much smaller base. I was more upbeat about our recent developments in Ireland and held out some hope for the future in relation to Canada: it had ended prematurely, but it was a successful pilot in a North American market, which we could potentially revisit.

Under a photo of a pale me surrounded by a pig costume, the highlighted quote read: "you only have one life, and you have to go for it." Indeed.

We're planning our 10th-anniversary celebrations with a series of events ranging from a joint birthday party with TGI Friday's – also 10 years old – to extra cinema preview screenings (a member favourite) and a client breakfast event. There's a series of new initiatives for our members too, most notably awarding Platinum and Gold status to our ten- and five-year members respectively. It's a lot of noise for very little cash.

———•———

Recently, I ushered a visitor from our offices with as much politeness as I could muster. His mission from his corporate masters: pick up an injured Pigsback for scraps.

Days later, in the early hours of a Sunday morning, I started contemplating where I find myself and the business I created. Not a good idea.

I reached for a pen.

'It wasn't meant to be like this.'

That is as far as I got. For all my self-belief, the truth is in the accounts, and it is no credit to me. Ambition is all very fine until it hits a wall, €12 million later.

I feel the pressure. Karen feels the pressure. Our marriage feels the pressure.

But we've survived, and I have the rest of this story to write. I wouldn't swap it. How sick is that?

6

Mega Deals

September 2010

Our search for new sources of revenue has not been in vain, producing one very interesting prospect. We have been grappling with the Pigsback Local service for about a year but were finding that local merchants such as restaurants and spas struggle to pay even very small upfront fees; a few hundred euros is too much for most.

Enter Groupon, a US company that recently acquired a German start-up called CityDeal. It operates in the hotels and local offers sector too, but with a critically important tweak: Groupon doesn't charge an upfront fee but instead takes a commission on every deal it sells. That one variation seems to make all the difference.

I've been reading more about Groupon's phenomenal growth in America. It has about five million subscribers to its daily deals service and was valued at $1.35 billion after a funding round earlier this year.

I soon learned about a new competitor, LivingSocial, also American, which is preparing to launch in Ireland. We have observed the endless marketing funds that Groupon seems to have and are now witnessing the same from LivingSocial, even before its formal launch in Ireland. Several Irish start-ups are getting in on the act too.

We are not going to step back and roll out a red carpet for Groupon or any of these guys arriving on our doorstep in precisely our space. Local and hotel offers are home territory for Pigsback. Over our first decade, we developed a range of interactive marketing products because we had no choice. We innovated in a big way in the FMCG space because those guys have the budgets, and we knew the space well from our early careers. There was no e-commerce to talk about in Ireland. But the original scribbled Pigsback concept envisioned online sales for clients, spearheaded by offers. This new 'Deals' business, as it has become known, is doing precisely that.

We've been busy working on our own Pigsback Deals offering. Johnny Mc and I have carved it up between us: he has taken responsibility for the tech and operations, and I have taken on the branding and commercial side of things. Within weeks, Johnny and the team had an initial system built. It hasn't got all the bells and whistles, but perfection can wait.

We know we can't invest in a new brand and don't need to. Instead, we have opted for a descriptive but punchy sub-brand: *Mega Deals from Pigsback.com*. It has a lot of impact and does the trick.

The initial system displays deals on a new Mega Deals section on Pigsback.com but also on the main homepage, the relevant section of the site, on Facebook and in email marketing.

We started with a daily email to everyone who signed up to the relevant categories – hotels, restaurants, beauty, etc. – but soon segmented that into separate emails for hotels and leisure. We left a prominent single-click 'Unsubscribe' button at the top of each email, just in case. We had NO complaints. This is what our members signed up to Pigsback for after all – targeted special offers, both local and national.

With Mega Deals, the merchant – which might be a hotel, gym, spa or restaurant – agrees to a deal to be sold through Pigsback, typically with 30% to 50% off the headline price. It might be a restaurant voucher for €40, which we sell for €25, for instance. We don't charge the merchant but we do take a 20% to 30% commission, depending on the business.

In return for the merchant's business, we email the offer to our members and place it prominently on the Pigsback site. Our members – or any member of the public who wishes to avail of the deal, for that matter – must buy it within 48 hours using a credit card, debit card or PayPal account. This urgency seems to matter. People are encouraged to tell their friends, and this 'viral' element seems to be really powerful.

The system can display a count of what is sold and manages the money flows back into our accounting system. That way, we know which merchants are owed what. We can trace all vouchers back to member accounts, allowing us to handle refunds and credits. That's a hell of a start.

In this model, everyone's a winner. The consumer gets a fabulous deal. The merchants get approximately 75% of the voucher value, as well as new customers and huge brand profile. They retain all of the 'up spend' (anything the voucher-holder spends above the voucher value), which we estimate could be equal to the value of the voucher again. Pigsback gets its commission, plus a partial benefit from unused vouchers, not to mention a heck of a lot of site activity and new members.

We're allowing our members to use their accumulated PiggyPoints to part-purchase deals and also to exchange unused deal vouchers for points. We appear to be the only company clearly offering a refund for unused vouchers. Our reward points have become Mega Deal credits, an arrangement that works for our members and for us. Our members can use points to get further discounts on deals. In this way, the points now serve us and not external suppliers of rewards vouchers, which is proving very beneficial from both a marketing and financial perspective.

Overnight, our Pigsback Local reps became Pigsback Mega Deals account managers, and we're adding to their number quickly. For a while, we found it difficult to retain account managers. Many were easily lured by the digital multinationals around Grand Canal Docks, but we've responded well by simply filtering out anyone in interviews who is showing that particular preference.

Encouragingly, Groupon ran one restaurant offer, which we also ran. They sold 340 vouchers, and we sold 460. We haven't got it all right, of course, and some deals are flopping but we are learning and have found an exciting product to plug into our brand, membership and sales team. There's nothing like competition to get a market going, something our traditional Pigsback offering has lacked in Ireland over the past ten years. Competition brings more noise, more consumer awareness and more investment; it helps to grow a sector, not just a particular company.

If we nail this down and secure a position as one of the two leaders in the space, Mega Deals could grow quickly. It should generate between €250,000 and €500,000 in gross profit next year. That's more than enough to compensate for the steady decline in the Pigsback Advertising business, which we simply have not been able to arrest. Much of the cream has gone from the market, and we have been battling for smaller budgets from more demanding clients.

From a branding perspective, the integration of Mega Deals under the Pigsback banner prompted a mini upgrade. We've dropped the name PiggyPoints, renaming them simply: *Pigsback Points.* We also decided there will be less of Curly across the site (but he will remain that eye-catching presence in our external advertising). There will be a bit less pink and a lot more black. It's all a nudge upmarket in readiness for the higher-end deals we are already targeting.

Email to Shareholders

Subject: November 2010 Update {Extracts}

Dear Shareholder,

It's been a game of survival in 2010 in the face of a horrible economic climate in Ireland that has heaped bad news on top of more bad news. We just don't know if it can get worse as so much confidence seems to have gone from this economy. We had a reasonably strong first half, in hindsight, but right through the summer and autumn, confidence was eroded [in our Pigsback Advertising business]. It's been about cost control, scrapping for revenue and trying new things.

There are distinct positives within that, but it is hard to counter the overall pressure on [advertising] revenues [resulting] from successive client budget cuts.

The positives have been:

- *Pigsback Mega Deals, our answer to Groupon's CityDeals, have generated €180k in gross revenue in about 10 weeks and are now generating a healthy contribution. At current run rates, these should account for €250k, at least in contribution in 2010. They are working well in Ireland but failed to take off for us in the UK, where the market is saturated.*

- *Empathy Research is up about 50% year-to-date*

- *Our site activity and membership are responding very well to the new site, Facebook activity and Mega Deals (membership and activity are both up 15% to 20% since about mid-year off lower marketing and rewards budgets).*

I'm hoping we will emerge with a strong market position in Ireland, a reformed low-cost business, a top 2 position in group deals (a huge trend being led by Groupon.com) and a strong and dynamic research business.

Michael

Despite my opening realism about the terminal challenges to our traditional advertising business, the overall message was a positive one. I also indicated an expected return to profit, which must have come as a welcome surprise, as I found myself in receipt of messages of support. We all feed off encouragement, and I realised how I had missed this essential nourishment.

It's an appalling economic climate, a depression. Ireland's public finances are in disastrous shape, hit with the triple-whammy of falling tax revenues, rising welfare payments (unemployment is through the roof), and the huge cost of bailing out the banks. In late November, the government agreed on a bailout from the International Monetary Fund (IMF), European Union (EU), and European Central Bank (ECB). The bailout from the so-called *Troika* amounts to €85 billion, with €35 billion of that to be used to fix the banks. For the foreseeable future, we will all be answering to the IMF, who wants us to tighten our belts.

The headlines say the collapse was caused by a bank-fuelled bubble of greed and economic waywardness, particularly in relation to property, but we grossly mismanaged public spending too: over €7 billion was added to the public service wage bill from 1997 to 2008. I was reminded, in an economic article I read recently, of one of the most basic principles of economics: *stuff is scarce.* Everyone can't have loads. Hard choices must always be made for the long-term economic good. Ireland lost sight of that one, and we're all paying the price.

One positive is that Ireland is regaining competitiveness. Private sector productivity is up 16% year-on-year, exports are up, there's a strong multinational sector and – although indigenous manufacturing has been hit hard in recent years – there are seeds of enterprise germinating and sprouting new life.

Back at the Pigsback ranch, recent weeks have been throwing up more challenges. First up, Nick popped into my office: 'Michael, the sheriff is at reception.' He was very tempted to laugh. *Does he have a gun?* I wondered. 'Send him in, Nick'

You couldn't make it up. Uncharacteristically – at least as far as our experience is concerned – the Revenue Commissioners pulled the trigger on a relatively modest late payment of about €50,000, referring it for collection to the Sheriff. It could have been worse, but it felt like a new low.

It feels like the "delinquent" and "thieving" headlines have led to a backlash within the Revenue and a blanket tightening up of their tolerance levels. This had never happened to us before and seemed like an overreaction. But they have been more than fair to us overall.

Our visitor was as keen as we were for a constructive conversation and only too pleased that we hadn't boarded up the doors like so many companies on his list. We didn't feel we belonged on such a list and couldn't wait to get off it, which was readily arranged.

No sooner had we dealt with one crisis than another appeared. This time, AIB threatened to pull our Mega Deal trading. Strange as it sounds, our success in selling deals has thrown up an unforeseen and potentially tricky problem.

AIB Merchant Services handles credit card payments and takes a small cut for its trouble. It must safeguard against an unscrupulous or insolvent deal provider or merchant going under, having taken consumers' cash without fulfilling the associated contracts. This could leave the bank with the liability. With our deals business taking off, this represents a new exposure in the bank's eyes. So they threatened to put an immediate and outright halt to our Mega Deals trading. Johnny Mc worked hard at this one and has got agreement that we will progressively build a reserve of €150,000 in a ring-fenced buffer account for the bank. That's a relief.

January 2011

Right now, I'm coming to the end of a good Christmas and New Year's break. As one year closes and a new one begins, it's the perfect time to regain perspective, reset objectives, recharge the batteries, and refuel the optimism tanks.

We spent New Year *en famille* in Roundstone in Connemara. Valerie and her family joined us here. We drank, ate, walked, read and laughed. Roundstone is a new destination for us. We are very fortunate that my brother John and his wife Natasha have bought and renovated a house at the foot of Errisbeg, overlooking the majestic Dog's Bay and Gurteen Bay beaches. They are more than generous with access for family.

We climbed Errisbeg, a desolate mountainscape with a 360-degree vista from the top, spanning Roundstone, Dog's Bay, Ballyconneely, Clifden. and the 12 Bens mountain range.

I did some running too.

I've stayed on for an extra couple of days to try to put some shape to these journals. I'll be heading home tomorrow, mentally and physically refreshed.

In the early weeks of 2011, Mega Deals are already the bright spot. We've struck a partnership deal with a group of radio stations, where we will exclusively supply our deals on a margin-sharing arrangement. This is a win-win: we get brand profile, membership, revenue and profit; they get a share of sales.

Our plan is to drive Mega Deals through Google advertising, partnerships and PR. We are projecting our Irish credentials strongly too, using the Guaranteed Irish logo and why not? We are an Irish business and employ about 30 people here.

The motto for 2011 is 'Get Ahead, Stay Ahead': let success breed success, put losses and cashflow problems behind us and deliver profits. Profits have been the missing link for far too long now. They are the key to a better future, peace of mind and maybe, in time, some respite in my personal finances. There's no time to delay.

———————◆———————

Last year's Emergency Round valued the equity in the business at €1.5 million or 10 cents per share (excluding options). Granted, the balance sheet remained negative post-funding to the tune of €1.3 million (much of that in EI's Prefs). Since then, I've set my own target of €1 per share on exit, whenever that may be. This would get most of our supportive investors out on top and would obviously give last year's subscribers a particularly good return. If anyone asks, that's what I tell them. All things considered, they should be happy, and I sure would be too. Yes, that looks like a huge stretch in the current economic climate, but I think it is achievable if we can stay alive and keep evolving. It's the only show in town for me.

———————◆———————

I got a tap on the shoulder from James McGuill, an old pal from my rugby-playing days in The Town. We were at an Irish rugby international at the Aviva Stadium.

"Biscuits, have ye seen Joe Duffy's autobiography?"

Biscuits, I should explain, was the nickname I acquired in Dundalk Rugby Club, playing for the very sociable 3rds and 4ths. I was heard calling for a 'bikkie ball', a signal that I was going to pick up the ball from the back of the scrum and run at the opposition. The club comic and local optician, John Leavy, found the codename – and the very concept of me running athletically through enemy lines – too funny. On the spot, he nicknamed me *Biscuits*. It stuck, if only in The Town.

A few days later, I bought a copy of Joe's autobiography. Sure enough, there I was in the middle of the tale of Chocolate Kimberley. Joe is an icon of Irish broadcasting, but back in the early 1990s, he was an emerging name. He launched the Workers Playtime segment on the Gay Byrne Show on RTE Radio with the aim of bringing talent from the factory floor to the airwaves. In addition to his successful morning radio programme, of course, Gay was the renowned host of *The Late Late Show* on RTE television. The slot on Gay's radio show shone a light on young Joe's talent.

A call came in to one of the factory managers in Jacob's to see if we would host the first Workers Playtime event. It was a perfect fit and the factory team was up for it. They knew I would be too and asked me to take it forward. The many and varied characters in Jacob's were quickly identified, with their songs, anecdotes and Dublin wit, including one lady with a booming voice, known affectionately to all as 'Bernie, the queen of the mallow'.

Joe charmed and cajoled the best out of each character and was rewarded with rich content for the segment. But the fun was only beginning. In the course of the programme, a listener phoned into RTE asking if Jacob's would bring back Chocolate Kimberley. Joe took up the campaign.

The idea of bringing back Chocolate Kimberley (discontinued as part of the move to Tallaght) was a popular request but had been met with resistance in Jacob's, which was starved of money to invest in the machinery required. Factory workers regularly took the normal, sugar-coated Kimberley biscuit, placed it on the chocolate enrober, then walked alongside the conveyor belt as the Kimberley first got coated in milk chocolate and then cooled on the refrigeration belt, ready for their lunch box. To my mind, no further market research was needed.

Well, Joe's crusade catapulted the project to an altogether new level of urgency. To get around the investment question, I proposed launching a Christmas tin of Chocolate Kimberley, confident we would secure the necessary price premium to cover the initial additional labour costs. Within weeks, the first tins of Chocolate Kimberley were delivered to RTE's head office in Donnybrook. There followed a celebration on national radio and television, with a live Saturday night prime-time feature on *The Late Late Show*. In his time-honoured tradition, Gay Byrne declared "there's one for everyone in the audience". Singer Sinead O'Connor wouldn't leave the studio without her Chocolate Kimberley and the audience phone-in was hijacked by viewers trying to secure a tin. It was a rip-roaring success. We were sold out in weeks. When desperate consumers heard that tin supply was the constraining issue, some wanted to drive to Jacob's, tins in hand, looking for a refill.

Joe recalled the story in his autobiography, and it's a measure of him that he remembered me: *"The greatest achievement of the day – and probably of my radio career – was that, while reminiscing about long-gone biscuit [days], an intense demand for the re-emergence of the defunct Chocolate Kimberley emerged across the airwaves. Jacob's at the time had a young, bright marketing manager, Michael Dwyer, who jumped on the idea and had tins of Chocolate Kimberley in the shops for Christmas. They have been selling like hotcakes, so to speak, ever since."*

April 2011

We have just closed the books on an excellent month of March and an excellent first quarter. We are up about €80,000 in revenue versus budget for the month and up €140,000 for the quarter. It's down to Mega Deals. If Groupon started this deals wave, we're riding it. We hit €235,000 in gross revenues in March despite a poor start to the month. We are doing it well and putting a huge emphasis on deal quality. Behind Groupon, we are vying for second place with LivingSocial, which is backed by Amazon, and BoardsDeals.ie, which is backed by Distilled Media, which also owns the very successful Daft.ie property website and the recently-launched online news site, TheJournal.ie.

I can see us hitting the number two spot with some more new partnerships, kicking off in April with RTE, the *Irish Daily Mail* and Oxygen, a student website. It feels like providence is on our side at last. We have been blessed to be able to plug Mega Deals into our business relatively easily. They have brought good revenue, profit and cash. They have re-energised us.

I was recently appointed a director and incoming chairman of the Marie Keating Foundation, the cancer awareness charity set up about ten years ago by the Keating family to commemorate their mother, Marie, who passed away far too young from breast cancer. Valerie, of course, is married to Gary Keating.

It's a new departure for me, and I am feeling a little trepidation. The Keating family asked me to get involved about six months ago. I pushed it out initially for business reasons. There's never a good time, but something tells me I'm ready for it, and I have no issue volunteering my time and energy. So far, I'm enjoying it.

The foundation has been well served by its directors and executives and by the huge commitment of the Keating family. Linda Keating has served as director of fundraising since the start and travels the length and breadth of Ireland every year to raise money and spread the charity's important messages. My own appointment is an acknowledgement that board rotation is one of the keys to best practice governance in charities.

So many families are benefitting from the service. It's a positive distraction from Pigsback and refreshing, too, with new issues, new perspectives and new people.

———◆———

I was a little concerned that, at age 46, I might not have the physical and mental stamina for this one. The Connemarathon, they call it, drawing in seasoned athletes, the unsuspecting, the dreamers and – this year – me. 'To run within myself' was the plan and, hopefully, finish in under 4 hours and 20 minutes.

The start is in remote Connemara, alongside mystical Lough Inagh, with views of the Maamturks and the Twelve Bens. The field thins by midway at Leenaun, where supporters offer their applause, marvelling at the leaders, encouraging the straining masses, pitying the ill-prepared, and offering words of comfort to the unfortunate injured.

Then the undulating roads lead to Maum village with its welcome and support, sweets and water, before the runners face into the long uphill stretch known for good reason as the 'Hell of the West'. Eventually, the crowd comes into sight at Maam Cross, in dotted lines first, lifting the spirits, the finish in sight now, then joy at the final stretch, arms aloft across the line in exhausted ecstasy, down to a walk, emotionally accepting the medal from a kind volunteer, before polishing off a 99 from a well-positioned ice cream van.

It was a 3 hours and 59-minute run but months in the making.

———◆———

Ireland is weary, battered by its bleak economy, banking woes, a deficit of silly proportions, and a national debt of insane magnitude. The marrow is being dried from the economy's bones. No one wants to take the hit – IMF, ECB, EU, the bondholders – and it's all left to the SMEs, the taxpayers, the masses in the middle, to grin and bear it.

The country needs some wins, small and big. We don't need dramatic conclusions or new economic bubbles. Lots of little wins might get us restarted. God knows the people have earned a break.

Perhaps as a reminder of what is really important in life, our eldest girl Kerry, aged 15, and the middle girl Nicky, aged 13, both had health scares.

Kerry took a bad fall when her horse fell on landing after a jump. Kerry was catapulted to the ground head-first, and her helmet came off on impact before the horse tumbled over her. She had a seizure and was still unconscious when I got the call at home.

As I set out for the nearby stables, praying to God to look after Kerry, I would have given up everything and anything I possessed. I arrived minutes later. Mercifully, she had regained consciousness and had movement in her hands and toes. She lay on the ground with sand and fibre remnants all over her. We couldn't risk moving her and waited for the ambulance. She recognised me and, although disorientated, the signs were encouraging.

The rest of the weekend was spent in the excellent care of nearby Naas Hospital and Beaumont Hospital in Dublin. After a few weeks' rest, Kerry recovered well and was allowed back riding. Then her own normally sure-fire pony ploughed through a fence, and Kerry was again knocked heavily to the ground. Once more, she hit her head, but the helmet played its part this time, and there was less impact. A long break was agreed upon and very careful consideration before she'll get in the saddle again.

Nicky, our middle girl, also gave us some worries earlier in the year with a bone infection which left her in intensive care in Crumlin Children's Hospital in Dublin for treatment and observation. She was kept in for a week and treated with great rigour and attention. She made a full recovery.

I count us very fortunate to come through these episodes. We have a lot to be grateful for.

For the first time in maybe a decade, I have truly felt the weight lifting. I am feeling fulfilled from a full and varied life with family, friends, business, sport and some gardening. God alone knows what is around the corner, but I am coming out of myself again and for that, I am very grateful!

Business-wise it has been very positive and exciting. I still have lots to be concerned about but it's easier when you're out of the bunkers with good results and a sniff of success. It puts a smile on the face and breeds positivity.

Mega Deals account for the turnaround. They will be the largest part of our business next year and may soon leave the rest in the shade. We are happy to follow in the slipstream of Groupon but with the advantages of knowing the local turf better and of bringing a very useful brand legacy, member following and service ethos with us.

Weaning ourselves off the old model and onto MegaDeals is a precarious financial balancing act. We can't just abandon the traditional Pigsback Advertising business because it is still important financially to us, but the reality is that we've been haemorrhaging revenues in this area since 2007, mostly to Facebook and Google. To many advertisers and their agencies, the gravitational draw to these monoliths is irresistible. They now dominate an utterly-changed advertising world.

October 2011

I may have spoken too soon. We have just got some concerning data on the deals market. Although we have grown pretty much every month since we launched in the Mega Deals space, the market has outgrown us in recent months.

It looks like we have underestimated the progress made by some rivals. Groupon remains a strong leader, with over half of the market, but the fight for the number two slot looks set to be vicious.

There is a new entrant called GrabOne, a joint venture between the Irish newspaper group Independent News and Media (INM) and APN in Australia. It is a formidable competitor all of a sudden and commercially aggressive too. GrabOne has a huge leg-up from INM with open access to its newspaper titles and websites to advertise its brand and deals. It is moving very quickly into the regions too and showing sales growth for its efforts.

Groupon and LivingSocial continue to spend literally millions of euros building their audiences in Ireland through every available online advertising channel. Other competitors like BoardsDeals and a couple of smaller local discount entrants are active too. The barriers to entry in the deals market are low; the upshot is that we are losing market share.

Can the market stay like this for long? No. It's hard to believe that anyone is making money right now except Groupon. That's unsustainable. The economist John Maynard Keynes once warned rather ominously that *markets can stay irrational longer than you can stay solvent.*

Long-term, I think two deals players can survive but hardly more. Our resources don't compare to Groupon, LivingSocial or GrabOne. But we know all about *Loaves and Fishes*, and we will have to try harder.

It is going to be some battle. Bring it on. I will do it for my family and for everyone involved in and around this venture.

———◆———

We had our AGM today. There were seven external shareholders, mostly the ex-Octagon directors, who have been consistent supporters of Pigsback from the start. It feels like a key juncture, and the vibe was guardedly positive.

We opened with another candid review of what went wrong: the UK investment now lost, recalling very good traction but poor timing and too much market resistance from agencies; the misfortune of Bell's withdrawal from our very promising Canadian joint venture; the economic tsunami since 2008 that almost wrecked our business in Ireland, and the steep and steady decline of the Pigsback Advertising business.

I reported that we were in the process of administering the final nail in the coffin of our UK-registered company. Good riddance. We have taken the two remaining employees into the Irish company structure, both helping with Mega Deals. One is finding new merchants for new deals in the UK, and the other is doing graphics and copywriting.

We discussed our mixed but encouraging trading overall: Mega Deals reached over €3 million in sales in its first 12 months, bringing in net revenue of close to €1 million, well ahead of the initial forecast. Pigsback Advertising continued its decline, but we still need its contribution to overheads and profit.

Overall, the business is profitable and growing again. We are predicting that 2011 net revenues will be up over 20% on last year. We explained how the competition is hotting up and our market share concerns, but also the path to more profit if we can win the volume and market share battles ahead.

Shareholders don't like seeing their investments go down in value, so it was gratifying to hear those present give us credit for our candour and honesty through the difficult times.

———————•———————

November 2011

I'm sitting at Manchester Airport with a pint of ale. It's November 3rd, my birthday. I am taking the weight off my feet, having just taken another weight off my mind for good. We have formally put the UK business into liquidation. It was a horror story, really, but a line is finally drawn under it now. I won't waste another ounce of positive energy on it.

———————•———————

This deals business is fast-evolving and fiercely competitive. We're trying to be chess-like with our strategy and tactics, knowing we just can't afford a wrong move.

Our strategy is to keep accentuating our more premium brand positioning. This is in response to hoteliers and restaurateurs consistently giving us feedback that our members are more mature and have more money to spend than those of our competitors. That's a very useful insight and competitive advantage. It's precisely the profile that the top four-star and five-star hotels want to see. Our members are all-round good to themselves: they move up the wine list, go through the menu courses, tip the staff and use the spa. That really makes a difference to our hotels. Not only do they monitor this so-called *overspend*, but they are very careful to attract suitable customers for their brands.

In a matter of months, we have become the sought-after deals site for these hotels, having run very successful deals for the K Club and Druids Glen Resort, both renowned five-star Irish properties. Groupon has burnt some bridges in this area by over-selling deals and by failing in its backup service to some hotels. The hotel breaks segment is ours to win and keep. That's a major priority.

Some restaurants use daily deals as a cash flow crutch. Our competitors, notably GrabOne, are paying them everything upfront, regardless of the refunds they might have to issue down the road. Looks like we'll have to play our competitors at their own game to get in on that action. We have little choice.

———————◆———————

There is a whole new market expanse emerging, meanwhile, in what we call the 'Goods Business'. It refers to products bought as a deal and requiring delivery, typically to the home. Our merchants have sold beanbags and watches, sunglasses and laptops, slimming pills and wine. We know that our range is too limited and our delivery timelines are not yet what they need to be, but we are moving quickly to improve these.

The Pigsback Goods business is being incubated by Rob Larmour, our last remaining UK employee. As it happens, many of the merchants are UK-based, so that works. We are getting good traction for these offers in Ireland. Rob seems to have a flair for trading, so we have let him at it, with Johnny Mc in support. We have some figuring out to do and need to very aggressively expand the range of offers, but we're here to play. The same people who are buying those K Club breaks might pop into The Harbourmaster pub for lunch on the way and come home to find their garden furniture delivered, all of it via Pigsback.com.

I'm hoping that the Goods business, created in the last salvo by our team in the UK, will help recover significant corporate value for Pigsback. That would be nice after all we've been through. We'll give it every chance.

———————◆———————

Groupon's IPO on the Nasdaq stock market raised $700 million for the company at a valuation of $20 billion. The shares rose 30% on their first day's trading. The doubters are flummoxed, the believers bullish. It feels like it can only be good for the deals market and, maybe, for Pigsback.

———————◆———————

Our former UK MD, Brian Harrison, whose departure to the Telegraph upset me initially, has now landed as MD of the second-biggest daily deals business in the UK: KGB Deals. Brian has recruited quite a few of the old Pigsback.com UK team, and they are willing to trade insights and tips. We took a small team to meet them in London.

The main conclusion for us was that we need to publish more deals on the site and get more Pigsback people on the road. Johnny Mc and I duly agreed that we are going to ramp up the number of local sales reps.

Back to basics, feet on the ground, knocking on doors.

———————◆———————

January 2012

Pigsback Advertising remains a very leaky bucket. In contrast, we're forecasting gross sales of just over €8 million for Mega Deals in 2012, from nowhere 18 months ago.

We have split the Mega Deals business into three units: Pigsback Hotels, Pigsback Local and Pigsback Goods. We have just appointed Barry McGrath, proudly home-grown in Pigsback.com, as head of hotels, which is quickly becoming our biggest and most important unit.

This week we welcomed three new Mega Deal reps. We won't get to number two in the market without them. With this expansion of the local salesforce, we have committed to a great deal with the car brand Fiat, which will see our fleet of white Fiat 500s grow to 12. It's a deal in cash and kind, ramping up Fiat's advertising on our site and on social media. With a huge pink Curly on the side of each car, that fleet will make for some sight. We are branding a commuter bus in Co Kildare, too, in another contra deal. It's bright pink, of course, and features Curly in a few guises, all very large. Quite unmissable. We are also doing a big 'Welcome Home' ad in Terminal 2 at Dublin Airport to match the one we already have in Terminal 1. It is a huge brand statement and marks a step up in our win–win partnership with

Dublin Airport. In addition, we have secured more contra advertising on radio and in magazines and have done a deal for a homepage position on the RTE.ie website for the year.

Finally, we are determined to crack Google and Facebook for our own use. We are starting to ramp up our spending to see what business we can viably generate through advertising on those platforms.

It's feeling like a dynamic marketing environment once again.

Kevin, our chairman, has sensed the confidence in the air again and is keen to get back to planning an exit. I'm not as keen. My gut feeling is that we need time to expunge the advertising business and replace it with something bigger and better in the deals space. Nonetheless, we had our first conversation with a potential corporate finance adviser last Friday in Dublin, and Kevin has lined up two more meetings in London.

———————◆———————

During our succession of crises, tribulations, half-fixes and fixes, cash deprivation, hope against hope, and tireless reinvention, myself and Johnny Mc strained like no others. We seemed to discover a kind of reserve tank that was untapped in either of us until then. There was a pleasure in discovering those reserves and a strange satisfaction in working under stress and – above all – surviving.

For long periods, every day was a hard fight. We knew we could lose any given battle, but we always felt that the war was ours to win. That's optimism!

In Moby Dick, the narrator Ishmael describes the whalers' peculiar thrill at the lowering of the boats from the whale ship, the Pequod, and the desperado humour at these times of great danger. Johnny Mc and I had our share of those ironic laughs - unexpected but welcome levity coming from the depths. Afterwards, when the danger has passed, the whalers miss the edge and the frayed nerves. For Johnny and myself, there has been more time and calm recently between battles. Weirdly, it can feel like something's lacking - addicts without our drug.

———————◆———————

As a growing proportion of our 250,000 members are now buying goods from us, this opens opportunities and threats on the supply side, which we must tackle. Our goods buyers want a bargain, but they see us as their fall-back if something goes wrong with the product or merchant. One merchant has just sold a large number of tablet computers in advance of delivery at a price of just €117. It's an alternative to the expensive Apple iPad and seems like a great starter tablet or laptop alternative for secondary school kids. But there are risks. What if this product turns up with Chinese instructions, not English language ones? What if it doesn't meet European technical or safety guidelines, despite assurances? What if the merchant takes our upfront payments and runs? What if there's a fault that causes damage to one of our customers? They are all obvious and serious questions which we are trying to address. We may need an alternative to dealing with it on an ad hoc basis with the importing merchants, mainly based in Britain. Getting closer to the point of manufacture, mainly China, may help us to ensure quality and be more competitive.

Personally, I have never been drawn to China. Frankly, I have been wary. I don't think my experience with Jacob's inflatable shamrocks helped, but I haven't felt inclined or ready to take on the cultural and business challenges there. But China has become the world's factory, and so many huge businesses have formed very successful supply alliances. It's time we explored the possibilities in more depth. To kick it off, Johnny Mc and Rob, our head of goods, are planning a visit to China. We have an Irish agent to advise us and accompany the lads. It is early days, but there is momentum.

With the battle for Bell in 2007, the sun set for Pigsback in the West. Could it now rise in the East?

March 2012

Kevin is actively on the prowl for an exit and has set up two meetings for us in London today. We arrived at Goldman Sachs, where our first meeting was scheduled with the very affable Hugo MacNeill, the former Irish rugby international and now investment banking dynamo. This is the London den of the *Masters of the Universe*. It is an imposing building with no branding and a big security presence.

"Sir, have you got the right building?"

I don't think the Occupy London protesters outside St Paul's Cathedral, only hundreds of yards away, would get beyond the doormat. We managed that, at least.

I felt like a bit of a fraud in this haven of wealth and corporate deals of the highest magnitude. Eighteen months ago, my injured enterprise was on the verge of insolvency, and at a personal level, recent years have given me a financial roasting. But up we went to the 11th floor and met Hugo and a colleague. There was no aloofness or condescension. Hugo was the gentleman we expected and hoped to meet. His colleague was keen to give us a steer or two but made it clear from the get-go that this was a favour for Kevin and that Goldman Sachs wouldn't be taking on Pigsback.com as a client.

We knew we were way too small for them but had nothing to lose by listening to their advice: "Make your numbers, develop your growth story and keep working on the new idea that propels you back onto the international stage."

It felt like an hour well-spent, and we moved on to meet a smaller and more suitable boutique corporate finance outfit. They certainly seemed to want to take us on and were talking about a valuation of "15 million to 20 million". I didn't want to ask if they meant euro or sterling, so I stuck to my poker face. What a turnaround in our fortunes that would be in a couple of years. They are selling their corporate finance services, which don't come cheap but, at those numbers, they should be able to add enough value for whatever fee they might charge. Kevin is buoyed up, the smell of exit in his nostrils. After everything I have been through, this is exciting but feels a bit too easy and somewhat surreal.

———◆———

I don't wake up these mornings worrying about Pigsback. For years, a cloud hung over me, my mind overshadowed by the worries, my personality weighed down by what might happen, what needs to be done, what's helping, and what isn't. And, of course, obsessing doesn't help. That cloud has moved on. Thankfully.

Groupon is having issues, and I find myself a bit divided. A strong market leader invests in a market, and that rising tide can lift all boats. As such, I welcomed their successful IPO. Groupon is a candidate to acquire Pigsback. But Groupon's share price has more than halved from its peak in response to accounting practices that the market didn't like. Their promoters hungrily took cash off the table too. I am probably old-school, but it feels a bit odd to me that promoters take cash off the table before a business is established and proven. Given Groupon's struggles, it smacks of greed and desperation. I can only conclude that this is what can happen when there is an oversupply of capital and an undersupply of enterprises with unicorn potential - those start-ups capable of creating prize pots of billions for investors.

I have to think clearly about what Groupon's issues mean for Pigsback. My read is that the deals business model is fundamentally a good one, but it must improve on some of its business basics, like customer care, merchant care and realistic pricing. For now, Groupon's weakness is our opportunity, but we must do better. How do we present ourselves as distinct from and better than Groupon? How do we ensure that we can sustain our growth without the big Groupon engine driving the market? What is certain is that unprofitable operators will die as the sheen goes off the deals market. I fancy Pigsback will be a survivor, led by our hotel breaks, with goods, and maybe fewer local offers, all wrapped up in a more upmarket, customer-centric brand and business.

Time will tell, but I think we're on the right track. We were never followers.

April 2012

I wonder if we could make the *Guinness Book of Records?* Yesterday, over 26,000 members fell for our good-humoured April Fools' prank. Our graphic offered '50% off Household Charges', the new and very controversial government charge, which isn't going to be discounted any time soon.

We did label it an 'Unbelievable Offer', which, of course, it was. We're a local brand without big corporate strictures, so we can have fun like this, not the type of thing Groupon or LivingSocial will be doing any time soon.

We're off on a week's family holiday now – and I won't be worrying about the business.

———•———

I sense it was a tough enough visit to China for Johnny Mc and Rob. Their time was spent mainly in the industrial southern province of Guangdong, a labyrinth of factories and traders' warehouses. On their return, it didn't take much discussion to conclude that dealing directly with Chinese factories is not for us.

The complexity of coming up with a wide range of reliable manufacturers across many categories – with appropriate quality assurance – is likely to be beyond us. Instead, we are going to put our efforts into filtering the professional merchants from the chancers and opportunists. The good ones earn and deserve their margin. We can and should stick to the knitting, getting the demand side right, making sure we do the front-end marketing better than anyone else, and choosing our merchants carefully. We may lose some profit margin, but it is more likely to lead to better quality supply and less complexity.

This is the best solution in a sector fraught with quality risks and where it's often easier to get it wrong than right.

The lads were unimpressed by the local fare, too: "not nearly as good as the Chinese in Thomastown," according to Johnny Mc. They were never so pleased to see a sign for a McDonald's restaurant on their last day. Home sweet home.

———•———

Recent challenges have led me to ponder what we've got right and wrong in recruitment. It's such a key process for any business.

We acted very quickly sometimes - even at the first interview. Conveying our confidence like that can really build someone's confidence and commitment. Overall, it has served us well as a strategy, and it's very gratifying when we're right and a good one comes through. But of course, it means getting it wrong sometimes, which can be painful.

We don't expect to employ the finished article. Of course, we'll invest time and money to unearth and harness someone's talents. We want progressiveness, room for improvement, and material to work with.

We don't want clones. Once the baseline intelligence and ambition are established, we are looking for a chink of light behind the initial appearances: character, humility, and a hint of something special.

Finally, we do want people to want us - people who believe in the company and brand. They won't need much motivating!

One mistake we have made a few times in the past (and I blame myself) was to back someone who was too individual to the point of being selfish. They are so driven as to be 'all elbows', pursuing their own ambition, their own objectives, their own need to stand out, and their own material progression above everyone else's. It's so tempting to let them keep bringing in the results because they will, but we've always ended up regretting it. Individualism is corrosive in organisations which are collectives, where people rely on each other, must work together to a common overall purpose, support each other, and should certainly not undermine each other. Be driven and ambitious, by all means, but get the balance right and work with others in your team and in the overall organisation! No *one* is more important than the team.

We've had our retention challenges too lately, as I've documented, but I think we've found a good workaround by targeting a different profile of candidate.

———————◆———————

June 2012

It's a mixed picture but a pretty clear one.

Research remains solid, albeit off a small base, and Pigsback Advertising continues its uninterrupted fall despite our best efforts.

On the deals front, the Goods business continues to show lots of potential, but painfully, in local and hotel deals, too many players are fighting even harder for market share. It can't continue like this.

Johnny Mc and I took a trip to London last week. We had four meetings over two days and plenty of time to consider what was right and wrong in the affairs of Pigsback.com in between. We spent a lot of time discussing the interest being shown by the National Consumer Agency (NCA) in the UK in the deals space. A week or so earlier, we had received a letter from the Irish equivalent of the NCA making certain enquiries. The same letter was sent to all players in the sector. It felt like an exploratory exercise more than anything else, but Johnny and Dave Foody replied within days to outline why everything we were doing was kosher. Our proactivity was appreciated, and no concerns were apparent.

As we landed in Dublin on Thursday evening, a message was waiting to contact RTE News, which was doing a piece on the NCA's review. RTE wanted a spokesperson for the industry. There's the power of the Pigsback brand again: we are not market leaders, but we are long associated with the market and don't hide our heads in the sand.

We headed straight for RTE in Donnybrook, and I pre-recorded a brief piece for the late evening TV news on RTE2. The following morning I was on Morning Ireland, the biggest morning drivetime radio show in Ireland, for a live interview with presenter Cathal Mac Coille along with the guy from the NCA.

Mac Coille grilled me, but I had customer service data which I cited, evidencing the very high levels of satisfaction with our service. I outlined the major benefits to merchants in terms of new customers, high profile, no upfront investment and high *overspend* from Pigsback customers. At lunchtime, it was Today FM, in the evening Q102, and, a couple of mornings later, Newstalk's early morning business show with Ian Guider.

It was a buzz. I thoroughly enjoyed the media work and was happy that Pigsback was getting the profile and was seen to be open and trustworthy. If we stepped into the breach to speak for the industry, that was our good fortune – and fortune, sometimes, favours the brave.

July 2012

This trip was JD's treat. He invited Harry and me to Las Vegas to mark Harry's 50th, a break planned to coincide with the World Series of Poker. We were brought up in a card-playing household, but there's a lifetime's learning in poker, and it requires lots of practice, where I fall down for obvious reasons.

I love tournament poker, in particular, and it suits me. With a tournament, there is a fixed entry amount. You know exactly how much you are staking, and you invest that upfront in return for tournament chips. The objective is to win everyone else's chips. It is buzzy, mathematical, and psychological. It requires patience, a level head, and aggression. It's about knowing the strength of your position from known variables: your cards, the community cards, players' chip counts, and betting patterns and from unknown variables: your opponents' cards, their propensity to bluff, and the chances of them making a mistake. Poker requires the player to make multiple quick decisions: to take no further part in a hand (fold), to invest in good cards (value betting), to invest in cards that have unfulfilled potential (semi-bluffing) or to invest in inferior cards (bluffing). But players must take into account their position at the table, the phase of the tournament, their stack size, their opponents' stack sizes, position, cards, abilities and mindset. The senses need to be alert, the sixth sense awake, and the patience and aggression tanks both full and at the ready. It's only a game, of course, but it's a game of warfare, albeit a sociable one.

We looked forward to Las Vegas for months, and it didn't let us down. We will be living off the memories for another few months. I won my section of a Shoot-Out event, and was knocked out just three places shy of the final table. A prize of $9,000 was a fair consolation, but there was a top prize of close to $1 million. That would have remedied an issue or two.

---•---

September 2012

Perhaps it's some of the negative publicity or shoddy service associated with the sector, but it's like 'deal' has become a dirty word. The excessive competition doesn't help. Every deal has several companies queuing up for it, and some of the later entrants are not resourced to handle the service required and the problems that can arise. Margins are falling, too, in a race to the bottom.

We are trying hard to maintain our pricing discipline but have to be pragmatic at times. The fizz seems to be going out of the market. Hotels have been holding back on deals in what feels like a concerted move to promote direct business. We have had to significantly revise our forecast for the year, which now feels like it was drafted in a different climate.

BoardsDeals, a significant competitor, has closed its doors in a vote of no-confidence in the market. The closure announcement had a swipe at competitive practices and unsustainable undercutting. No wonder! We had BoardsDeals at fifth place in the market, so its closure won't make a huge difference. The tactics of the top three are of far greater concern, in particular INM's GrabOne, which joined the market with nothing new to offer. Instead, it attacks with a price-led strategy. Unfortunately, INM needs a digital success story and seems happy to fund a bunch of losses to get it. It's painful. It has been more of the same in recent months, and I sense the collapse of one, maybe two, high-profile players at this rate.

I am very focused on putting brand distance between us and the daily deal people, and fast. That means continued accentuation of our premium brand positioning and of our older and more affluent audience. We have finally resolved to remove the Mega Deals brand, indeed any mention of 'deals', from our business. It's a longer-term play and is not without risks. We are now all talking about our 'Exclusive Offers' and our 'Premium Brands'.

We have also retreated from the all-things-to-all-people Local Deals strategy we were pursuing. Instead, we have retained a small local team focused on the higher end of the market, better quality restaurants as well as beauty and hair salons. We are majoring on short breaks, at the premium end in particular, and on the goods sector, where we are encouraged by developments.

It may have taken a few hard knocks from an overcrowded market to articulate what distinguishes Pigsback from the crowd. It's difficult, but it may not be a bad thing for us in the long run.

7

Exit Tension

January 2013

We closed out 2012 at just over €4 million in net revenues, up 17%. We invested in our growth, and this resulted in a small and disappointing net loss. We estimate our market share at 17%, which is satisfactory, albeit we only measure the top four sites. And we certainly consolidated our leading position in short breaks.

We are forecasting low single-digit growth in 2013, but an operating profit of €600,000. Our cost base is already tight, but we'll keep looking for further efficiency.

Kevin continues to press the exit agenda hard, despite a lack of progress since our meetings with advisors. As chairman and significant shareholder, he's well within his rights, but I'm still not feeling it. I don't think our numbers are good enough, and I can't see the value in the business right now. I have faith given time and would prefer to focus on winning the market than on pursuing an exit.

———◆———

We have been working on a strategy to develop upmarket channel-specific sub-brands. First up was the launch of TheDiningRoom.ie focused on quality restaurants. We invited restaurateurs and press to a lunch in the Michelin-star restaurant, L'Ecrivain, to mark the launch. The restaurant's owners, Derry and Sallyanne Clarke have been very supportive of this new avenue for our business.

Tom Doorley, the well-known restaurant critic, has agreed to act as our restaurant and wine contributor. He attended the launch along with a host of Ireland's top restaurateurs and some celebrities who had submitted posts under the heading 'My Favourite Restaurants'.

There was excellent coverage of the launch in newspapers and magazines. The same restaurateurs who were previously reluctant to be on Pigsback.com are embracing TheDiningRoom.ie. That is the value of a focused and premium brand and community.

Not a week later, I was back on media duty, this time on TV3 to defend our offers against an attack by the Restaurants Association of Ireland (RAI). The RAI's chief executive is against deals, full stop. He is not engaging to discuss the pros and cons. My main point was that restaurants have a lot to gain if they understand the 'how, when and where' of using offers. We have many restaurant clients who do not agree with the blanket dismissal of deals, and I was not prepared to give the RAI a free run with its negativity. The presenter, former Fine Gael minister Nora Owen, made all her guests feel relaxed and welcome, and I must say, I enjoyed the buzz of the TV studio.

July 2013

We're at the midpoint of another year, and the going is tough. The economy seemed to groan audibly in May as the first Local Property Tax payment, a new annual charge, fell due. When will this austerity stop? FMCGs, once our golden goose, are being squeezed further as the discounters continue to win market share in the grocery market. The upshot is that any effort to stem the decline of Pigsback Advertising is futile. My friend Paul Duffy chose the right words for it: "It's hard to catch a falling knife", he said as he encouraged me to keep looking beyond the failing model. I should listen to Paul. Few people have looked out for me more than he has. A few years ago, sensing my pressures, he invited me to consider leaving Pigsback for a role in the large international company that he was heading up. I gave it some thought. It was good for my confidence and good to feel that there might be a fallback. In the end, I felt I had no option for all concerned but to hang in with Pigsback.

Johnny Mc has taken the finance function under his wings. With Kevin and Tom McCormick both on our board, he has plenty of accounting and finance advice available to him. He won't need much.

Right now, we are back in the trenches, managing working capital to a daily schedule. It's a critical occupation but not one I would choose. There is a lot of negative stress in it, and the main satisfaction is simply getting to the other side. Our creditors are waiting longer than we would like, the bank overdraft is regularly up against its limit, and we are back negotiating a seasonal payment schedule with the Revenue.

We expect to get respite in September, with increased hotel supply coming on stream just as many members are thinking of getting away with their partners or friends after a summer spent with the kids. Then, from October, the first gifts will be purchased and squirrelled away by members, well ahead of the bumper Christmas season. We hope!

We continue to adapt. TheDiningRoom.ie is going down well since its April launch, attracting more premium restaurants. We have wasted no time in launching TheBeautyLounge.ie, our bespoke offering for the beauty segment. It was impressive to watch a small team, led by Valerie, getting an identity and design together, planning and commissioning content, making a huge effort to get merchants on board with their offers, and planning a launch party, all in a matter of weeks.

We are exploring new sub-brand concepts for premium hotels, for our shopping proposition and potentially even for a food channel.

It's altogether a more exclusive execution.

We might yet prove Darwin's view that 'it is not the strongest of the species or the most intelligent of the species that survives, but the one that is most adaptable to change.'

———————•———————

I'm on a flight home from London, a welcome change. I've missed airports – the 'me time', space to think, to read and to write, as the world hurries by. When travelling, it's easier to find pockets of time for my journals in an unforced way or to read random articles in papers or on social media.

One such random article featured two professors debating whether good entrepreneurs are products of nature or nurture. For my money, it's nature with a bit of nurture. However, an entrepreneurial nature easily gets suppressed by the cycle of life and careers, buried under the weight of responsibilities and daily pressures. This is where the 'displacement factor' comes into play, something I heard about in college many years ago. Some people need to be jolted out of the comfort of their everyday lives if they are to achieve the level of motivation required to launch a new business. This could be a redundancy, a death of a loved one, a breakup, or a move from one region to another. Even the most naturally entrepreneurial individual can need a catalyst.

I enjoyed the visit to Lonor don and walked extensively as I usually do, this time through Hyde Park, Green Park and St James Park. London felt edgy, positive and flush. The city seems to have put recession behind it, and I was glad to enjoy it with our UK business stresses behind me now.

I was there to meet Groupon's vice president for Europe, a meeting I prompted but he readily accepted. Sure, Groupon is a competitor but it is also a potential acquirer or partner of some sort for Pigsback. We spent around an hour together. I wanted to emphasise that we weren't another follower and that we were around a full decade before Groupon and tried to pioneer where we could. To his amusement, I showed him a copy of the 1999 newspaper on which I jotted the concept for Pigsback. He liked what he called our 'verticalisation strategy'. We parted, agreeing to have a pint together on his next trip to Dublin.

It is an important part of any CEO's job to get around within the industry and meet the key players. It's about a potential exit, for sure, but also about being networked for when opportunities arise and being tuned into the latest thinking and developments.

Johnny Mc and I met our landlord, a North American bank, together with its letting agent. The office space in Citywest is simply too big for the slimmed-down Pigsback, and the expensive and lengthy lease makes no sense.

We need a rent reduction and a concession on unpaid arrears. Ironically, the arrears we have built up are helpful in making our problems and demands real. We faced a very stern audience of four. With no chit-chat, the man from the bank opened: "You're €55,000 in arrears. Could you explain that, please?" I gave it to him lock, stock and barrel, with emotion evident in my voice: "We're facing unprecedented economic and market difficulties, as well as the demise of our traditional business. Add to that, poor seasonal hotel deals supply in a very hot summer, and it's even worse. Our balance sheet is very weak, despite the long list of cost savings we have achieved. We don't believe our brand and corporate reputation could survive the damage of a formal restructuring."

This was code for an examinership, a temporary court protection for a business from creditors under Irish law, or the more drastic options of receivership or even liquidation. Any of those options would be bad news for the bank.

"What do you want from us?"

It was a blunt retort, but encouraging.

"We're just trying to come to a fair arrangement to exit an unsustainable contract. We have defined an affordable level of rent for our business based on its new reality. We need forbearance and cooperation in achieving this, as well as a compromise on outstanding arrears." My response was factual.

"You'll need to write to us with your latest accounts and your view that you are facing a restructuring if you don't get the concessions. If we agree to your request, we will issue you with a Deed of Renunciation and you will have to pay the new affordable levels of rent until we find another tenant, as well as charges. All of this is without prejudice."

We were pretty sure we had got what we came for. I sincerely thanked them for the meeting and for their constructive approach. I assured them we would waste no time in sending a board-approved proposal to them. We shook hands and left.

When a safe distance away, I glanced at Johnny Mc. "That went well" he smiled. We were fortunate to have a receptive party opposite us. It could be a big building block to a secure future.

———————•———————

Dealing successfully with our office lease brings another major liability into focus: Enterprise Ireland's Prefs and accrued interest, totalling €700,000 between them. They weigh like a tonne of bricks on our creaking balance sheet. The Prefs are a legacy of a different era and what now feels like an entirely different corporate project. As we launched Pigsback internationally, they were a welcome and important part of our funding. We undertook to invest in our product development and our marketing as we embarked on our hugely ambitious launches in the UK and North America. We did all of that and found ourselves near death's door.

We could have opted to restructure, which, if completed with due process, would have raised no issues with EI. Instead, we've tried to hang in to give all of our stakeholders another chance: staff, creditors, customers, shareholders, and the state agency too. Everyone took a lot of pain as we sought to cut costs to a realistic level: shareholder loans were converted to equity, salaries were cut, my accrued pension was lost, shareholder stakes were diluted (none more than my personal stake) and key creditors like our landlord and our email provider agreed concessions.

Granted, there is no pressure from EI to repay, nor will there be any time soon, but a better balance sheet would give a lift to the business in several ways. The Prefs hangover makes us way less attractive as a company to invest in, and less motivating a place to work for anyone with equity as part of their package. If our competitors took a good look at our balance sheet, they could portray us as a risky trading partner.

So, all in all, it feels like a reasonable case for a write-down or even a conversion of the Prefs to ordinary shares. But EI is standing firm, however, claiming to be technically and legally hamstrung. They may be afraid of laying the preference share system open to abuse or even litigation.

I regret being the awkward client, but I have my responsibilities to my company and however difficult a position I put EI in, mine is worse. One day we will probably repay the state agency in full, but that's not the point. Right now, I must first and foremost seek to do what is best for my company.

EI certainly helped us as we were scaling, for which I will always be grateful. A little more flexibility in helping us to wriggle through the choking knots to recovery would be welcome right now.

———◆———

Our hyper-aggressive competitors are riding roughshod over our fancy brand positioning and new sub-brands with their lower commissions. With the cashflow pressure comes a focus on increasingly elusive cost savings: our marketing remains low in cash cost and high in invention; our technology has served us well, and we're down to a very small team; we have outsourced our IT management and moved most of our office services to the cloud; and our salespeople all pay for themselves and more.

We plough on, with an eye all the time to the future, hoping for a normalised market with fewer participants and more order. It can't come quickly enough.

We have launched LuxuryBreaks.ie as a specialist brand for premium hotels, manor houses, country homes and the like. We are adding a 'Golden Key' feature, an invitation-only VIP offer for top-end properties, which will kick off with Ashford Castle in Mayo and Dromoland Castle in Clare.

We have been working on a new mobile site and app too, called Pigsback Live. We're trying to fuse old and new together. We need to deliver on the 'live' piece with plenty of exciting fresh content and offers. The latest offers will be published to the Live stream as we go.

Competition has forced us to define a new strategy by reference to our competitors. We've learned where our strengths and weaknesses lie. We've upped our game. There are too many competitors. That's painful. Everyone appears to be losing money. Someone's got to blink soon. But some have very deep pockets. Some of these are international players. But this offers sector might yet be one where local advantage matters. So I tell myself. Glass half-full. Again.

November 2013

I have needed a calm head lately, most recently after a data theft at Loyaltybuild, a Co Clare company recently acquired by an international group. The personal and – in some cases – credit card details of customers gathered and stored by Loyaltybuild were stolen, with a potentially detrimental impact on the brand reputation of the affected partners.

I had been watching on from a comfortable distance for a few days until, out of the blue, Pigsback.com was mentioned on the *Irish Times* and RTE websites, and then on the main RTE News at 9 o'clock. We were one of many parties affected even though we haven't done business with Loyaltybuild for a few years.

Our own systems were not breached and we had not given any data on our members to Loyaltybuild. But they had legitimately gathered their own data on our members and held that on their servers, which were breached. It looks bad for Pigsback, even though we are entirely blameless and helpless in the situation.

Lots of big companies were affected by the breach, including Supervalu, Axa, ESB, Clery's and Stena Line. Our PR adviser wanted to issue statements and comments. We differed on this one. Pigsback did nothing wrong, and I felt that a calm, low profile was the way to go. It blew over quickly, but not before my mother-in-law Nora quipped: "You're in very good company with those big brands".

————————◆————————

I expected another faller in the deals market by now but the competitive pressure has actually increased. One of the lesser-known brands, DealRush.ie, is winning volume in the market by taking lower commissions from hotels. It means operating margins just continue to tighten for the deals companies, and that includes us.

Kevin, JD and other investors, I'm sure, look on wearily at the uncertainty and meanderings of the business. They would like an exit. I get it! But I have to keep focused on the business and make sure there is something left to sell whenever that time is right.

I am trying to give myself more elevation. It's a nuanced change, but potentially an important one - I have given Johnny Mc the day-to-day reins as MD of the business as I take a more strategic role as CEO. I will try hard not to get in his way. I want to use the breathing space to look to the future inside and outside of Pigsback.

————————◆————————

January 2014

It's been a poor start to 2014.

We lost one of our biggest hotel clients because GrabOne undercut us. On top of their discounting, they are throwing free advertising into the mix. Our premium branding arguments didn't stand up to a five-point reduction in a commission rate. We are between a rock and a hard place. If we give way, we can wipe a quarter off our hotel commissions – and who says it stops there? It is galling to suffer at the hands of a competitor that is racking up losses, subsidised by a parent company busily spinning yarns about a digital turnaround.

Mercifully, we have had wins too, including the five-star Castlemartyr Resort in County Cork and the very popular four-star Killashee House Hotel in County Kildare.

Meanwhile, Johnny Mc has not been 100% health-wise for a few months now. He is keeping fit and running lots, but he's tired. Ironically, work is his refuge.

All told, it's hard to be bullish about the year ahead. It's been feeling like 'one step forward and one or two steps back'. We beat on and sometimes I despair a little. *Me and Willy Loman*, I think. It's then that I try to remind myself of all the old positives in Pigsback: the brand, the audience loyalty and quality, the great team, the technology platform, and the legacy. These are the factors which have convinced me, time and time again, that we can prevail. If I feel I need it I add a dose of higher purpose: *the nobility of free enterprise* and the *brave place of the SME*. And, when a clincher is needed: *someone's got to show that these multinational heavyweights can be beaten.*

June 2014

After initially challenging me on the wisdom of abandoning a hard-earned senior seat in the corporate world, with its inherent financial security, my father-in-law Gerry became one of my biggest supporters. In his heyday, Gerry was a formidable businessman, working his way from the ground up to the very top of one of Ireland's leading financial institutions. He became a great mentor to me.

He has seen the highs and the lows on our Pigsback journey. As a mature investor, Gerry primarily wanted success for Karen and me. He was excited in those early years as he watched us achieve profitability in Ireland, take on the UK and partner with Bell in Canada.

He was fond of Johnny Mc too and took every opportunity to give us credit for longevity and any signs of progress. "Business," he regularly reminded us, "doesn't run on rail tracks," citing "unprecedented times" as we faced our 2010 restructuring. As business picked up with Mega Deals, he wrote with typical brevity: "Spirits should be lifting; keep up the good work! Adversity can be stimulating and rewarding."

Sadly, Gerry has been slipping away from us. We were aware that something was not quite right for quite a while, but the formal diagnosis of dementia is relatively recent. A long period of apparently harmless forgetfulness descended quickly into a phase of full-on confusion. Watching him wither visibly has been hard on Karen and on her mum Nora.

It is a long and particularly cruel goodbye when someone we love is still there but not.

———◆———

Meanwhile, I have just handed over the reins as chairman of the Marie Keating Foundation to Thérèse Rochford, who, as well as being a most capable corporate lawyer, is one of life's all-round decent skins. She is a sure pair of hands for the coming few years. As a cancer survivor herself, Thérèse has extra motivation. It's more of the board rotation that is important in voluntary bodies – come in, do your best for a few years, and then move on after paving the way for fresh blood.

During my time as chairman, Ireland's charity sector came under the spotlight with alleged unapproved salary and pension top-ups to senior executives in some non-profit organisations. The spotlight moved right across the wider charity spectrum. Thankfully, at the Marie Keating Foundation, the ratios of service spending to administration and fundraising are well managed, reflecting how tightly the foundation has been run.

There have been new appointments to the senior management team, too, notably the new CEO, Liz Yeates, also a cancer survivor and massively committed to the cause.

The Keating family continues to play its oversight role, and Linda Keating continues to lead fundraising. It is a strong triumvirate of board, management and family, which will ensure that the founding vision and ethos are protected.

———◆———

August 2014

We have launched a new feature for our hotel clients, which the team has called *Concierge*. Paul Finnegan, our very talented chief technology officer (CTO), has developed the back-end booking system to handle bedroom quotas for hotel clients, who have fed back their frustration at the prevailing manual processes to handle bookings and changes from the deals sector.

This latest innovation was driven by the sales team and their clients, and it's going down very well. None of our competitors has anything this effective, and it may make a big difference, given time and further development. It is all part of the continuing focus on where our business is strongest, hotel breaks.

We have also developed a new advertising campaign and strapline, also focused on hotels: *Pigsback.com – Enjoy Luxury for Less.* We will be using it in online and magazine advertisements, portraying some of our top properties. It hits back at GrabOne and others in a premium way. The message is that we are Ireland's premier source of quality short breaks, but that we also have fine dining offers, as well as the best in beauty and leisure.

Commercially, business remains gruelling as our competitors just seem to discount their way from one customer to the next. As if any extra pressure was needed, we have also had a frustrating financial reporting challenge to deal with. Having asked Johnny Mc to make the finance function his own, he has done precisely that. Unfortunately, not all of his conclusions are in our favour. We need to take a hit to the balance sheet to the tune of about €300,000 to reflect falling rates of voucher breakage, much of it relating to our leniency in giving credits to members for unused vouchers.

Coming on top of a write-down in a tax credit and some substantial restructuring costs, our 2013 statutory accounts are going to make grim reading.

———•———

We hit another cash flow bump and looked to AIB for a short-term debt facility. Our request was approved, but I broke a promise, personally guaranteeing a €75,000 overdraft top-up. It is the first and last time I will do it. I had no choice, and Karen is with me as ever.

Kevin gave a further €50,000 bridging loan. There was simply no point in asking other shareholders: most would walk away from their holdings rather than pony up.

———◆———

Trading has been incredibly tough. We're at about breakeven this year at an operating level, but we will record a loss at the net profit level. Working capital is at its worst right now, just before hotels start releasing availability to us for the autumn.

Hoteliers have enjoyed successive warm summers where Irish people have holidayed at home. With good weather, many hotels don't need us or our offers. Now Ireland is enjoying an Indian summer on top, extending the trading challenges faced by Barry McGrath and his hotel team into September.

———◆———

Last week I met a friend, now a partner in an insolvency company. I wanted to make sure that I understood my obligations as a director, the board's obligations and the company's options. It was unofficial and off the record. These are our options: trade out of it (we're trying); shareholder support (it won't be welcomed and probably won't work); an examinership or receivership (a last resort, and still requires new funding – but either would allow the new owners to wipe much of the overhang of the past); a liquidation (terminal, no coming back).

My friend was pressing me towards the examinership or receivership, but I am not prepared to suffer the price in reputational damage for the business, the brand and me.

There's plenty of advice coming at me too.

My brother JD is one of the most able and hard-working people I know and has the career success to show for it. His advice is: "Get out, sell, don't risk your reputation any further. You still have a decent career cycle ahead." I understand where he is coming from and I know it is well-intentioned. He has selflessly supported me and the business through troubled times. Objectively, he may be right, but we are on such different planets right now.

There are others offering similar well-meaning advice too. I hear them. I try to see the other side, but sometimes I wish they would just leave me alone. There may well be tidier and less stressful options out there, but I have given so much to this venture. I'm in deep, financially and emotionally. I have unfinished business.

Yes, I'm stubborn, and yes, I'm emotional, and maybe part of me doesn't want to listen. Maybe I'm not even seeing clearly?

Reading about Neil Alcock recently struck a chord. It was Alcock who conceived of and initiated the noble and massively progressive Msinga rural agriculture project in South Africa. As it was failing, he wrote to his former supporters asking: "Why have you abandoned me to fatigue, inefficiency and failure? Why me alone?" He got no replies.

———◆———

September 2014

Yesterday was September 11th, and I thought Pigsback was finally about to come crashing down around me. I walked around the Citywest business campus with Johnny Mc at mid-morning. Walking helped.

I was on the very edge of my nerves, and for once, my optimism seemed to betray me. I was struggling to see a way through. Sales were too slow; the weather was too good, so several of our big hotels held back capacity from us, delighting in their direct bookings.

There was one reason after another as to why this offer or that offer wasn't going live, was cancelled, was delayed or was lost to a lower margin from a competitor. Our creditors' list is too long, and our progress in normalising it feels too slow.

I sat down on a bench near the tram stop at Citywest, looking down at the unyielding concrete. My fingers were tugging at my hair, and I felt sick in my belly. Johnny alluded to our directors' responsibilities, and we went as far as to discuss the trigger points for a formal restructuring. But I was more focused on what it would take to get us over the hump and go again: *how do we trade out of this? What revenue can we fast-track? What forbearance can we expect on the payment due to the Revenue within days?* I felt there was a way through and wasn't ready to throw my towel in any time soon.

Johnny looked weary, his appetite and energy for the fight waning. I felt for my exhausted friend and colleague, seemingly at the end of the road, but we would have to return to that later. For now, I was on my own, confronting the entrepreneur's lonely truth: the buck stops with you.

I called Barry, our head of hotels, and asked him to join us. Barry was in the firing line of the competitive pressure. He held the levers.

"Let's do whatever it takes to secure whatever business is out there," I declared as my opener.

"If you cut the margin, it could cost us 200k annualised," Johnny interjected.

He had a point, technically, at least, but this was my battle now.

"We'll get it back through higher volumes," said Barry.

His confidence was helpful as both Johnny and I knew that Barry was closer to the sentiment among our hotel clients.

"The hotels are on our side for our brand and customers. Our service is better too, and they're loving Concierge. A few small concessions will do it," Barry continued.

He left to brief his team.

I got a notion almost straight after and met with Declan O'Reilly, the relatively new boss of the Empathy Research business. I put it to him that he should consider buying his business unit. We tested selling this business a few years ago, but there was no serious bite. But Declan expressed a keen interest, showing his hunger and ambition. It's early, but I think he could pull it off. We would miss the €100,000 or so in annual contribution from Empathy Research, but a lump of cash from a sale would go a long way to stabilising our business and even propelling it forward. Declan went off to do his research, his interest piqued.

I had scheduled lunch in Dublin with a mentor and friend, Brian Delaney, in Matt the Thresher. Divine intervention! Brian was in his usual bubbly form, recounting his projects and enviable life balance. His positivity was infectious, even as my stress simmered just below the surface.

Then it was my turn. Brian listened as I downloaded it all: the pressures, the worry, the fear that I was at the end of the road. I couldn't have wished for a better audience. He immediately brought perspective.

"You and most of Ireland's SMEs," he said. "You have an exaggerated sense of reputation damage among your creditors – you're probably in much better shape than most SMEs out there. Don't worry about the Revenue; they know what the economy is like and are reasonable. Your case is far from hopeless."

But he wasn't letting me off without a hard message: "Get ready to move on. Go explore mergers. Wrap this up with a healthier acquirer." I took it on the chin. Brian has my best interests at heart. But then the clanger: "You're better than this!"

Coincidentally, I had a meeting scheduled on my way back to the office. It was with a competitor, a potential merger partner. They had made the initial approach, which I welcomed. Again, it was early days, but Brian's words were now ringing in my ears.

By the time I eventually got back to the office, Barry and his team had concluded three new hotel deals. The biggest one was an exclusive 12-month deal, cutting out all competition in return for a modest margin concession. Barry had been given the ammunition and was delivering.

Typical of Johnny Mc, he had brushed himself off and got on with his own challenges. He filled me in on his discussions with the Revenue, matter-of-fact and a reasonable arrangement reached. This was progress too.

Sales for the day were also lifting. With the new offers about to break on the site, we could be back on track quickly.

But the day wasn't over yet.

That same morning, before all the drama, I encountered Tim Ryan, a marketing manager with Glanbia, our neighbour at CityWest, and we exchanged a bit of banter.

"You owe me a meeting and a new campaign," I said, laughing.

"I'll see you in the afternoon," he replied, then disappeared.

We have done a lot of business with Glanbia over the years and know them well at all levels. Our biggest partnership was in the development of the MyMilkman.ie concept and platform (codenamed

Project Doorstep at the time). It has gone on to win several awards and is now an important part of the Glanbia business in Ireland.

Guess what? Tim showed up to the office at 4.30 pm and agreed there and then to a €20,000 campaign for Avonmore Slimline Milk, very welcome revenue on the day that was in it. Good neighbours.

In the evening, Karen and I went for a walk around the Punchestown race track near our home, always a head-clearer, before meeting with Gabriel and Pam, owners of Grapevine. They too know the pains of enterprise.

Gabriel is using Linked Finance, a crowd-funding solution for SMEs, for the first time. Any member of the public can go in and take a slice of the loan Gabriel has sought. No personal guarantees are required there.

"Do you think they'd give me €200k?" I asked him.

He laughed good-humouredly. Good friends.

It had been a long day, but the early darkness had given way to brightness, a new dawn, I hope.

November 2014

I recently completed my tenth marathon in Dublin. On seeing me looking quite exhausted at the finish, Karen expressed her concern about the toll it seemed to have taken.

A few years ago, a friend commented in front of Karen that I could get a heart attack out running. "That's true," I replied, "but if that happens, I wouldn't blame it on the running."

Running has been my haven, but Karen is right: marathon-level exertions take a heavy toll, and notare getting any easier. For my 50th birthday on November 3rd, she presented me with my ten marathon medals, beautifully mounted and framed. A nice gift, subtly delivering its intended message of completion.

I have spooked a few of my pals by suggesting we need a 30-year plan. Let's face it, that's about as many healthy years as a 50-year-old male can reasonably expect. It has changed my perspective. As soon as I accepted and assimilated this '30-year life' ahead, I quite urgently wanted to call time on this conveyor belt that I have been a slave to for almost 15 years. I realised too that the same conveyor belt could cut that remaining life even shorter – and that didn't feel fair. Integrating more quality and less stress into my life ahead has become very important indeed.

It may reek of a late mid-life crisis, but *now* is the time for balance, not later. *Now* is the time to look after all things health-related – physical and mental – not later. *Now* is the time for family and friends, not later. *Now* is the time for me too, for the 'me' who is not the Pigsback boss. I'm bored with myself – *now* is the time to change that, not later.

Following a lot of reflection, I have ended up with this more elevated view of my life across work (graft), family and friends (gang), my own interests and pursuits (games) - sometimes shared with Karen and the girls, sometimes not, and gratitude for how lucky I have been despite a few setbacks, leading to contemplation on how I behave in this world and should give back to my community (good). *Graft, Gang, Games and Good: 4Gs* to think about and balance – for at least 30 years, I hope!

December 2014

It is 7.20 pm on December 8th. I have hesitated to write here over the last while. I think it felt like tempting fate, but here goes: I am waiting to hear from a potential acquirer, a big media player in Ireland with a business in our sector. I have no doubt maligned the same company in these pages, but hey, business is business.

I was contacted a couple of months back. We met and got on well. We talked for a long time about our common experiences, and both agreed that our sector needs consolidation. It makes sense to look at coming together, and I came across as being open to either Pigsback being the acquirer or being acquired. The resulting efficiencies and synergies are obvious and worthwhile. We left it at that.

We later agreed to explore what shape a deal might take and met on three subsequent occasions, progressing to a plan for them to buy Pigsback. We each put the proposed plan to our respective organisations to get the necessary buy-in. Both parties signed the draft Heads of Terms document for the transaction. It outlines a fair deal for us and would be the makings of a strong combined Irish deals entity, nicely profitable and vying with Groupon for overall market leadership.

It may be a small transaction in the scheme of a bigger business, but it's a very important one in tidying up my life and, perhaps, opening up a new chapter. It will be complex enough to execute, so we need to plan well.

Progress has been sluggish since, however. There was even a suggestion by one of their senior directors of push-back in the valuation of Pigsback. I have conceded nothing and don't like the smell of it. The many layers involved in the structure of the potential acquirer make them hard to figure out. However, they have signed the outline terms with a view to due diligence – a detailed examination of our operations and finances – in January.

We have traded well in the meantime, enjoying a strong supply of hotel offers to meet the demand for Christmas gifts. Yesterday we set a new record of €75,000 in the day, with a single promotional hour doing €16,000 worth of business. December should be a record month. It's well-earned respite.

———————◆———————

January 2015

We are just back from a sunny week in Tenerife. It was the break that was needed; I exercised, wrote and read a lot. Karen and I walked a lot too, and of course, enjoyed the food, wine and a few beers. We are both feeling better for it. I hope it helps over the next few weeks.

I'm back to work tomorrow, motivated and with a big to-do list.

The pace of progress towards our deal slowed before Christmas, but we did get a signed Heads of Terms document, and my interlocutor messaged me this morning saying they are ready to proceed with due diligence on Pigsback.

———————◆———————

Released from our lease in Citywest, we have moved into new office space in Park West on the outskirts of Dublin. A fresh start. We like the new office. It's about 2,500 square feet, which is all our slimmed-down business needs now. It is opposite a gym, and we have negotiated membership for our staff - another contra. The buzz is better in Park West, with restaurants and shops close by. We like the lease too: it's about 20% of the cost of the previous arrangement at Citywest.

It's been a good start to the year's trading too. Looks like we'll meet our early targets.

We've been busy with the merger project, completing a very detailed due diligence process. It appears to have gone well: our technology platform came out of it with flying colours and, with it, our culture of quickly pivoting the business to where the market is at or where it is moving to.

It's approaching D-Day for the deal. My gut feeling is that the transaction will happen. I'm expecting a final negotiation in the next few weeks, a swipe at valuation probably, which we'll resist, and that should be it.

Together, the merged entity is significantly profitable. I don't know where my future lies if they buy us, but I am excited about the new possibilities. There's no point speculating much further for now.

———◆———

May 2015

Dear Diary,

The media men wasted our time and money. They tell us there was an eleventh-hour crisis of confidence. We had gone well past the time for that. I had met with their senior executive twice, a decent man, I thought.

We thrashed out a deal he was happy to recommend, but his overlords said No at the very end. I asked them to sell us their business. They said NO to that too.

———◆———

I've had plenty of time to think in recent months.

Firstly, I'm sick and tired of the pressure to exit. There is nothing to exit right now and focusing on exit is not helping me to run and develop Pigsback. I have engaged the CEOs of the five most relevant potential acquirers of our company. There is no one out there interested or willing to acquire us at any kind of reasonable valuation.

Secondly, I am fed up overseeing a company hovering tortuously around breakeven. I am determined to push the company into profitability and well beyond, whatever that takes. I believe we have a real and rightful future in this sector and that our repositioning work will pay off. I have a plan, which is to take out the few remaining costs at group level (mainly the fees that are still paid or, more accurately, still accrued, for board members and advisers); to once again review headcount and all overheads; to sell Empathy Research to Declan; and, with those funds, to drive the Pigsback Offers business forward.

Thirdly, and urgently, I need to do what it takes to lock my key managers in. Right now they have no reason to say 'no' to the next recruitment agent who comes calling. Our CTO Paul resigned recently and was literally on his way out the door until he was hauled back with a lot of extra love by way of salary and bonus, combined with a promise of significant equity in the business soon. Paul leaving was a terrifying prospect, given our excessive dependence on him.

The Goods business is now under the management of Dave Foody, one of our original recruits, who has turned his hand effectively to a few roles at this stage. It will be Dave's biggest challenge thus far, and it has already brought out the commercial beast in him. The Goods business requires many more offers in many more categories than the hotels business, plus a lot of experimentation. Dave has the ability to manage and analyse the associated data, and then to bring automation to the offer production and evaluation processes. This has a lot of potential all-round.

Dave and Barry, our head of hotels, are completely in control of their respective business units, utterly reliable and professional managers. I can't even contemplate losing either of them, so I need to keep them energised and lock them in for a few years.

The only currency we have left to play with is our equity, the shares in the company, and these guys have negligible holdings. This is simply wrong given their commitment and their salary and bonus sacrifices over the years. When the day comes that the company is doing well from their efforts, they must feel that they have done well too. It's only fair, and it will keep them in place and motivated.

My personal shareholding has been diluted across several funding rounds, notably in 2010, when I also lost my pension. In looking after my colleagues, I am not prepared to take another hit. We have been more than fair to shareholders, who we have kept in the game despite many simply watching from the sidelines since their first investment. Now shareholders need to be fair to the team and to me to keep us all on board and motivated.

Johnny Mc is exhausted, and I'm trying to give him breathing room and a better outlook.

I've been giving some serious consideration to a couple of options, including a management buyout (MBO). I have spoken to a corporate finance adviser, who is confident of securing the cash, probably via a UK mezzanine fund that is active in such transactions. The interest rate on the funds would be high, and there would be an exit payment on top. They will not ask for a personal guarantee on the debt, but they would own the brand and business if we default.

Whatever the outcome, I am not prepared to leave the status quo.

I'm calling it *Project Encore*, our encore and last chance.

———•———

I approached my four most senior managers. Johnny Mc was first. After recent events, I could anticipate where his mind was at, but I wasn't proceeding without this courtesy to him, at least.

He has no appetite at all for the MBO route.

"Do you really need the stress of this?" he asked.

I had no doubt that his concerns for me were heartfelt, but he could feel my energy for a new solution. "An MBO is very risky at a personal financial level for you," he said, "but it is a deal Kevin should accept and bring to shareholders."

He concluded: "Wherever you've got it from, you've found a new energy. I'm tired and can't find that in me right now."

Johnny has been playing his cards face-up since our walk around the park at Citywest back in September. He is tired after 15 years of Pigsback, the grind, the commute from Kilkenny, the kidney stones, cashflow battles, constantly trying to find positives – and of me too, I suspect. He deserves a rest, and I promised to explore his options.

In the following days, I spoke to Dave, Barry and Paul. They're all up for what might unfold and seemingly okay with the risk that could come with an MBO. The status quo is the least attractive to them. The consultations confirmed to me that if I can lock them in, re-energised, I can absolutely rely on them to run and develop their areas of the business.

Karen gets it, senses my new energy and is supportive. I have already contacted Kevin and requested a meeting in London. He knows we're at a crossroads, so I just told him we would talk it out in person.

———————◆———————

June 2015

We arranged to meet at Pizza Express in Charing Cross. Kevin opened by asking if I was sure an exit was not possible. I assured him it was not, adding: "It's exhausting for all of us, constantly trying to manage a business on the precipice of failure."

I had invited JD, knowing his presence would be welcomed by Kevin and helpful to both of us. Having trained and worked together as accountants, the guys trust each other. They're two of my biggest supporters, the first I sought advice and support from ahead of the Emergency Round in 2010. That time we met at the Groucho Club; this time, we were meeting in the less salubrious surrounds of a pizzeria basement.

Kevin is a friend, too, so this was going to be a tough conversation. Neither he nor JD knew in advance where this was going.

"We need to acknowledge where we're at. It hasn't worked, has little to no value and has no future without an entire reenergisation. That means making some further deep cuts, selling Empathy Research, taking the exit agenda off the table and agreeing on a lock-in equity deal for the management. If that means me making an offer to buy out you and the other shareholders, I will find a way to do that." I opened.

The best route I could see was an MBO, I explained. To achieve it, I would need to engineer clear-cut profitability fast by cutting out the few remaining non-operating costs, including any remaining directors' fees – which include Kevin's – and the monitoring fee we paid to the investor group Connection Capital, formerly Hotbed.

There would have to be significant operating cost savings too. No part of me felt good about the name 'John McDonald' on that list. We would seek to sell Empathy Research, probably to Declan, as part of this package and would compensate elsewhere for the loss of its annual contribution. These measures, I felt, would give me enough to sell the MBO story and secure the necessary funds.

JD brought his usual elevation and perspective. He expressed concern for me and for the prudence of my personal plan. His own investment didn't come into the equation. His biggest flag was my historic over-optimism. He feared that any kind of share buyout or MBO could land myself and Karen in even deeper waters financially.

Kevin was more circumspect than normal. Fair enough! The cutting of non-executive and consultants' fees was no issue to him. I indicated the level of offer I thought was feasible: in his case, it is the equivalent of about 30% in the euro on his total investment, upfront, with a share in a later exit beyond a certain threshold (all of which would apply equally to all shareholders), plus the return of his director loan.

But today wasn't about a formal offer. I certainly wasn't ready yet. If Kevin were prepared to take it forward, a formal offer would follow. I would have to secure the funding, resign from the board, and let Kevin, as the senior director, write to all shareholders with the offer details and the board's recommendation.

He understood my predicament, but I sensed he wasn't warming to the MBO route, and, for better or worse, he wasn't happy selling his shares to me. If that was his prerogative, he had paid handsomely for it.

Without Kevin's agreement, the MBO won't get out of the starting blocks. But with the choking status quo, he'll need to come up with a viable alternative.

———◆———

In a sign of the times, Amazon has acquired the former Jacob's biscuit factory in Tallaght as a site for a new data centre, where it will host countless web businesses in the so-called cloud. The Pigsback site is hosted by Amazon Web Services in exactly the kind of facility planned for Tallaght.

It is headlined as a boost to the local economy. You can't halt progress, and there is a certain serendipity about this turn of events. Having left Jacob's in 1992, after all the fun of Chocolate Kimberley and Shake a Shamrock, I am set to make my return with Pigsback hosted in one of the racks of computers that have replaced racks of biscuits. From bites to bytes, you could say.

--------●--------

Kevin has been back. He is not in favour of an MBO. He has a counterproposal, however, and is happy to put it to shareholders. Of course, he accepts the proposed group and other cost cuts. He also accepts that the commitment and forbearance of the senior team require an exceptional response in equity. Giving up shares now, he believes, is his and the shareholders' best route to realising value in the medium term.

The proposal is in two parts. The first will be a lock-in sale of equity to the director managers. These shares must be purchased now but at a nominal price. The message is: "Simply stay and commit to Pigsback, and these are yours". That's a very helpful start.

The second part is a new share option scheme across the team, replacing the existing one with about 15% of the equity at a 5-cent strike price (which equals the last transacted price on our share register). The old share options are 'underwater' – meaning the options were priced above the company's value – so they were ineffective as a retention or motivational tool. It is a fair bar but will be meaningless without significant trading progress and, in time, an exit. Across the two new schemes, about one new share will be issued for every three existing shares, but these replace the existing share option scheme (equivalent to about 17% of ordinary shares).

For the management team, there is still a leap of faith. The company remains loss-making, and the balance sheet is negative to the tune of about €2 million, so selling Empathy Research, as envisaged, is still key to avoiding an unwelcome cash call.

Kevin will now take his proposal forward and take soundings from other directors, past and present, followed by a full discussion and – hopefully – ratification by shareholders at the AGM.

Kevin - more than anyone - will see his shareholding diluted, but this is a win-win formula: if we succeed in re-energising the business, the share value increases for everyone. If we don't, the shares have no value.

———•———

Kevin has been actively moving on the proposal and first spoke to Tom McCormick. This is right up Tom's alley as he has a history of incentivising his management teams well. Despite losing its monitoring fees, Connection Capital is supportive, welcoming any plausible route to profit and stability. We've run it all past KPMG and our lawyers Whitney Moore. Kevin is getting more feedback before a final airing with shareholders at the AGM.

Already board and shareholder support are looking assured. If I'm honest, I am relieved not to have to go off to raise money for a risky MBO. It wouldn't have been easy, and I could do without putting more pressure on myself. Kevin's proposal is a good compromise. Under the new arrangement, all staff members get share options. This time I am protected against dilution: Karen and I will gain a net 3% on our family shareholding, going some way to making up for years of equity and pension sacrifices.

It's the only employee dilution of any note in 15 years in business. It was in a similar vein that Ryanair founder Tony Ryan issued his young chief executive Michael O'Leary a 25% profit share in the airline. Any recovery was good for Ryan, and it proved to be one of his best business decisions. I hope – in our more humble world – that the same will be said of Kevin's move in the future.

The reenergisation strategy is working already, with Paul's feet back under the CTO desk and a noticeable shift in the mindsets of Barry and Dave too. They are ready to commit to the business and add every bit of value they can, as any business owner would.

Kevin hopes we can build back to a value of 20-25 cents per share over time, which compares well to the 10 cents of the 2010 Emergency Round. I hope we can do better, of course, but I know this is exactly the tonic that the whole company needs. *Encore* it is, and I don't want to hear any talk of exit.

8

Molon Labe

July 2015

The message from the team now and for the foreseeable future to all comers in the deals market is *Molon Labe: if you want us to lay down our weapons, come and take them.* We're going nowhere.

The Irish economy has made a great recovery. The people deserve it. The crash was savage, and the ensuing depression was harrowing for many business owners. Pretty much everyone took pain, mostly suffering in silence and getting on with it as best they could. The troika played its part. Politicians, this time, deserve credit. Many self-employed have little to no safety cushion of their own, or from the state, for some, that was just too much. I don't think we should be begrudged this bounce. Weren't we the best pupils in the class, paying unsecured bondholders, guaranteeing banks and taking more pain more silently than any other nation – with the possible exception of Greece? Employment levels are right back up there again, but the worst legacy of the crash may prove to be the property crisis. Astronomical price rises during the so-called Celtic Tiger left even starter apartments and houses out of the reach of young people. Now, with so many builders and property developers forced out of business in the recession, there are very few new homes being built. High property price inflation, when all is said and done, is bad news for society.

The improved economic backdrop may have helped Declan O'Reilly secure his funding, and we've agreed terms for the sale of Empathy Research. Declan has shown the courage of his convictions. I wish him well. It's a cracking opportunity for someone of his ability and ambition. He's buzzing with energy, another manifestation of that transformative power of ownership. We still have to cross a few legal and tax hurdles, but we'll get there. The sale of Empathy Research will improve our balance sheet by about €550,000, less some costs, but foregoing €100,000 in annual profit drives the remaining business into a net loss despite recent savings. But with this injection of working capital, we can pay hotels and restaurants quicker than our competitors, and we can invest in new advertising campaigns. I'm betting on our Offers business delivering. It feels right.

———————•———————

August 2015

A first look at market shares in the deals sector for July shows a market under a lot of pressure, but we did grow our share significantly and are second in the market behind Groupon. That's progress, indeed. However, there's clearly an ill wind blowing through the market, and we can't expect to be unaffected. I feel we have anticipated this, and can only hope that our work to reposition the Pigsback brand will sustain us.

I was in Belfast to review a potential acquisition, TreatTicket, a small but similar business to our own, which is open to discussion right now. We have a limited legacy audience of perhaps 10,000 active members from our launch in Northern Ireland in the early years of the business. From that, we know that people in Northern Ireland purchase a lot of short breaks in the Republic. Combined with the much bigger TreatTicket audience, it could make for something viable.

We had lunch with our hosts at the Titanic centre in the city's docklands, once the home of shipbuilding and now an impressive tourist destination in peacetime Belfast. It all left a very pleasant impression, far removed from my early memories of working in the north Belfast meat plant just after college.

As far as the business of the day is concerned, we won't be rushing it. We have barely received the cash from selling Empathy Research, so we will leave it to rest in the bank account for a while.

———————•———————

I read another one of those social media debates about entrepreneurs. This time the distinction was being made between company founders who are *entrepreneurs* and those who are *artists*. Entrepreneurs, they said, are committed to the exit, are looking at the next venture already, and may be involved in multiple ventures. Artists are more likely to be wedded to the success of their work, no matter what. Kevin would no doubt say that I'm an artist. I'm not sure.

September 2015

A year ago today, I came as close as I have ever come to throwing in the towel. It was a day that improved as it progressed. It marks the point at which we came out more determined than ever to fight our competitors and take the necessary measures to see that fight through. We had let them undercut us for too long.

A year on, it's not all roses, but I think it's fair to borrow the famous line that *the long arc of the competitive universe [may be] bending towards us.* At last. The funds from the sale of the research unit are giving us oxygen. Gone are the day-to-day cash manoeuvrings and the occasional financial support from Kevin and myself. Kevin got his short-term loan of €50,000 back, and my €75,000 personal guarantee is now rescinded, to my relief and Karen's. A worry removed and a concrete sign of progress.

Our UK shareholders' investment was originally negotiated and later overseen by Hotbed, an independent investment company now under a new guise as Connection Capital. They have long been negative about the investment in Pigsback. Why wouldn't they be?

They invested in the promise of the UK and further international expansion of the business. We struggled after a promising launch when our UK roll-out hit a severe British recession from 2006 and then the global credit crunch from 2008. Our foray into Canada failed too, quite misfortunately.

Over the years, Hotbed's quarterly investor updates made for the grimmest reading. They could do little else. We were heaping bad news on top of bad news, so they heaped one downgrade on top of another. I found their updates clinical and, at times, even felt a bit of shame. It wasn't that the commentary was unfair, but it was light on extenuating cyclical and economic context. It all read to me like a failure of my management.

As Connection Capital, they've continued to attend our board meetings and partook in all key decisions, but it now seems like they have had enough of our struggles. They want out of Pigsback and recently asked Kevin if he would consider making an offer to buy out their shareholders. Although not a seller of shares, Kevin declared that he wasn't a buyer either. He has more than enough at stake. I was very keen to tidy this one up and remove the monitoring fees paid to Connection Capital. After convincing Karen that we should take this final chance, I set about finding the funds. I responded with an offer, which Connection Capital passed on to its investors. About half accepted, and the other half will now be managed directly by the company.

That's it now! Karen and I are well and truly all in.

I am four weeks into a memoir-writing course at the Irish Writers Centre in Parnell Square in Dublin city centre. I'm trying new things, as I continue to grapple with those 4Gs of Graft (work), Gang (family and friends), Games (leisure) and Good (giving back), seeking to identify a new balance. It's working. There's a positive energy in my work, my family time, my leisure, my reading, my learning and writing, my curiosity, my exercise, and my sociability.

Last night it was my turn to read to the class; I had kept my head low for long enough. It was a daunting experience, ridiculously so, with only eight classmates present and a fair bit of public speaking experience behind me. I had earlier listened as one member read a harrowing story of what led her to attempt suicide. Another wrote in lyrical prose about her idyllic garden in Co Mayo. The more I listened, the more my middle-class tale of corporate challenges seemed shallow and unimportant. Everyone has a story.

I got going anyway, reading a journal entry about the day I faced our banking woes in December 2009 and the stress that caused me. To my delight, I got lovely feedback and encouragement from my classmates and from our tutor, Henry Mc Donald, the Ireland correspondent for the *Guardian*.

It is a positive forum, I grant you, but suddenly the decision to get out of my comfort zone, pursue the course and go through with my first public reading from my journals felt so worthwhile. They described my writing as "businessy but personal, sincere and showing the caring face of business". It conveyed a naivety, as well as a sense of 'what on earth is happening to me?' The existence of a business or someone running a business with a caring face was a revelation to most of this group, and that, in turn, was a revelation to me.

There were a few pointers from Henry on style and structure. The class encouraged me to do an audiobook. They've certainly given me the enthusiasm to continue.

————•————

November 2015

Today was our AGM, later than normal. I had prepared a slide on our financials since the Emergency Round in 2010. It was a bit of a reality check. Leaving out adjustments for tax movements and voucher breakage, our annual losses since 2010 read -€386,000, -€60,000, -€25,000, -€6,000, -€233,000. Unfortunately, there's likely to be a small loss in 2015 too.

I recapped on Project Encore in detail, starting with its simple but critical objectives: give us one more chance (an 'encore'); lock in the business leaders; remove insolvency and illiquidity worries; improve the balance sheet, deliver €500,000 in net profit by 2017. We outlined Kevin's proposals to lock in the team. The re-energisation was welcomed and unanimously rubber-stamped.

There was a very positive but realistic tone at the subsequent board meeting too. While the short-term picture is improving significantly, there was a wary caution as well, given the known volatility of deals. All of a sudden, Dave Foody, who had exited the afternoon board meeting, returned, laptop in hand.

"We're number one, ahead of Groupon!"

"Wow. Are you sure?"

"Yes, there's a margin of error in the data, but I'm happy that we're number one."

I was off like a child, wandering between the boardroom and the open-plan offices. I couldn't restrain my joy, wanting to shout it from the rooftops.

"Pigsback is number one. Did you hear that, everyone? We're number one. Wow! Yes! Well done team!"

Dave qualified it: "it's only one month, and the deals market had a bad month."

Nothing was going to take the shine off this very proud moment. Groupon came to eat our lunch in 2009 – and very nearly did – but here we are in 2015 eating theirs! We have worked so hard to set ourselves apart from the deals players; this is the first evidence we might be out-staying them.

By coincidence, it was my birthday. No gift could match this.

I spent this very day, four years ago, in the north of England, finally and officially liquidating our UK business. It was a line through the most challenging and expensive chapter in our corporate history. As one chapter closed, another one opened, another long fight, but we seem to be finally getting on top.

———◆———

I was sitting with Johnny Mc, poring over budgets, when the news came through on WhatsApp: 'GrabOne is closing!'

Well, good riddance! I said.

How quickly the dynamic can change in a market. It was sudden and clean. The 24 staff seem to be well looked after. Pigsback has been winning market share in recent months, a tailwind bringing us to the number 1 spot, albeit for just a month. Now the company that targeted us most directly has finally folded. I am very proud that we dodged the endless bullets aimed directly at us, but what a waste of time and money!

It's a Monday in early November. A year ago, we would have happily taken €25,000 in gross sales. Today we could hit €50,000.

———◆———

It's November 30th, Cyber Monday, a few days after Black Friday. I don't think I had heard of either of them a few years ago. Now, these American promotional days mark the biggest sales season of the year for e-commerce on both sides of the Atlantic.

We began promoting our offers a week ago, on the Monday of Black Friday week and will ease up after today, Cyber Monday. In that eight-day period, we had sales of nearly €500,000. In November, for the first time, we will break the €1 million mark in monthly gross sales; it looks like we will finish November at €1.2 million, nearly 25% better than our previous best.

We celebrated the moment with a glass of bubbly, and Grapevine delivered a bottle for everyone to take home. It has been a long time coming. We are rolling with the positive momentum, but we will need to keep doing what got us here. That means executing well.

———•———

December 2015

'Off the back foot' was the rather kind headline on journalist Colette Sexton's feature article in the *Sunday Business Post*, with me in my customary pink shirt. I looked like I could do with one of our breaks.

Colette didn't gloss over our challenges.

"After an influx of global competitors with huge budgets, an unsuccessful launch in new markets and cutting staff to a quarter of their peak, Pigsback is starting to bring home the bacon again."

Much of the remainder of the article talked about the repositioning of the brand over the last few years, and the development of sub-brands like LuxuryBreaks.ie, TheDiningRoom.ie and TheBeautyLounge.ie. I talked about saying 'no' to the lower-end three-star properties and conducting marketing campaigns that would make luxury companies confident about our brand and environment.

The article concluded: "Pigsback will not be looking outside Ireland and will stick to *home sweet home*", quoting me saying: "We've taken on board enough risk for any one company in its lifetime."

Never a truer statement.

———•———

It's December 22nd, and I am sitting at one of the pine tables in Le Pain Quotidien bakery and restaurant in the Kildare Village shopping outlet. I have just had lunch with our middle daughter Nicky, who is working in one of the outlet shops as part of her gap year. The restaurant is very bright and airy, which somehow befits my mood.

I have given myself the rest of the year off. I will enjoy watching our sales dashboard – which gives a live update on sales by category – and the banter in the management WhatsApp group, but I'll try to cut all of that off from Christmas Eve. We're all a bit hooked on the dashboard. It's hard not to press 'refresh' every few minutes during peak sales periods. I can't be too hard on myself or the team for that! Our cash balances are healthy after selling Empathy Research and after some strong Offers trading.

The market is indeed swinging our way. This is the high season, which can make or break the year. The outcome for the full year won't seem that rosy after our rougher ride in the first half of 2015, but the positive recent trajectory is evident in our customer conversations and, particularly, in our hotel market share. It feels like we are bossing that sector right now, with GrabOne out of the picture, Groupon out of favour and LivingSocial gone quiet. The discount operators, DealRush.ie and Escapes.ie, continue to emerge as the others fall back. We have a very close eye on them.

It's as if hotels have decided that deals are bad - wait for it - but that Pigsback is different and is good. *Yes!* So we are asking properties for exclusivity, extra availability and integration with our Concierge bookings system, which they love, in return for a commitment to filling their rooms with quality guests.

As the year-end approaches, Pigsback has just over 500,000 active members, 130,000 Facebook fans, and when we pay for it, we are regularly reaching well over 1 million Irish adults through booster ad campaigns on Facebook. It's quite the machine.

As we forecast next year, reflecting the gains made in the second half of 2015, we really should achieve that elusive net annual profit at last.

Roll on 2016.

———◆———

January 2016

I hadn't slept well and I got up within minutes of my new radio alarm sounding at 6.45am. I had arranged an early morning meeting with Roland Bryan, the CEO of Wowcher, one of the large UK players, which is backed by private equity. He was in Dublin to visit the Irish operation of LivingSocial, which Wowcher has recently acquired.

I was happy to focus the agenda of the meeting on trading opportunities, mindful there was potential for a bigger alliance down the road. There was a sense of uncertainty about Ireland for my UK counterpart, a headache he could do without, I hoped, as he focused on the big prize of the UK market.

In the mode of a busy and assured man, he jumped quickly to his view of the world and to the options at hand. He felt there was no big play in Ireland for his company, and was interested in us joining forces in Ireland, a merger. It would be, he said, a quick route to clear market leadership. I headed back to the train station, intrigued. For some time now, we have bought into the view that a bit of market consolidation is overdue. We're all a bit jaded from years of fighting tooth-and-nail in too small a market. So, on balance, it seems to make sense to merge.

It has been several months since Johnny Mc left after the implementation of Project Encore. We have kept in touch, of course. If our trading and market position have improved, Johnny deserves much of the credit. If we are to hit a continued growth phase and consider this merger, I would be keen on getting him back. He is getting a proper break and it's doing him good. I'll bide my time, but I felt it reasonable to bring him into the picture.

February 2016

We have been busy over the past few weeks. I am heading to the heart of London for a lunch meeting with the private equity company that is the principal owner of Wowcher, with whom we are now in advanced merger talks. The proposed merger would create a new joint entity, and our shareholders would have the majority of the equity.

There is a 'but', however, at least in my mind. The market momentum has belonged to Pigsback in the past few months; we have passed these guys out and might just leave them behind altogether if we keep the foot to the floor on our own.

I asked Johnny Mc to meet Wowcher's operations team as a favour. He was happy to take a trip to London again. The welcome he got was underwhelming. He felt their team was preoccupied with the bigger immediate issue of integrating a new UK business they had just acquired.

The next day, I met my contact from Wowcher's private equity company at their reception area. My counterpart suggested we "grab a sandwich", so there was no question about visiting the office or meeting any of the private equity team. My host walked along beside me, laden with legal papers. In the café, chair space was tight. I wasn't comfortable. With minimal delay, my counterpart proceeded to outline how the new company would be run, how new management contracts would be drawn up and how I could be dismissed at their sole discretion if targets were missed.

"This is all standard issue," I was told.

"Let me go away and think about it," I managed.

I met Johnny Mc for a pint, and we headed home. There will be no deal now, but we don't need to burn our bridges. I will keep in touch with Roland, who I warmed to and who I feel I can work with down the road.

———◆———

May 2016

Pigsback is showing exceptional growth for the first four months of 2016, up 55% versus last year. All of the other main players are suffering in a deals market that is still challenging. That market weakness concerns me, of course. I can't be sure of what's in store in the second half of the year and in the next couple of years. I feel we need to push on again, somehow, to put an even greater distance between us and the deal players whose days may well be numbered.

During the lean years, we reduced our team to the bare bones. Granted, we had made a lot of technology investments in previous years, which we could lean on for a while, but we almost paid the highest price a few months ago with the threatened departure of our CTO, Paul. That over-reliance was a mistake, albeit we had little choice. Now we do, and we have recruited one senior developer and are sticking our necks out with another. It means we will have tripled our investment in the tech team in a matter of months. We are already planning quite a bit of catch-up on tech maintenance and development, and we have a bit of bandwidth for what we hope is coming down the tracks.

I am so thankful for these recurring revenues, which continue 24/7 whether I'm working or not, whether we're awake or asleep; for the growth we are enjoying and for the cash and headspace it is giving; for the profit we are at last earning. I won't take it for granted. We will continue to improve by investing more in our people and across our business.

———————◆———————

This week, I have been ill and succumbed to a doctor's visit. I am starting a course of antibiotics and am confined to my office at home, where I can recover in peace without bothering or infecting anyone.

It's a good time for a new and very interesting opportunity to arise. I took a call from Peter Clarke in DealRush, a competitor that has been a thorn in our sides but whose progress has stalled. I have gone out of my way to nurture a relationship with Peter, and we have spoken on several occasions. I find him an intriguing character, an ex-tennis pro, and an energetic, if somewhat restless, entrepreneur. He seems to be consumed in a new wedding business, and from what I can gather, DealRush is suffering.

From our call, it appears that Peter would prefer to focus on and invest in his new business. I made it clear that I was interested in DealRush but also that I would have to be prudent; I can't dig a new hole for our business now that things are finally going well. We discussed some pricing parameters. The door is open.

The attraction of acquisitions is obvious. In my time in France, the company I worked for twice merged with other Danone businesses. It required detailed planning. In those cases, revenue was protected, but duplication of staff and overheads was slashed. In theory, if we add another deals business onto ours and even just maintain the additional revenue at our current gross margin levels, all of that can flow to the bottom line, less only any extra costs in the people or overhead that we take on. In addition, by adding a new channel to the acquired business – our Goods offering to DealRush, for example – we could grow revenue and margin.

The trick would be to run the acquired business on our technology platform from the get-go while retaining the acquired brand and its colour scheme initially, at any rate. We know our platform works. What's more, we are confident that our user experience is at least as good as any of our competitors. There should be no need for any extra staff, so we maximise efficiency. Our team will rise to the extra volume in areas such as member services.

There are risks, however. We could upset merchants or customers who are used to other ways of doing business. For some unforeseen reason, the transfer to our platform could fail; migration problems happen - we know that from our own experience with V3 and with Pigsback Live.

In terms of the market, it is still ridiculously overcrowded, so any consolidation will make for less gruesome competition and, perhaps, in time, improved margins. The acquisition playbook is obvious, but we have no margin for error.

Above all, I need to make good decisions right now. I have got better at saying 'no,' but opportunities are coming my way thick and fast. The challenge is to find a gilt-edged one.

There's no rush.

July 2016

It sounds bizarre, but I'm bored. It's true. Everything is going swimmingly. The business is trading well, and we don't have to force the pace.

I have got much better at listening to my more prudent self and to my counterbalance, Johnny Mc, who has been back in the Pigsback fold since April and enjoying his work again. I need him and his experience around me as we grow significantly and evaluate opportunities that are coming our way.

In the past six months or so, we have examined and said no to an investment in a struggling deals business in Northern Ireland and to the merger with Wowcher's LivingSocial. I've also just sent Peter off to think about a lower asking price for DealRush - it's risky, but I think he'll be back. On top of that, we've been very slow to engage with an Asian trading company seeking a UK and Ireland alliance because we simply know too little about them. In addition, we have assessed but drawn back from an affiliation with a major media buying agency to push display advertising to our sites via an automated so-called 'programmatic exchange' model because it doesn't feel right.

None of these I regret. Pigsback is going well right now, and I'm nervous about anything that could disrupt that even keel. But I'm itching. Just ticking over isn't my thing. I'm missing the bumps and spills.

In the meantime, we are smashing targets. Our deal revenues are up 57% in the first half of the year. Our market share is growing rapidly as we disproportionately attract GrabOne's customers. Our members are well engaged and are buying across the board and increasingly from our Goods business.

We have completed preliminary forecasts for 2017 showing us hitting €1 million in profit. It assumes we complete the Deal Rush acquisition and nail it. Now that's exciting!

No matter what we do, we can't stop the fall of the Pigsback Advertising business. It's small enough not to worry us anymore, and it won't be included in next year's budget at all.

From hero to zero in ten years.

I met with our old Pigsback colleague Gareth Lambe over a few glasses of pale ale. Gareth is now in a senior leadership role at Facebook in Ireland, overseeing Europe, the Middle East and South-East Asia.

As ever, he was generous with his advice and wisdom. Gareth has been very loyal to me and to Pigsback, and he takes a genuine interest in our challenges and progress. Facebook advertising is becoming an increasing part of our own marketing efforts and continues to work very well in delivering sales and new customers. So we continue to invest more. There is a mighty marketing machine behind all those smiling faces and photos.

Generally, Gareth advised, those companies that spend big with Facebook also spend big with Google. It hasn't worked as well for us to date, so perhaps we are missing a trick.

The day after my meeting with Gareth, we pulled together a new group, grandly named the Digital Marketing Task Force. Its challenge is simply to increase the Pigsback customer base and demand for our content, with a particular focus on cracking Google. With introductions from Gareth, we met the Facebook team to discuss our challenges there. We're off to look for the same access to Google.

———◆———

Internally, we have firmed up a few pretty progressive arrangements. We have a new scheme that ensures every one of our staff, at all levels, gets a monthly bonus when we beat our targets (unless they are already on commission). We are doing better now, so we should. It has been appreciated.

I know it takes a bit more than money to make us a better company to work for, however. We have always tried hard to treat everyone like a responsible adult – unless we're given a reason not to, which is rare. I'd say there's a *mature trust* in the organisation. We know we are only one part of people's lives and that we all need a reasonable balance.

So, for example, there's no point telling a mother or father that they can't tend to family matters when required. There's no point telling people who have to brave the vagaries of Dublin's M50 traffic that they must do so at peak times; why not reduce a journey's duration by half at off-peak times? We have put in place very flexible work patterns, goal orientation and buy-in to what we are all trying to achieve together. The latter is important as voluntary positivity about your work and its 'project' takes away the need for undue oversight. Some of our most effective people are unlikely to have thrived in a tightly managed, suited-and-booted office environment. They are best left to make their choices as to how they work and what role the office plays for them. This culture, in particular our flexibility, is very helpful in retaining people.

We all meet regularly to share feedback and direction in management team meetings, functional teams, and in multidisciplinary steering meetings. There has been a long-standing tradition of the Monday morning briefing, which we encourage as many people as possible to attend. Monday is the one day we're likely to be tight on desk space.

These briefings are highly interactive. A team member from each area of Pigsback is nominated to update us all on what's going on, where the challenges are, and how we are doing. In that way, we all become accountable to each other. It's a good buzz, as people draw energy from each other. It's generally an atmosphere of encouragement, but with a recognised interdependency across the company, any pattern of slacking or bullshit gets called out by the team. It's simple but very effective.

Setting clear goals always helps people know where they stand: are they under or over par? Not surprisingly, we have good data and reports across the whole business, so we tend to spot weakness pretty quickly.

I'm not in favour of too much short-term pressure on individuals. Everyone and every business goes through good and bad phases. We have to support individuals through the ups and downs as they learn to adapt. Encouraging someone who is off-target can be critical because it's then that they need to feel belief and support more than at any time. They'll thank us for it afterwards.

I admit that I don't like managers or staff who need micro-management. It does not suit my management style, and I find it draining. I'll do it when required, but that's always a bad sign. Share a strong vision, give people a clear view of their path and targets, make sure they have the knowledge, skills and tools, and be supportive. It means finding the self-motivated and those who are flexible and determined problem-solvers. Our conversations get to the 'what if?' and 'wouldn't it be great if?' rather than a box-ticking, picky review of the minutiae of their work.

We have allocated business responsibilities clearly across business and service units. Officially, the business unit leaders, Barry and Dave, report to me, and the service units, Paul in Tech and Erin in Accounts, report to Johnny Mc. In reality, we keep it very fluid. With these guys, it's light touch – far more about supporting than controlling. And it just wouldn't be the same without a no-holds-barred culture of slagging.

As a result, we now have an organisation with a distinct sense of its mission, its own personality and culture, as well as an unmistakable positivity. It also leaves me with time to hover, think about things, network and find a better balance. I have even started to play golf again after 10 years, and I'm loving it.

———————◆———————

I arranged a dinner in London with Roland, the Wowcher CEO. I just wanted to ensure there was no hangover from our aborted merger talks and, ideally, that the door would be open for another discussion when the time was right.

It helped to be greeted and looked after like VIPs by Richard Corrigan in Bentley's, dining alfresco on Swallow Street on a very warm Central London evening. We happily talked business for the night, ate and drank well and were the very last to leave at 2 am.

I think we both learn a lot from these encounters, where lessons and experiences are exchanged in a relaxed way. I don't think it would work if either of us were too guarded. An exit to Wowcher may yet come to pass, but we completely avoided the subject, and Roland knows I'm in no hurry.

———————◆———————

October 2016

What a day! This time last year, we sold a business. Today we bought one. Our first. DealRush agreed to sell. Peter Clarke indicated he was ready to improve the deal, and I was prepared to pay a fair price. We both acted quickly, and the closing process took about three weeks. Once the Heads of Terms document was agreed upon, there was no messing, no silly tactics, and both sides got on with it.

I never thought I would buy a business from a guy I had never met, but that's what happened. Johnny Mc and I did meet Peter's fellow director, Trevor. We now own the DealRush business and assets. Perhaps only we would have done it this way. I look forward to meeting the mysterious Peter someday.

My gut feeling and hope are that the deal is a particularly good one, potentially paying for itself in a matter of months, adding somewhere in the wide range of €500,000 to €1 million to our bottom line.

Johnny Mc played a blinder and was in his element, working through their systems and technology and briefing our guys on their tasks. I have asked myself a few questions repeatedly.

Is it risky? Yes.

Are those risks managed? Yes.

Is it a good deal? It could be a great one, but it's unlikely to be a bad one.

It's the kind of asymmetric risk we should be taking. It's a 'bolt-on'. In the case of DealRush, we bought the assets, not the business, so there is no overhead coming with it.

I'm so happy now that we scaled up our tech team when we did. It's a decision that looks to be paying big dividends now, as Paul and his tech team have integrated DealRush onto our platform without a glitch.

Merchant reaction has been very positive, and we're preparing to get all of our offers in front of DealRush members fast.

It has been quite a rush for the whole team. Johnny Mc is smiling again from ear to ear.

November 2016

Big things have been happening on my birthday in recent years. Today, November 3rd, we sent our first email to the DealRush audience, and it will be very telling. I await the outcome with interest: the higher the member engagement we achieve and the higher the sales conversion, the more likely we are to get a quick return on our investment.

DealRush aside, Pigsback's Offer sales are now up by 58% year-to-date. We are taking yet another hit on our Pigsback Advertising business – the last time that will happen – but it won't take away from an otherwise excellent year. Operating profits are likely to land at around €700,000. More importantly, with a fair wind and given the addition of DealRush, they could be more than double that next year.

The integration of DealRush has been a home run on all fronts: technology, member engagement, sales conversion and profit flow-through. I am moving on quickly.

Escapes.ie is not unlike DealRush. It is a lower profile player run by a thrifty and shrewd young entrepreneur, James Donnelly, originally from Sydney, and his Irish wife, Gill.

Escapes.ie is an emerging threat to Pigsback in the hotel space and is very effective commercially. It would be a perfect bolt-on for us. It has a sister site called Pamper.ie, very similar to our site, TheBeautyLounge.ie.

My initial contact with James wasn't met that warmly, far from it. He viewed us with some scepticism, having read our unflattering annual accounts. It led him to ask who should be buying whom.

However, my persistence, assurances and, above all, the completion of the DealRush acquisition seem to have got James to the negotiating table. He is biting, but his expectations are at the higher end of my price range. His new advisors have asked for proof that we have the funding. We will get over that one, and money might just have to talk in the end.

There's no deal for now, but I'm hoping there'll be no escaping for James!

———◆———

Amazon kicked off Black Friday early; if it's good enough for them, it's good enough for us. Yesterday we hit €106,000 in daily gross sales, a new record, and that's before the big sales day itself.

We are on our way to Singapore to see Kerry, our eldest daughter, who is spending her exchange year at Singapore Management University. I have been looking forward to the trip enormously. What an experience this is for Kerry. She is enjoying the Singapore college experience and making the most of her time, with extensive travel around Asia in the planning. I am visiting the Far East for the first time and expecting quite a culture shock. Kerry tells us that Singapore will ease us into Asian culture before Hong Kong ("Singapore on steroids," says Kerry) and later Thailand. It's an immense privilege to take a trip like this, particularly being able to travel in the knowledge that the business has never been on a better footing.

I am planning to use the travelling time to reflect, write a bit and give some time to tidy up my journals. What started with scraps of paper, then little notebooks, later phone notes and emails, is turning into a tome. I went with it, as the very exercise of reflecting and writing down my thoughts, experiences, and emotions was calming and seemed to help me to gain perspective. The value of the record will be for others to judge, but I know that it has helped me considerably along the way. In many ways, it has held me together. I am glad to have the record too. I read back at times and am reminded of previous events and challenges. The Pigsback journey has taught me so much, and while I wouldn't advise the level of risk the younger me took on, I feel pride at the resilience and reinvention.

To anyone who is up against a life challenge, particularly an enduring one, I would recommend writing it down.

I have delayed a planned digital detox for a day. I couldn't keep my eye off our sales tracker today, Black Friday. It has been some sport. We have beaten last year's record sales by a factor of three and comfortably topped the €200,000 in sales for the day. What's more, DealRush was a big factor, contributing about a quarter of all sales, and it looks like paying for itself in just a few months.

It has been a bumper time for sales of Goods, which will easily top the €1 million mark in revenues in November. Last November, we celebrated the milestone of topping a million in revenues in a month, going on to record €1.2 million. We were happy, and rightly so! This year, November will hit double that.

We are leaving Singapore on an afternoon flight to Hong Kong. Singapore was an eye-opener and an impressively structured society and economy. The temperatures were a bit high for me, and the air was too hot and heavy.

I am expecting something altogether more chaotic and fun in Bangkok, with some wind-down time in Phuket before turning home.

The Pigsback team is only getting out of bed in Ireland as I write. They have had an amazing November with the DealRush integration, Black Friday, Cyber Monday and Giving Tuesday (a new initiative we got on board with yesterday, where we gave 10%

of all gross sales from 8 pm to midnight to charity, in our case to the Simon Community).

With this momentum, we will be at a whole new level going into 2017. And it's all happening without me!

9

Magical Momentum

January 2017

"We give a shit."

This is the team's new mantra chosen at a recent away day in Galway. We've posted it big and bold on the office wall. It's about doing the right thing by our members, by our clients, and by each other. In every aspect of the business, at every level of the business, from Johnny Mc to our latest student recruit, 'giving a shit' is what is helping us win the market right now and be a better business.

It was an incredible close to 2016. The acquisition of DealRush in November seems a long time ago now. The integration was smooth and was achieved without adding any extra people. DealRush now accounts for 25% of our sales – all extra, pretty much – and there may be better to come as we apply improved email technology and customisation for our members.

In the meantime, we have purchased a small golf deals business called JustGolf.ie. We did a deal at the first meeting. JustGolf launches for us on March 1st and could bring an additional €1 million in gross sales in its first full year, as well as breathe life into Pigsback's golf audience.

The Christmas season – all the way from Black Friday – was incredibly strong. We're clear market leaders, and there is now a magical momentum in the business. We're rolling with it. With six days to go to the end of January, we have already beaten the budget for the month. We weren't far off the €1 million profit mark in 2016; 2017 should leave that for dead.

———◆———

Nick Coen, my friend, colleague, and fellow punter, passed away on January 30th. His life was never destined to be a very long one, but it was a shock, nonetheless.

Nick's parents, Patrick and Ellen, gave him a great life with a can-do attitude, encouraging him to indulge his main passion, horse racing, whose community of trainers, jockeys, owners and fans all added tremendously to Nick's life, just as he added to theirs.

Johnny Mc and I had the honour of delivering a joint tribute at a special service to celebrate Nick's life. There was no shortage of racing and Pigsback stories to draw on for the address: memories of Nick selling his wheels to the National Stud for advertising space; his memorable rendition of *The Fields of Athenry* at a Pigsback night out; his determined completion of the 5km route when the official starter for the Pigsback.com run for Marie Keating; his secret last-minute trip to Belmont Park as a guest of Aidan O'Brien when St Nicholas Abbey romped home (of course he did!).

At Pigsback, we were all big beneficiaries of our friendship with Nick. He accompanied us through the many highs and lows of the past decade or so. He added to each and every day with his cheeky smile and divilment. The office will not be the same.

March 2017

In a great start to the month, we have just bought Bite A Bargain, the company behind Escapes.ie and Pamper.ie. The price is a chunky enough, €1.2 million. We could not have dreamt of paying that much even six months ago.

The business has been built up stealthily by James Donnelly, a formidable young entrepreneur and negotiator. This is the first time we bought a trading company rather than just the assets, requiring more onerous legal and commercial due diligence.

As we waited in the lawyers' offices for a final agreement to sign, we needed to pass the time and break the tension. I had a laugh introducing James and his wife Gill to the games of *Spoof* and *Pitch and Toss*. We signed much later than expected but had enough time for a late drink at House on Leeson Street. Johnny Mc and I had left thoughts of food far too late, and we crowned the evening with takeaway curry chips on Baggot Street. Bite a bargain, indeed.

Pigsback is buzzing as we welcome four new team members from Bite A Bargain, including James, who has an oversight role for a few months. Barely two days after the acquisition, Paul had both Escapes.ie and Pamper.ie up and running on our platform.

A couple of weeks in, and it's already looking like another excellent bolt-on. We have just rewritten our budget for the year at €24 million in gross sales and over €2 million in profit. I am quietly confident on both fronts.

What an acquisition roll we have been on, and all in just six months.

April 2017

I'm writing from the snug at the back of O'Dowd's bar in Roundstone. I'm enjoying a Connemara Gold Ale, brewed not far away, near the Coral Strand in Carraroe. I've fond memories of our very early family holidays in Carraroe and two later stays at the Gaeltacht there as teenagers. Back then, it was all about the *céilí* and the *cailíní*. But there's always been something special for us about the landscape and air of Connemara. Today, it was a trek up Errisbeg. It was a bit windy on top, blowing straight in from the Atlantic.

This is a short break, but I'm planning a much longer one this summer. I feel I need it and have earned it. Pigsback is on track for a huge year.

In this new phase, we're planning to consolidate in a few areas, mainly tech, before we drive on again. We've got a big upgrade agenda encompassing our software, our server architecture and security, and our cloud-based IT systems. We're also planning a thorough review of our member communications to try to reduce our dependence on bulk email in favour of personal messaging and notifications from our site and app.

It's a big agenda and more critical than ever to deliver, as we have our new-found scale and profitability to protect. Being an Irish business, we're close to our customers, which puts a certain moat around the business, but we must continue to keep up with the high pace of change in technology and in marketing tools.

The big looming corporate question is whether there is more growth on the horizon or whether we have eaten up all the market share we can. If we are facing a plateau or, worse still, a decline in sales in the coming years, then that four-letter word, E-X-I-T, could be making its return – at my instigation this time. There's a lot of shareholder value at stake. Stick or draw? I'm torn, but on balance, I think it's high time I wrapped this up. I have done my best and am grateful that the last few years have restored such value. I'll try to steer it home now.

———◆———

It's all going swimmingly, which makes me anxious. There's been immense satisfaction in getting to where we are, particularly after all we've been through, but hanging out at the summit isn't that much craic. Just ticking over nicely is not for me. But nor do I feel a huge urge to take the cheque and walk away into retirement. The last thing I want is to be sitting in some tax haven or at home scratching my butt, wondering on Monday mornings, in varying degrees of depression, what I'll do for the day. I've been that *man in the arena* for so long, and I'll miss the edge, the daily battles, the conceiving of ideas, shaping them into business models, making calls, having a go, making mistakes, reassessing, then going again, taking real pleasure from watching a team and its individuals enthuse, grapple, and, hopefully, eventually thrive. I'll miss that *arena*, but I will try new things, and I will find triers to back.

———◆———

October 2017

Our letter to accompany the annual AGM pack to shareholders read well. How things have changed in the past year or two. I'm sure our shareholders welcome the continued change of fortune. For many, the question no doubt arises as to whether a return on investment can now be offered. I felt it was time to broach the question but was non-committal, referring to *a review of liquidity options*, and managed to avoid the exit word.

My enthusiasm had been tempered by some soundings on exit options I recently took from a Dublin corporate finance house. They say that prevailing valuations are still suppressed at an average multiple of 4-6 times annual earnings for companies at our scale. That's not very attractive. I would prefer to work on the business and take my chances of increasing value over time than accept that. Anyway, there's nothing on the horizon.

———◆———

The last quarter of the year, including Black Friday, accounts for 40% of our annual sales and 50% of our profits. This year we've decided to invest about €100,000 in a real-world or *above-the-line* advertising campaign. We spend enough on Facebook and Google. We debated lots of options and decided on a campaign targeting the captive commuter audience on its way to and from work and colleges in the major urban areas of Dublin and Cork, with lots of ads on Dublin Bus, on Dublin's suburban rail routes (the Luas and Dart), on rail platforms, and in the concourses of major rail stations. We hope that our ads will prompt commuters to have a look at our offers. We're using the new strapline *Give the gift of luxury for less.* It strikes a nice balance between quality and value.

November 2017

We have just acquired MyDealPage, a brand and service aggregating deals from multiple platforms for consumers. We have been talking on and off for some time, but the deal was finally agreed upon at a Monday morning management meeting and executed 60 hours later. Content from our brands is already more prominent. That's some credit to Johnny Mc and to Paul, our CTO.

In November 2015, we celebrated the milestone of €1m in monthly sales. In November 2017, that number could hit €4 million.

Board Meeting - Corporate Overview 20/2/18 {Extracts}

2017 was a landmark year for the company with the successful [integration] of 4 acquisitions and 5 brands: DealRush, Escapes.ie, Pamper.ie, JustGolf.ie and MyDealPage.ie. Gross sales after refunds grew from €15m to €26m, up 71%.

In total, we had 193k unique purchasers, up from 117k, spending €133 each, up from €127, on an average of 2.5 items, up from 2.36.

We believe we now make up over 50% of sales in daily deals. This sector is otherwise stagnant (if not declining) and we are [now defining] our competitor set and market opportunities by reference to both the broader hospitality market – in particular, Irish hotel accommodation booked online – and the broader [market for] e-commerce marketplaces.

2017 EBITDA [operating profit] will be €1.9m, and we are now projecting a 2018 EBITDA of €2.2m.

———◆———

January 2018

Life goes on at Pigsback, and 2018 is starting well. The buzz continues, and it's a pleasure to be part of it. The team is getting stronger with a very capable middle management layer emerging, with the likes of Annabelle Quinlan and Philip Kelly in the hotel team, Aiden Cronin in dining, Barry O'Meara in golf, Kevin Rooney and Cillian Nolan in marketing, and Karena Flynn-Thai and Jonathan Townshend in Goods.

We are working on more commuter advertising for Mother's Day, encouraged by the positive feedback to the Christmas campaign. It's good to be back advertising in the real world too.

The team is also busy getting ready for the new EU General Data Protection Regulation (GDPR) laws coming into effect in May.

I am not as busy as I once was, and I'm more effective for it. For too long, I worried about all the details. These days, I don't get in the way. I limit my intervention to the weekly team and management meetings, some key customer meetings or when input is asked for on any significant issue that arises. Other than that, I steer the corporate ship, manage board consultations and meetings, and meet the bosses of companies in our sector. The upshot is a clearer focus on the major strategic opportunities and challenges ahead.

———◆———

Jocelyn Davis's book on the subject of management, *The Greats on Leadership,* sets out lessons from philosophers, novelists, playwrights and poets, delving into such diverse sources as the Iliad, the Bible, Jane Austen, and Shakespeare, which she blends with modern management theory along the way. Her conclusions ring true for me, and the rich literary references elevate and colour the subject.

I have drawn a few conclusions on management from my own 35 years of experience in organisations, most of it managing teams.

Credit to Jocelyn Davis for influencing some of these, but you'll have to read her book for her version.

On Management

- There must be a very authentic people focus
- Leaders must go first ('lead') at key times

... consult others of course, consider the data, but trust in their decision-making, and get it right much more often than not

- Charisma and extraversion are overrated
- Create an environment where people can grow
- Shine a light on the people around you
- Accommodate people's lifestyle needs
- Be highly attentive to emotions
- Set achievable objectives
- Define clear areas of responsibility – no fudges
- Give people the right tools
- Let people feel your confidence in them
- Performance measurement should clearly tell people how they're doing – over par or under par
- Feedback should be consistent and continuous – no surprises or waiting
- Give people a fair chance but don't tolerate sustained underperformance. When all has failed, be decisive, clear and fair, accepting your share of the responsibility
- Have fun
- Share the fruits of success

May 2018

I slept poorly and just about made this morning's early CityJet flight from Dublin to London City Airport, sleeping for most of the journey. I was meeting Jean-Charles Lacoste, the UK MD of Secret Escapes, an international player in the premium travel deals space. Jean-Charles reached out to me a couple of weeks ago. Having initially binned his email after only a very rapid scan, I thought better of it, read it closely, and picked up the phone. Jean-Charles introduced himself and gave me the background to Secret Escapes, explaining how the company was pursuing acquisitions and forming commercial partnerships internationally too.

He thought Pigsback, with its strong and premium position among Irish hotels, would be an ideal fit for Secret Escapes. He had done his homework. Secret Escapes, he said, could supply its international travel and accommodation content to Ireland, and Pigsback could supply its Irish hotel offers to Britain and other markets. A win-win.

Jean-Charles was friendly and convivial. We talked about France, and we conversed a little in French too. It didn't take long for him to get to the point: "Would Pigsback consider selling to Secret Escapes?" Wow, this had escalated, but I wasn't too surprised by this turn in the conversation. I gave the correct answer: "No." I continued: "We have been through a lot and are enjoying a strong trading period with excellent growth and profitability. We have no thoughts of exit right now."

He persisted, whereupon I added: "I guess everything has a price."

We agreed to meet in London today: May 2nd, 2018. I arrived early to the Holborn offices of Secret Escapes and was duly impressed by their 'Concierge' (reception), their awards cabinet, an array of upmarket travel magazines and a warm welcome. Out at lunch with Jean-Charles, he made it clear that while a commercial partnership between our companies was interesting, an acquisition was Secret Escapes' preferred route. The directness was softened by a Gallic charm.

We joined a large group back at the Secret Escapes office on Hatton Wall, including Tom Valentine, one of the co-founders. Tom, too extended me a very warm welcome and got his Irish credentials on the table at an early stage, pointing out that his grandmother was from Co Cork. I wouldn't have guessed it: Tom is quite posh and intellectual, endearingly shy and self-effacing too. I produced a few

Pigsback stress pigs. They all claimed to have been given one or to have seen it before, recalling our London launch. It cost a few quid, but we left our mark!

Alex Saint, the other co-founder, joined the meeting with a burst of energy, a big smile and a bigger handshake. He reminded me that we had met during his days at the Daily Mail Group when we agreed on a co-branded partnership for Pigsback under the Metro and Evening Standard brands. That felt like aeons ago, but it was a well-made connection.

If their objective was to put me at ease in their company and with their culture, it had worked a treat.

The meeting went through the formalities of the commercial partnership set-up and structure, but we circled back to acquisition. Tom took the lead: "We understand that acquisition was not something that was on your agenda, but would you consider it?"

I thought briefly and answered: "I won't rule it out, but it took us a long time to get into such a good place, so we're in no hurry. We'd have to talk about valuation parameters first before we waste any time."

We then did exactly that. I heard enough. It was good progress for a first date. We agreed to leave it at that for a few weeks.

This suits me as we need a little bit of time to implement a new booking fee for hotel deals. It's a common feature for hotel bookings online, but we resisted it up to now for competitive reasons. Barry feels it's time; I'd like it in our profit projections.

Culturally and in terms of the business model, I got a strong sense of *fit* with Secret Escapes.

Tonight, on the other side of London, I am meeting Roland from Wowcher. I am hoping he is prepared to sell us his Irish business this time. At the right price, it would be another very nice bolt-on, potentially adding a lot more profit in the nick of time.

———◆———

Dinner with Roland was relaxed, and Bentley's was top class, as ever. Richard Corrigan once more went out of his way to say hello and exchange a few stories. Roland and I refound our level with ease. This time I took the initiative but was rebuffed firmly:

"We won't be selling you our Irish business. It's not a big business, but it's worth keeping, and it's simply worth more to us than to you."

A bit disappointing, but I was in no place to argue.

He continued: "We should explore the merger of our two companies, not just the Irish entities this time, with a view to an IPO or trade sale. That would help give both sets of investors the exit that is their ultimate goal."

I hadn't expected that, but it was worth acknowledging with reciprocal positivity. Having done that, I managed to allude to the interest in our business without giving too much away: "...another party showing interest ....an outright acquisition..."

I also made it clear that going down the IPO route was not our preferred option:

"Going down a paper route together, with a whole new journey which I won't be in control of, is not something I want to sell to my shareholders, particularly at a time when there is a solid cash alternative at a fair price."

We left it at that. I would be very happy to get Wowcher to the negotiation table, not least for the competitive tension it could create.

I have known Roland for quite a while now, and we get on well. He is a complete professional, a figurehead in our industry, and has a progressive and inquiring mind. Moreover, he has consistently shown an interest in our business. He knows and gets on well with Johnny Mc too. He won't want to miss out on this opportunity.

It was after midnight as I strolled through the streets of central London from Swallow Street up to Welbeck Street and my hotel. Nothing in the fashion or art shops of Bond Street or in the department stores of Oxford Street could distract me. I was gripped by the possibilities ahead. I thought of Kevin and chuckled. He will too. Exit is back on the agenda. A good day's work.

———◆———

Less than two weeks have passed, and I'm heading back to London tomorrow for meetings with both parties. I have invited JD. It feels serendipitous. JD recently left a very senior role at PwC in the UK. He is particularly commercial for someone of such a strategic background. He has always been strong at building relationships in business, seamlessly merging the business and social with clients and colleagues. I am proud to bring him along, as a recently appointed non-executive director of Pigsback, as a corporate finance expert, and, as it happens, as my brother.

I don't know what the day will hold, and part of me is still a bit hesitant about an exit, whatever the price: it's hard to sell your own creation; it's hard to move on; it's hard to imagine an owner over your shoulder for whatever length of time that may be; it's hard thinking of the void beyond. Karen is more resolute, of course. As I left for the airport, she could sense my anxiety, smiled, but wished me luck. She has been playing her cards face-up on this matter for some time.

———————•———————

It's a balmy Tuesday morning in early June as we await the departure of our Ryanair flight, leaving a hot Dublin for the even hotter Italy and France. After a night in Pisa, we'll take a train to the coast and across the border to Menton, later to Nice, and finally to Antibes for the last five nights. It's our DIY holiday and one that Karen and I, our youngest daughter Ella and her pal, Rachael, are all looking forward to. It has been all-go since that London visit. Both meetings went well. The Secret Escapes team took up where they had left off, positive and decisive. They have been in acquisition mode for some time, see a strong fit with Pigsback, and want to buy us. It's not very complicated, and we agreed to progress to the next steps.

We met Wowcher over dinner at the Groucho Club in Soho, the Dean Street venue once again associated with a key juncture in the life of Pigsback. Our guests showed a determined front, raising the ante considerably since my dinner with Roland at Bentley's. They too are committed to buying Pigsback and see strong synergies between our businesses. They see me involved in helping them, but not full-time.

There is much to like about both parties. It could be a nice dilemma.

I will happily tune in and out in the course of our holidays to keep the process moving.

In my absence, both parties have advanced to sign non-disclosure agreements (NDAs), permitting us to exchange confidential data mutually. We now have every chance of achieving a full price for the business. A few factors are currently in our favour: we're now a strong number one in hospitality in Ireland; we have gaps in our offering that seem to present extra opportunities for both parties; we are significantly profitable for our scale, which points to a model and know-how that both parties can learn from; both need top-line and bottom-line growth with their own exits in mind; both are active in Ireland and would want us to run their Irish operations.

They're both buying into me being involved on a part-time basis, although it seems to matter more to Wowcher than Secret Escapes. It's helpful to have someone as strong and experienced as Johnny Mc at the helm. Any buyer will also want to nail down Barry, Dave and Paul too, who each have a lot to contribute above and beyond the Irish market.

While it's all very exciting at one level, I'm torn and anxious at another level, personally unsure about letting go and about what lies ahead in my mid-50s. Since I first sold a share in the company to raise money, I've known an exit would be the inevitable outcome. Is this the right time? I may not get this chance again. I can't be too greedy. It will be emotional, but yes, it's time.

We have circulated a final Investment Memorandum to both parties, and both have confirmed visits on my return from holidays. We expect offers soon after. If we ultimately accept, there will be a due diligence process for a couple of weeks in July, and contracts will be, hopefully, exchanged by September.

There is a risk for all of us that any significant delay would bring us into our high season from late September, when, believe it or not, the Christmas season begins.

Our managers and team are all focused, positive and – if the truth be told – licking their lips at the prospect of a payout. It could be financially rewarding beyond expectation for all staff and shareholders. We burned through millions of euros in the early years in Ireland to get going and then much more in the UK, a lot less successfully, followed by that consistent drip of losses and incredibly tight squeezes up to and including 2015.

It has been some turnaround in our fortunes.

And Michael will agree to the deal. And Michael will support the acquirer. And Michael will begin to move on. And Michael will get over his fears. And Michael will work on for-profit stuff and not-for-profit stuff. And Michael will chill a bit and develop new interests. And Michael will finish his account of the Pigsback years. And Michael will enjoy freewheeling downhill for a while. 1

July 2018

Dad passed away on July 21st, 2018, after a long illness. He was an inspiration to all who knew him and a particular inspiration to me on my entrepreneurial journey. Education was his passport to a better life, and his commitment to family, business, community, and the arts made it a very good one.

As we set up our own families, we valued his relationship and role no less, a much-loved and good-humoured dad and grandad. He enjoyed sharing a few life values with his kids and grandkids alike: *be decent and as good as your word (integrity); put in the work, and don't fear enterprise (work ethic); be kind by sharing, in your everyday encounters, in your time for family and friends, and in your good fortune (kindness), when you make a mistake, acknowledge it and learn from it (humility).*

The local newspaper headlines said it all: 'Alf Dwyer was a towering influence for good in Dundalk', *Dundalk Democrat*; 'Corkman Alf Dwyer made a big contribution to life in the town he loved and made his home', *The Argus*, in a piece written by long-time editor and Dad's long-time friend, Kevin Mulligan. Both are online.

10

Bringing Home the Bacon

August 2018

Tomorrow marks ten weeks since my meeting with Secret Escapes and the dinner that evening in Bentley's with Wowcher. It was the day when both parties confirmed their interest in buying Pigsback. But corporate wheels grind slowly.

Sales were flatter than expected during the first half of 2018, as we battled an unseasonally harsh winter and early spring, followed quickly by a heat wave. Neither extreme is good for our business. It was a good chance to catch up, consolidate, and now carry on into a second half of sales growth as we launch a new app, new advertising, and personalisation improvements.

We have made another acquisition: TreatTicket, the small Northern Ireland business that we met back in 2015. It's an extra string to our bow for a small outlay, and we think it could do its job nicely for us as we try to grow in Northern Ireland again.

With all the acquisitions, we have ended up with a few too many brands. We're confident that the core Pigsback brand has the legacy, the historic investment, and the profile, so we've started to transition our secondary brands under it. First up was DealRush, whose audience is now under the Pigsback.com brand. There were a few stages to the process and no resistance from members. We are actively preparing to do the same with Escapes and TreatTicket.

———◆———

It's all go on the exit front again all of a sudden. After some to-ing and fro-ing, we have received both offers, each valuing our business from €20 million to a potential €30 million, payable in stages and subject to performance. That's encouraging. If it comes to pass at these levels, I might just beat that €1 per share target I set for myself all the way back in 2010, despite all the trials and tribulations.

The ink had hardly dried on the offers, however, when Johnny Mc asked to meet me at my house. He had started the annual exercise to reconcile unused Pigsback vouchers. We have tended to leave this exercise as late as possible, usually when the annual audit is in its final stages, giving us the fullest possible visibility of vouchers used and unused from the previous year.

It turns out that we are doing too good a job: more vouchers are being used, so fewer are expiring, leaving us with an inaccurate accrual (an assumed amount) in our accounts, affecting our 2017 profits, 2018 projections and our forecasts for later years. These are already contained in the Information Memorandum we sent to both prospective buyers. It's annoying, and I fear it reflects poorly on us. However, we have grown so quickly in recent years that something like this could easily fall between the cracks. We had already recognised this gap in our resources and have been planning to hire a new financial controller to report to Johnny Mc later this year.

Johnny completed the analysis a few days later, and the number is at the wrong end of the range, but we have plans to compensate for the hit. I brought it up without delay. Both parties have been empathetic. We are all in similar businesses with similar challenges, so everyone is curious to learn anything they can. I'm pretty sure that neither party is going to be deterred by this. They certainly aren't doubting our bona fides. It helped that we commissioned an urgent independent verification by accountants EY.

After getting the *mea culpa* out there, my line to both parties was hard to contradict: "It's better to buy a business that is built on customer satisfaction with great experiences rather than one built on customer dissatisfaction with unused vouchers."

It's true, and thankfully, they are accepting it. We are completing revised projections, and won't be too far off our forecasts when all is said and done. Strong sales in June are a useful reminder of all that is good about our business.

———◆———

It's been a full month since Dad passed. We booked a weekend city break *en famille* in Barcelona, which was very welcome. We walked a lot, but more than anything, I enjoyed parking myself in a café or bar with a beer or coffee and a bit of quiet reflection. I messed around with a few sketches and wrote a few words before meeting up with the gang again along the way.

I spent a bit of yesterday and today preparing some answers to questions asked by Secret Escapes. There's nothing we are concerned about, but it feels like that nervy stage where suitors could easily fall out. We are trying to keep both parties simmering, but I don't want to drag Roland and Wowcher out any more than is fair if they are not going to be the ultimate choice. I need to guide both parties to the finish line now, then pick a winner.

I am very fortunate to have a couple of pals outside the business to consult for objective and experienced views. Paul McKeon, a shrewd and experienced investor, has me focused on what portion of the proposed buyout payments is upfront and legally committed, tending to discount the potential earn-out elements. Michael Mc says: "Sell while the going is good," adding that matters beyond our control can change so quickly.

I'm listening.

Of the two bidders, I have my preference for now, anyway. It's a close call, and there isn't unanimity around the board table. For me, Secret Escapes moved first with conviction, which must be acknowledged. So far, they have walked the walk at every turn. I have no reason not to trust them nor to believe that our business and team would not be in the right hands. Their offer ticks every box for us. In addition, their very similar culture, hotel focus and premium brand positioning all help. Secret Escapes is happy to let me move on within a year. There is support for Wowcher, too, around the board table, perceived by JD in particular as having fewer 'deal risks.' I listen carefully, but I know that the whole board will back my call on this one.

November 2018

The deal looks like going the way of Secret Escapes, who are preparing a Letter of Intent. This will outline the essential points of the acquisition agreement – both commercial and legal – and, therefore, form the basis of an exclusivity period. During that time, they will complete due diligence (a deep dive into our financial and legal records), and we'll use the time to agree on the final share purchase agreement (SPA).

It has already been slower than I'd like, but the deal could still be completed in December. I really don't want any further delays, as I am nervous about our trading performance this month and next. That is mostly in our control, but we rise and fall with the vagaries of consumer confidence and spending, and there are growing fears about the impact of Brexit, which is just around the corner.

Getting this sale to the finish line under the circumstances will be good work.

————◆————

Johnny Mc has enlisted Valerie, and they have formally notified our investors of a possible deal. We want to tee them up to complete the signing process efficiently. Valerie's role is to update all shareholders' contact and bank details. It's an important and painstaking job.

The reaction from shareholders has been one of *a nice surprise*, with a flood of goodwill and positivity at the prospect of a deal. Fingers are crossed that we stay on track and get the transaction over the line. Share certificates are being dusted down. Of course, everyone would now like to have had a bigger share of the 2010 Emergency Round, struck at 10 cents per share, which looks like yielding a minimum of an 11-fold return. These were risky and critical funds when funds were hard to come by. The extent of a shareholder's participation in that investment round was always going to be one of the single biggest determinants of their final outcome. The shareholder register tells the full and complete story of every investment round in Pigsback's long fight. It is the bible, legally and commercially, the only show in town when it comes to settlement day.

The prospects of an imminent deal continue to create a stir in the office. I will be delighted for our team, whose sacrifices and forbearance will reap just reward. That may be the most satisfying part.

————◆————

I got up to join the team for a 7 am start at Tara Street train station in Dublin city centre. We were doing a commuter promotion, part of the brand MO, since 2000. I was pretty sure it would be my last, so I wasn't going to miss it.

We split into teams, covering Tara, Connolly, Heuston and Pearse stations. As the morning progressed, we would move on to target the bigger office blocks. Our commuter advertising campaign is also in full swing at all of the stations and throughout the commuter transport network, so we were building the brand profile even further.

We had a target of giving out 10,000 stress pigs to commuters. It was a miserable, wet morning, but we put a lot of smiles on a lot of faces. It was fun and energising work, deserving of a bite of breakfast in Bewley's Café on Grafton St afterwards.

The sales graph is rising strongly as October and November progress. I'm pleased, of course, but on days like this, I do wonder as I feel the business and this kind of team spirit and buzz slipping through my fingers.

———◆———

A bit of humour lightens even a long and grinding process like this. It started when I answered the phone to Johnny Mc, who was with our lawyers.

"Hello, Ardee Gardaí," I answered in my best county Louth accent.

Later one of the finance guys in Secret Escapes asked for "a bit of colour" on a historical tax matter. Johnny Mc responded: "Most of the issues are green, and one has a light shade of orange, but there's no red."

To which the reply came: "I don't know my Irish history all that well, but I don't think orange and green mix terribly well."

It got a laugh, but not too many concessions.

Meanwhile, one of our UK shareholders, with the appellation 'Sir George', no less, responded to our investors' email. He laughed as he seemed to be quite unaware of his investment in our business, apparently made on his behalf in 2006. Johnny Mc took him off very well and all in good spirits, of course: "no one told me I had shares in a piggery in Ireland."

———◆———

December 2018

It's mid-afternoon, and Johnny Mc and I are lodged in Whitney Moore's boardroom, awaiting another draft of a warranties document. Johnny Mc has become part of the furniture. There's a calm in the air. We have been discussing our respective holiday plans next year and how we will cover for each other in February and March. We just need to get all the i's dotted, and the t's crossed. We're chilled out and hope to stay that way before, during, and after the big 'final issues' call at 4 pm with both sets of lawyers.

Secret Escapes are well into the exclusivity period. I had my conversation with Wowcher, advising them of our initial choice. It wasn't easy, but Roland could not have been more graceful and kept the door open.

It has already been a long and intense process. The finish line is in sight, but deal fatigue is kicking in. I am feeling it! An enterprise is hard to get going, harder to keep going, and exceedingly hard to exit.

———————◆———————

January 2019

One shareholder has written to us, purporting to represent two or three others close to him, though he leaves it ambiguous. I called them friends once. Now they are threatening to hold up the sale process. I could see this coming from as far back as the Emergency Round in 2010 when one member of the group – in choosing not to reinvest – unleashed his criticism at me. I didn't argue with him; his mind seemed made up, and his tone was spiteful. None of them took up their share allocation then, falling into a deafening silence about the business, waiting, I sensed, in the long grass. These are savvy, experienced, and wealthy investors. There is nothing naive about them.

Our records are very good. Like all shareholders, big or small (in their case), they were given audited accounts for every year since the business began, were invited to every AGM and EGM, and were given every chance to participate. They attended none. They showed no proactive interest in the business. Now they pounce, with me at my most vulnerable, the deal at its most critical and sensitive stage. They are seeking a review of pretty much everything since pretty much the start: an impossible request, as they well know. To the extent that they are entitled to answers, they have been given them in full. But a review is not what this is really about. It won't get them anywhere.

I wasted no time in talking to Alex and Tom, the cofounders of Secret Escapes. They have been around the block in this business and others, and have had many shareholders come and go. They were fully expecting something of this nature, given our very fragmented shareholder base.

We shared the correspondence and history with the Secret Escapes legal team, who quickly completed their review. They were fully supportive, calling the communication "spurious and opportunistic". Johnny Mc had other words for it and pulled no punches: "Pure nasty!" Kevin, as usual, is unflustered, confident in the oversight and governance he brought since 2001.

Our lawyer Thérèse, who has overseen everything we have done, every step of the way, is foursquare behind us. Just in case anyone felt remotely inclined to do any kind of deal to make them go away, she declared: "There can be no special treatment for any one shareholder or group over another."

She needn't have worried. If we need to 'drag them', as our constitution allows, we will. This simply means invoking a clause to force them to accept the deal, provided more than 70% of shareholders have accepted it, which is a formality. We're as sure as we can be that all other shareholders will sign.

Above all else, at a personal level, it feels very sour and disappointing. I don't like falling out with anyone. I don't seek conflict, but I will defend the integrity of every move we made and of the board's oversight at all times, whatever that takes. Right now, it means putting on hold any regret I may or may not feel at lost friendships.

———◆———

The endless to-ing and fro-ing of the legal process is tiring and has slowed down ahead of the Christmas and New Year period. Such is life. I can't fault our lawyers, who have done their best to keep the pace up. Still, it's frustrating, so I get edgy, the board gets edgy, and that just makes me edgier. It doesn't take much to throw me at this stage, with my nerves raw from two decades in the trenches. My colours are well and truly nailed to the Secret Escapes mast now. I have placed a lot of trust in Alex and Tom and still have every faith in them.

Right now, I'm putting the finishing touches to an email I'll be sending out to our shareholders with the offer letter as soon as contracts are exchanged. I need Kevin's input and sign-off for this one as chairman. He has been fully engaged in every part of the process. He is matter-of-fact, professional and more stoic than me.

What a loyal and supportive investor I got in Kevin all those years ago: he has supported me to the end, through thick and thin, and I hope we remain friends for a long time to come. He was instrumental in shaping Project Encore, which energised the business when it was most needed, and now is proving its worth for all investors and staff too. I know Kevin has enjoyed the journey. He will miss Pigsback; he'll miss the craic during his trips to Dublin with myself and Johnny Mc, the interaction with the team and the unknotting of challenges together over the years. That said, he will, of course, be very happy to exit his investment so well.

February 2019

Our middle daughter, Nicky, is doing an exchange term at Melbourne University. It runs from February to July. It was planned for a long time that I would accompany her for the first two weeks and help her settle in. We're here now. I'm loving the quality time with Nicky. It's a rare chance too to meet some old friends and discover some of Australia (this is my first visit). I even got to play one of the events at the Aussie Millions Poker Festival (that took some planning!).

Of course, the plan was made assuming that our deal would be done and dusted. It isn't. This is due to unexpected delays with Secret Escapes funding, which is causing a lot of restlessness around the board table. I am taking Alex at his word all the way and telling everyone to breathe and wait.

Alex was insistent that I make the trip to Melbourne. He knows I'm monitoring everything and am available at any time at the drop of a hat. Karen was keen I went too. No wonder. Apart from putting Nicky first, she's happier with me in Melbourne than obsessing at home.

Melbourne has quickly become one of my favourite cities. What a city! And what a privilege to have ample leisure time here. It is a city at ease with the arts and culture, indoors and outdoors. It has the facilities to match: the Arts Centre, the National Gallery of Victoria, Federation Square and Melbourne University itself, with its blend of the old and new. I'm enjoying the graffiti streets like Hosier Lane and the distinct vibes of the city's urban and suburban districts from St Kilda to Fitzroy to Balaclava to Brunswick. That's not even to begin to get into the riverside parks and walks, coastal Melbourne, and the city's ample leisure facilities and famed sports grounds.

The trip couldn't have come at a better time for me. The delays in the sale process are frustrating but beyond my control. The board is super-alert to the risks. Brexit is like a dull weather system moving into our picture. I'm afraid it could still scupper progress.

Last Tuesday, we sent the offer letter with a note from myself and Kevin to all shareholders, albeit subject to the exchange of contracts. We just need Secret Escapes to sign.

———◆———

Earlier today, I went for a run along Saint Kilda Beach south to Elwood Beach. The sea air worked its wonders in clearing my head. Later I hopped on a vintage tram from our hotel into Melbourne, stopping off at the National Gallery for Julian Opie's superb exhibition of large bright, mainly digital artworks.

Right now, I'm sitting in the Abbey Road cafe and bar in Saint Kilda. I'm minding my own business. Nicky is back at the hotel, asleep after a long day and a night out. She has taken to Melbourne like a duck to water. Why wouldn't she?

I'm on edge. The Shiraz is helping, but it's a little lonely. My mobile battery is running low. So am I. It's February 4th, and I am expecting news of the exchange of contracts by midnight local time. A journey of 20 years, trying as hard as my mind and body allowed, is down to this. And it looks like I'll have that moment on my own.

In order to give effect to their new funding, Secret Escapes need to get their documents notarised by their subsidiaries in the Czech Republic and Germany. I've just been told that the notarisation process has been delayed by a few hours, so I'm going to head to the hotel and try to sleep.

It's 3 am in Melbourne, 4 pm at home, and I can't sleep. I just put a call into Alex, paranoid that something is amiss. He's adamant that all is proceeding, just more slowly than anticipated: "Go back to bed, Michael," he insisted, "the delays are nothing to be concerned about."

By the time I woke, word was through from Thérèse that the deal was signed at 7 pm Irish time today, February 4th, 2019.

All that's left is the formality of us gathering signatures from shareholders. Then the cash transfers take place. The deal, as initially negotiated, has remained intact, with Secret Escapes paying €22 million upfront plus another €3 million withheld for warranties, which will be released in phases. We could potentially get up to €8 million extra in a profit earn-out, depending on how the business trades for the rest of 2019. In the unfolding climate, no one is banking on the extra payments.

It's a cracking result and a fair price. It helped that we traded well at the end of last year and, of course, had two bidding parties at the table.

It's 19 years to the day since the incorporation of the business - a long time in some ways but no time at all in others.

I eventually tapped some tired words in an email to my senior team:

{Extracts}

Big congratulations!

A very proud moment for us all. We survived the carnage of 2000-2010, won the deals market over the last eight years, and now we get rewarded with a great exit. If the process was frustrating at times, so what! We have the right owner. I've been convinced of that since way back. Huge respect for Johnny Mc's stamina. He deserves massive kudos! But every one of you played your full part: amazing platform developments and robustness under Paul, a dream position in hotels, seriously well-managed by Barry ... decent dining & beauty positions too, unbelievable growth – gross and net – in Goods under Dave, acquisitions we had the balls for, great brand and audience from 19 years of work, and a great culture.

It wasn't long ago we were pulling our hair out walking around Citywest. I am delighted that you are all getting your just rewards!

MD

My respect for Johnny Mc's stamina was heartfelt. We've dovetailed well. On September 11th, 2014, he commented on the energy I had found "from somewhere", as he put it, and how he was exhausted. Well, the tables have turned. I used up all my energy on Project Encore, on the acquisitions since, and on teeing up this deal. Right now, he's the one with the new energy. I am sapped. I do feel content, but I am too mentally exhausted for any jubilation or urge to celebrate. It's just a relief.

Letter to Shareholders 5/2/2019 {Extracts}

RE: Sale of Empathy Marketing Limited to Secret Escapes Group

Dear < >

Message from Michael Dwyer, CEO and Kevin Watson, Chairman, Empathy Marketing Limited

We are very pleased to inform you that we have concluded a deal to sell Empathy Marketing Limited ("Pigsback") to Secret Escapes Group, a leading European online travel company, headquartered in London. Secret Escapes approached us in April 2018, recognising our market leadership in Ireland and the premium positioning of the Pigsback.com brand.

We had another interested party at the negotiating table up to October 2018, which makes us confident that the price being offered of up to €1.53 per share is a very fair price. This is made up of €1.002 per share upfront and potential deferred payments of up to €0.532 per share.

We believe this is a very satisfactory outcome given our uniquely volatile journey over the past 19 years. It's worth a recap:

Pigsback.com launched in 2000 during the dot-com crash. The brand was very well received, but internet household penetration in Ireland lagged behind Europe at about 15% of households, nearly all narrowband. We made ends meet in the early years by creating new revenue models like Empathy Research, Empathy Communications and Curly's Coupons.

We undertook a major launch in the UK in 2005, which was initially very promising, recruiting over 1m members and working with many major national brands. We quickly exceeded €1m in UK advertising revenues. The impact of the credit crunch on advertising expenditure heavily impacted our UK business, and we were eventually forced to withdraw.

We launched in Canada in 2007 under a joint venture with Bell and beat all initial targets in a pilot launch in Calgary. However, a takeover battle at Bell resulted in the closure of all of its new ventures, including Pigsback.com in Canada.

We found ourselves back in an Ireland, depressed by banking and economic woes. We completed an emergency funding in April 2010, converting Loan Notes and issuing new shares.

The economic environment and the emergence of Facebook and Google AdWords were putting extreme pressure on our original business model, and in August 2010, we began the repositioning of the Pigsback.com brand into the premium end of the deals business. We went on to launch premium sub-brands – TheDiningRoom.ie and LuxuryBreaks.ie in 2012 and 2013 – to accentuate our positioning.

Progress was stop-start in a very competitive and overcrowded marketplace. We were only 4th in the market behind Groupon, LivingSocial and GrabOne, with the discounters, DealRush and Escapes snapping at our heels. Meanwhile, various efforts to revive the original Pigsback.com advertising fee-based model had failed.

We remained loss-making for most of the years from 2010 to 2015 and struggled with a weak balance sheet. The loss of some of our top management to a thriving digital sector was seriously threatening the business.

We consulted widely, and after a presentation at the AGM in November 2015, we signed off on the multi-faceted Project Encore plan. Encore stopped the talent exodus, secured a final round of cost cuts and teed up the sale of Empathy Research in late 2015.

With critical breathing room, we began to make market gains and made our first acquisition, DealRush.ie, in November 2016. The bolt-on model was a huge breakthrough, and we quickly went on to make five more purchases: Escapes.ie, Pamper.ie, JustGolf.ie, MyDealPage and TreatTicket.

EML's gross offers revenues grew strongly from €8.8m to €29m from 2015 to 2018, and underlying operating profit went from zero to €2.6m in the same years.

The directors, representing 74.5% of the outstanding share capital, have indicated their acceptance of the deal. We would be grateful if you could sign and return the enclosed documents without delay. We believe that the outcome is a very satisfactory one and are confident that the business will be in excellent hands with Secret Escapes. John McDonald will take day-to-day charge of the business, and Michael Dwyer will remain as part-time CEO for 2019 (the trading period on which the deferred consideration depends).

Finally, we would like to extend our sincerest thanks to all shareholders, employees (at all stages and in all markets), directors and advisors over the years, all of whom supported us in so many ways through an incredible journey.

Michael & Kevin

———◆———

The takeover news wasn't supposed to break in the media until Secret Escapes' announcement this coming weekend. But two days after signing, I got a text from a former colleague congratulating me on the deal. He read about it on Sky News online with the headline 'Secret Escapes plots Irish getaway'.

We're not sure how it got out, but Secret Escapes are comfortable with it, which told me all I needed to know. There followed a series of telephone calls with journalists and a couple of excellent articles in the press in Ireland, notably in the *Sunday Business Post* and the *Sunday Times.*

Gavin Daly, while at the *Sunday Business Post,* had written a feature article on our turbulent journey back in 2010. He addressed both our ups and downs but was very fair. I was happy to speak to him, now at the *Sunday Times.* His headline read 'Pigsback boss Michael Dwyer tickled pink by €25m buyout'.

Once word got out and around, my phone started to ping and kept on pinging for quite a while. There were numerous calls and messages from directors and staff (past and present), shareholders, clients, and friends. They could be summed up with respect for the perseverance and gratitude for keeping it all going and keeping their investment alive.

It's hard to imagine that I need any kind of lift right now, but every message I received meant so much to me and gave me more energy and satisfaction than the prospect of monetary reward. I have no doubt I'll be grateful for that in time too.

———◆———

I visited a church in Melbourne today, something I occasionally do for a bit of contemplation and peace. I found myself reflecting with gratitude on the deal and on this chance for Karen and me to move on. I lit candles, a comforting ritual, for Dad, Gerry and Nick, who we lost along the way.

I am increasingly aware of the impact of years of stored-up stress and, lately, grief. For 20 years, there has been no question of feeling sorry for myself. Now, angst is looming as I prepare to let go of Pigsback.

Just as I was preparing to leave Nicky on the other side of the world, having spent these memorable and momentous weeks together, the emotions tipped. A lot had built up behind those eyes over a long time. It all just welled up and came out.

There I was in tears, sitting on a bench, of all places, on a busy shopping street in Melbourne. I was waiting for Nicky, trying hard to regain my composure. A concerned lady approached and expressed support; how kind people can be.

I gradually recovered. Nicky returned, briefly alarmed, but soon our talk and thoughts moved onto the long journey ahead of me and to all that awaited at home.

———◆———

Today, February 20th, 2019, we formally completed the sale of the business to Secret Escapes. The headlines had it right at about €25 million. All shareholders signed in the end.

Enterprise Ireland's preference shares and interest were first to be settled, which was preceded by my very sincere note of thanks. The distribution to shareholders is happening today. It's a big relief to finally bring home the bacon.

I am so pleased for all of our team. I recently read an Indian saying: 'You are nothing; you stand on the shoulders of your team.'

My team hung in with me and drove home our success. Every staff member did well from the deal, and the long-term managers did very well, like Johnny Mc and his capable lieutenants: Barry, Dave and Paul. The office is abuzz with talk of deposits for houses and renovations. What a privilege to have played a part in that.

I am pleased for our shareholders too. The goodwill has been overwhelming. It has been a stop-start journey with a good outcome. I can say, hand on heart, that we did our best and that the split of the spoils is as fair a reflection of our journey as we'll get. The investors who supported us most in troubled times did particularly well. They deserved to. Some others found themselves somewhere in between, on the slightly right or wrong side of returns, depending on the mix and timings of their investments. They too have been grateful and gracious. Those who decided not to follow their money or who couldn't follow, or who followed to a bare minimum were at least kept in play despite our troubles. They got most of their money back. I am proud of that. Several of these shareholders have contacted me to express their gratitude for a return despite their passivity. This was very much appreciated.

It is a good day for Secret Escapes, who are our type of people. They have bought a business that is in a great place now. They won't tamper with the culture.

I often anticipated this day, yet it is strangely anti-climactic. It's not like some warm feeling of success has come coursing through my veins all of a sudden. Apparently, this is the way with deals. They are all absorbing for a long time but get so dragged out that all sides are tired. I am certainly tired, emotionally drained, and strangely apprehensive about the future. I expect that will pass.

Right now, I just want to chill.

April 2019

True to their word, Secret Escapes are light on intervention and are essentially leaving this transition year to Johnny Mc. He took his planned and well-earned month-long break, featuring his annual pilgrimage to the Cheltenham Festival. He's back now and facing the rising challenges from Brexit and a Vat increase in Irish hospitality, hurting hotels and restaurants.

The team is already sharing learnings in a two-way process with Secret Escapes; Pigsback is launching Secret Escapes international holidays in Ireland, and Secret Escapes is launching Pigsback Irish hotel deals on its platforms in Britain and Germany.

Trading is solid but tough, with Brexit angst growing, causing consumers to worry and tighten their purse strings. Although we'll leave nothing behind, any additional earn-out from 2019 profit growth is looking less and less likely. Frankly, I'm very grateful to have secured the €25m in the emerging uncertain climate.

For 18 years, through thick and thin, I felt alive in the Pigsback office. As a sure sign that I have reached the end of the road, I am finding it extremely difficult to spend any sustained time there now.

It's like my whole system has just had its fill. I don't need to be there much and have regular meetings with the team in the coffee shops on the plaza where the office is located.

I'll do whatever it takes, but I am a background figure now. Pigsback is in new hands. Its future is bright.

───●───

August 2019

With my rucksack, plenty of sunscreen, and water, I set off to walk the 6km coastal stretch from Cannes to the picturesque village of La Napoule. I sat down, enjoyed a couple of beers at the square, and took the chance to write these words, reading a few pages of Michael Harding's book *Hanging with the Elephant.*

I have found myself in public places in tears of laughter or sadness at the raw honesty and emotion in his efforts to 'tame the elephant'. The elephant, Harding explains, is the Buddhist metaphor for the mind. Like an elephant, the mind can be managed if you have the right ropes and the know-how to use them.

The book is rich in Buddhist references, but Harding's own simplifications work best for me. Meditation is like 'dossing', a bit like the daydreaming we all fell into at school. It's when you let your mind switch off from its habitual racing and go off wandering to mull over the mundane: clouds, breath, a flame.

The 'internal weather' is the state of the mind that, for many, can change in a day, like it changes around Harding's mountainside cottage in Co Leitrim.

Two decades of Pigsback, culminating in the whole exit process, took a toll, and a few nerves got exposed. Over the years, I found my own ways to tame my elephant through running, poker, mindfulness, play and activities with the girls, reading and writing, and holidays. Still, Harding's book is a timely read, and I hope to embrace dossing to help me heal. I could get used to dossing in the south of France.

───●───

Pigsback was fuelled by optimism – my optimism mostly. I persisted, with little choice, time and again, for me, for mine and for many. I had Johnny Mc at my side from start to finish, the yang to my yin, helping to make sense of it, my friend and fellow adventurer.

Good fortune and friendship brought me Kevin, a proud Englishman but an honorary Irishman surely for his friendship and his commitment to Pigsback, the team, and to me, through thick and thin.

It was a Dwyer family affair too. Valerie had a huge influence throughout, and JD was always a selfless supporter. Harry, too, had a couple of key interventions, notably that Christmas walk on the beach at Seapoint in 2009. Geraldine was responsible for finding two of our senior managers, starting with Dave Foody back in 2000. I know Alf would have been proud and that Elma is.

Above all, throughout this marathon journey, I had Karen to rely on: my rock, who steadied me, us, and our family, keeping it all real and relative.

And here I am, oh lucky me, at last, on the Pigsback.

Epilogue

"It was just relief. I think the biggest gift you receive in victory isn't the trophy. It's the relief."

– Pelé on winning his third World Cup in 1970

It has taken me time to shed the stresses and anxieties of a two-decade rollercoaster. For many of my 20 years with Pigsback, I was obsessed with the business and its challenges. It's what entrepreneurs do, but what they also must somehow control. Years ago, I read the legendary entrepreneur Anita Roddick, founder of The Body Shop, saying that entrepreneurs can suffer mental health issues when exiting their businesses. I couldn't relate to it back then. Now I can. I found myself stressed from the sale process and, yes, from the separation and the void.

I decided to fight against that insecure voice – the one that's nervous about what awaits in the void: the pent-up stress, the loss of purpose, and perhaps even a touch of suppressed regret at my own progress arrested for that middle decade in Pigsback. I decided to say 'no' to any corporate commitments, not just because they could tie me down, but because I didn't want to do more of the same and don't feel a need to prove anything to anyone on that front. I want to try new things, and for that, I want to retain control of my time, surely one of the greatest gifts that money gives.

To borrow again from Roosevelt's famous speech: I am losing myself in new *great enthusiasms* for hours on end: podcasts, masterclasses and ebooks, walking or running, exercising the body and brain.

Karen and I have moved to Monkstown village in south Dublin, a more suitable suburban life for a couple whose children have flown the nest. We love being so close to the coast. I relax a lot out walking and running.

We're beginning to spend more time in Connemara, too, from our base in Clifden. It's all working.

We bought a small premises in the heart of Monkstown, which Karen renovated, and we're launching as the SeaRooms Gallery. It's a modest affair and hosts mainly local artists. I love being surrounded by the art and the randomness of who might pop in - an entrepreneur brimming with enthusiasm, an artist with a vision, or a visitor from a locality rich in its characters. John Nolan is the main artist we exhibit at the SeaRooms. We go back a long way. To celebrate Dublin's millennium in 1988, John, a very young artist at the time, completed a set of sepia drawings of Dublin's writers and landmark buildings for the side of a new Jacob's biscuit assortment called Gallery. We have been friends ever since. John has immense talent. He is generous in sharing his knowledge and techniques at his classes in the SeaRooms, which I've been lucky to attend. The SeaRooms is a peaceful hang-out when pursuing my other occupations. I'm always happy to sit in silence, surrounded by John's colourful jazz-inspired abstracts, letting, as Kandinsky put it: the "psychic vibration of colour" work on my soul. I can testify to the results.

From the SeaRooms base, I've been investing in some start-ups. Some will win, and some won't. It didn't take me long to move towards the higher-tech businesses, and am enjoying some informal advisory roles. I have met entrepreneurs in crisis, too, knowing I have some experience to offer. I have shared our Project Encore approach, where I deemed it appropriate, and it seems to have inspired at least two companies to reorganise and reenergise.

I am pleased to have passed the entrepreneurial baton to the next generation. At the time of writing, in early 2023, Nicky is busy founding her start-up under the brand name *Drobey* in the fashion rental space. She has lured her sister Ella back from a successful spell in the fitness industry in Australia as a co-founder. Kerry is immersed in the start-up space, too, bitten by the entrepreneurial bug. She is currently assisting numerous start-ups and early-stage companies in Britain and Ireland to find funding through her work with Swoop Funding. Remarkably, Kerry finds herself based in Dean St in London, within 100 metres of the old Pigsback office.

A chance encounter in Café du Journal in Monkstown sparked a new interest. I was introduced to a neighbour, Brian O'Beirne, who turns out to be a most erudite individual, particularly well-informed on the emerging technology known as "blockchain." Since our first meeting in the SeaRooms, I've found a new *great enthusiasm*. I later met and learned lots from Lory Kehoe and Eoin Connolly, two well-informed and experienced players in this space in Ireland.

My timing was mainly fortunate, but I have had to learn to HODL (hold on for dear life) in very volatile cryptocurrency markets. Although these new technologies are very much in their infancy, they seem to have the potential to impact many areas of our lives: finance, insurance, legal, taxation, gaming, social media, and no doubt a lot more, in ways that have not yet been discovered. Blockchain is helping many people worldwide who are "unbanked" (have no banking facilities) and may not even possess an official identity. What chance do they have of progressing in life? Now, with a mobile phone connection, they have an identity of sorts and access to digital wallets. This allows them to store currency and to send or receive it at minimal cost in seconds. Their labour, sold nationally or internationally, can be paid for in Bitcoin, which for all its volatility may be preferable to some local currencies susceptible to huge devaluation under crooked regimes.

I have smaller interests in early-stage disruptive blockchain start-ups. These have such wide-ranging missions as one that aims to bring greater trust to media buying and another aiming to create a marketplace for personalised health based on our individual genetic data. Like all seed-stage projects, they are intriguing and risky in equal measure.

Blockchain is another far-reaching technological revolution with echoes of the early Internet years - no wonder I am drawn in!

I've been having plenty of fun too! I joined a couple of horse-racing syndicates and experienced great communal joy when one of our horses, Champers Elysées, moved through the grades from Handicap to Listed to Group level. Incredibly, she won the Group 1 Matron Stakes at Leopardstown. If Pigsback's success came painstakingly slowly and was riddled with stress, Champers Elysées' win in the Matron brought everyone in the syndicate, our families and friends, instant and unbridled joy. It was the stuff of dreams: a small miracle that a horse purchased for relatively little could go on to win in the most exalted thoroughbred class of the sport of kings.

There's a National Hunt or jump racing syndicate too, with Colm Murphy, who trains in Wexford and knows how to train a Cheltenham Festival winner. That's the dream.

If my old pal Nick was around, he would surely have had honorary membership of both syndicates.

On the poker front, I had time during the pandemic to bring my game up to scratch again, with some coaching, a few new books and online study. I felt I was improving, then won a small but decent tournament at the Victoria Casino in London, and went on to get a few placings at live events. In July 2022, I got my best live score yet, placing 267th out of 8663 players at the main event of the World Series of Poker in Las Vegas. I rather liked the unofficial accolade of *Top Paddy* (the last surviving of 50 or so, mostly professional, Irish entrants). In September, I repeated the feat, this time at the World Series of Poker online championships, coming 49th out of 4984 entrants in the main event. I particularly enjoy the challenge and competition these large poker tournaments offer.

In the type of people we recruited at Pigsback, in the simple fact that they were drawn to us, and in the culture we collectively created, it's of no major surprise to me that so many went on to make their mark in the corporate world, some as entrepreneurs.

Cillian Barry, who I met at a media conference (offering him a job on the spot), had a big impact during his time in both our Dublin and London offices. He went on to set up SportsCaller, which became a world leader in sports prediction games before being acquired by US casino group Bally's Corporation in October 2021 for a reported €40 million.

Jenny Taaffe and her husband, Alan McGovern, set up an international digital agency, iZest Marketing, and Jenny was named Image Digital Businesswoman of the Year in 2018. Sadly, Jenny passed away in August 2019 from pancreatic cancer.

Colin Hetherington set up one of Dublin's first and most successful digital advertising agencies, Zoo Digital.

The Londoners weren't going to be outdone in the entrepreneurial stakes by their colleagues in Pigsback Ireland, however. Stephen Rapoport has become something of a serial entrepreneur, initially as cofounder of CrashPadder, which he started in Pigsback's Dean Street office, where he got a free desk in return for a part-time sales role. He sold CrashPadder to Airbnb in 2012.

Also out of Dean Street came Jessica Butcher, co-founder of the augmented reality technology business, Blippar, which achieved unicorn status, and Tick, a social video platform. She was awarded an MBE.

The former Pigsback UK MD, Brian Harrison, went on to set up Swoon Editions, an online furniture retailer, with his partner Debbie Williamson. Another Pigsback alumnus, James Horwitz, set up Two Times Elliott, a creative agency. Rob Larmour, the man responsible for getting Pigsback Goods up and running, left to set up HiyaCar, a car-pooling business that is going from strength to strength.

Of the Canadian team, meanwhile, Rob Kenedi served his time as a co-founder and has gone on to make his mark in podcasts, coaching and mentorship.

Some of these businesses were inspired in some way by their founders' experiences in the Pigsback culture or by our Empathy suite of products and services, but none competed directly. Enterprise begets enterprise.

Other Pigsback alumni have gone on to notable success in the corporate world, including at global level. In Gareth Lambe's case, it was with Facebook, where he would ascend to the very top echelons as a VP, heading its international HQ in Dublin.

Rory Duggan's move into the hotel business with Fitzpatrick Lifestyle Hotels bore fruit with the eventual sale of the hotel chain in 2016, after much restructuring led by Rory. Jo Malvern became the general manager of a large Hong Kong-based logistics company. Alan Gilson returned to the food industry and these days is on the lookout for acquisition opportunities at a private equity company. Darragh Doyle has become a notable community manager and blogger in the digital space in Dublin. Folu Merriman-Johnson has become a leading creative executive in the UK's entertainment industry, most recently with Netflix. Our former Canada marketing manager, Kristina Hayes, has gone on to the highest ranks of the global advertising agency BBDO Worldwide, based in Toronto. I could go on, but there are too many to mention.

What do I **not** miss?

- The 5.20 am alarm clock
- The 5.28 am alarm, after a snooze that was no help
- Not trusting my old Land Rover to start
- Early morning security queues at Dublin Airport when time was tight
- The neck strain from the head flop when the headrest doesn't do it (there's a market need)
- Small hotels - in fact, any hotels - near Paddington
- Rushing to and through Heathrow
- Feeling faint in meetings from trying too hard
- Recruiting senior salespeople in London
- The media-buying world
- Making friends and trusted colleagues redundant
- Having to be the resilient one all the time
- Long Powerpoint presentations (and I was guilty at the start)
- Sweating cashflow projections on spreadsheets
- The realisation that there were long years of grind ahead
- The grind turning me grey – and my life grey too – for a period
- The month-end sweats
- The drained feeling of being undercut, again, by another daily deals business
- Personal credit cards stretched
- Reorganising our finances time and again
- The threat of coming off our interest-only tracker mortgage
- Ringing Kevin for another dig-out
- Telling Karen we're part of the dig-out
- Johnny Mc's pallor when kidney stones struck
- Energy-sapping pedantry in legal negotiations

- Tensions with any shareholder

What do I miss?

- Ste rallying the troops for Friday drinks in Brown's Barn in the early years
- Any Pigsback bash
- Johnny Mc, guitar over the shoulder, belting out the tunes
- A round of Skittle Brew
- Beachhead clients: John Rooney, Sarah Power, Robert Jordan, Brian Kitson, Maresa Cagney, Ciaran Butler, Jackie Brannigan, Paul Reenan, Aiden McGuinness, Jane Manzor, Paul Wiseman, Brendan Murphy, Adrian Walsh, Jack MacGowan, Dave Robinson, Dick O'Sullivan, Pat Keogh, Paul Mullan, Seamus Leahy, and their likes. Too many to mention, but they understood Pigsback early and supported us
- The fast-tracking of bright young talent
- Nailing a new Empathy Communications contract
- Getting a new edition of Curly's Coupons away
- Formulating the weekly Pigsback Poll in the early years
- Seeing the early pattern in the first 20 responses of an Empathy Research survey
- The early morning Americano and almond croissant from Butlers in Dublin Airport
- Writing my journals in notepads on flights and holidays
- Jo rallying the gang for 'just the one' in the Wargrave Arms
- The buzz of Dean Street
- A pint of London's local ale
- Hummus and naan bread with a lamb kebab around London's Edgware Road
- Running around any of London parks
- A poker tournament in the Vic with all comers

- The creative buzz of London
- The Marylebone Hotel and all around it
- The Tube and the common purpose of commuters
- Tea and a KitKat on the Aer Lingus flight home
- The optimism of the early Canadian trips
- Sean O'Leary's positivity, all the way
- Knowing Johnny Mc 'got it' and would rally the tech team
- The Welcome Home ad featuring Curly in Terminal 1 at Dublin Airport
- The creative energy of brain-storming sessions
- The energy of shared purpose
- Brand engineering
- Reflecting hard about consumer messaging
- Cracking Facebook and Google ads, in the end
- Using early-stage Irish technology companies like Intercom and Xtremepush as suppliers and watching these companies take off
- Our Pigsback alumni faring so well
- The goodwill of UK alumni, despite our failure, and their eagerness to share experiences – none more than Brian Harrison
- Making traditional advertising work for us again
- The positive energy at an occasional lunch with Paul Henderson of the Irish Daily Mail
- Seeing the newest ad concepts from our agency, Fabrik
- The regular AGM attendees, rooting for us
- The chat and a pint the night before board meetings
- The energy from member workshops
- When Dave Foody went off inspired by some insight gleaned at a member workshop

- The commitment, above and beyond, of people like Dave Foody

- A lively Monday morning staff briefing

- The best of shareholder relationships: encouragement when down; our AGM attendees; the pleasant surprise that we kept going, kept everyone in and got there; gratitude from staff past and present; the balm of the many kind and appreciative messages

---

I wake up these days counting my blessings. I am indeed lucky. It all feels good again, with exciting possibilities ahead. Whatever the future holds, I am grateful for a life so far full of love, purpose and fun: at home, in my work and enterprise, and among my friends and my former colleagues.

These journals have already served their purpose. The story doesn't need a moral, but maybe one is jumping out: challenging and unpredictable as the road will probably be, life is ultimately better if we follow our dreams, give full expression to our talents, embrace our interests, old and new, and allow great enthusiasms to engulf us.

Thank you for allowing me to share my story with you. May you too, enjoy a life full of *great enthusiasms.*

Tribute 1

To my father, Alf Dwyer, who inspired me in life and in enterprise.

A Hard Act To Follow

A tall man, you strode out, saying big popular hellos.
We scurried to keep up, to be part of your greetings.
It seemed like most of Dundalk wanted a piece of you,
Of this confident, humorous, compassionate man.
You didn't let them down.

When you took to the stage
As Danger Mullaly, the Hiker or the Bird,
The Town Hall was in the palm of your hands.
We sold programmes and sweets at the interval.
We knew your lines and songs.

At the Albert Hall, a crowning moment,
You paused to let the laughing exiles recover,
Then set them off again with another of your yarns.
They had come to hear a great Irish tenor
But lapped you up as stand-up and compère.

You took us racing and enjoyed a punt,
Then you told us punting was for mugs.
When it came to the green baize,
You had the respect of Ireland's poker best,
A record we try hard to sustain.

You got a taste for enterprise,
And although you left it late,
You took your chance, pushing open doors:
Alf Dwyer – Tax Consultant, Fixer,
And Hearer of Confessions.

And still, you gave of yourself unsparingly,
When a peace march sought
To tell the world what Dundalk really felt,
When fundraisers needed help,
There you were: organiser, committeeman.

And suddenly, you had to slow the pace.
Your brain still sharp,
Your mind always cultivated,
Your way with people undiminished,
Engaged, to your brave, brave end.

Fear mór, fear uasal.

Tribute 2

I started this poem around 2009, probably on my Moby Dick voyage. For all my struggles on the business journey, I've always been a bit of a romantic in my view of free enterprise. With tongue somewhat in cheek, I put the finishing lines to this poem in 2022.

I dedicate this poem to all you never-say-die entrepreneurs out there and to your noble pursuit.

An Ode to Captains

It's in the demeanour, the look in the eyes,
The fire in the belly, the obsession inside.
No thoughts of failure, defeat or loss;
Just be in control, be their own boss.

True to a vision, they define a course,
Develop a product, recruit a workforce.
Rebels at heart, *a touch mad,* some say,
They put it all on the line; work night and day!

Whatever the weather, they keep her afloat,
And if they hit rocks, they'll be last on that boat.
Captains for the journey, never-say-die,
Bearers of the pains of enterprise.

Should the day come when they do reach port,
An *exit,* they call it, *the point of the sport,*
They might later wonder why they chose to alight
When what they loved most was the thrill of the fight.

Author's Note

I always kept good records but only actually started writing proper journal entries in early 2005. Most of what is contained from 2005 onwards is direct from and true to my journals, some of it verbatim and much of it edited by necessity to make for a better read.

I wrote 2000 to 2004 in a memoir format originally but rewrote it in journal format, a bit of artistic license to avoid a jarring switch between styles. I hope it has enhanced the read while remaining true to my recollection and records of events.

For discretion and out of respect for anyone who would prefer not to be part of the account, I have deliberately not identified some parties.

Throughout, I worked hard to be rigorous in my journals and in my recollections of events and facts, using all records available to me as an officer of the company and preserved by me personally. A complete record, of course, would be impossible and boring.

Acknowledgements

To Karen, Kerry, Nicky and Ella for their patience, encouragement and love always.

To Johnny Mc, Valerie, Kevin, JD, David Foody, Barry McGrath, Paul Finnegan, and every staff member, board member, investor, advisor, client and member of Pigsback since November 1999: thank you one and all. You all played a part in getting me to my finish line and in creating this proud and most resilient brand and company. To those still on that journey, I wish you continued success, enjoyment and fulfilment in Pigsback.

To John and Natasha, for the generosity in letting us all stay in *Mara*, an inspirational place to pull my early writing together. Extra gratitude to Natasha for her caring and excellent commentary on a very early manuscript.

As editorial assistants, additional thanks, in particular, to my daughters Kerry, Nicky and Ella.

For proofreading in part or in full, at various stages of finish, in addition to those already mentioned, my sincere thanks for all your efforts and contributions to Gabriel Cooney, Gareth Lambe, Jo (Malvern) Challis, Cillian Barry, Leo Kearns, Thérèse Rochford, John Kennedy, Barry McGrath, Brian Delaney, Patrick and Ellen Coen, Conor Horgan, Peter Murnaghan, Paul McKeon, Paul Duffy, Joanne Lynch, Conor Griffin, Brian Whyte, Noel Hayes, Kevin Mulligan, Willie O'Reilly, Brian O'Mahony, and Jim Donnelly.

Thanks to Alan and Justyna in Hacketts in Dun Laoghaire for the great service, printing, and binding of many proofs along the way. To Micheline Egan, who I met in the SeaRooms and who gave me some useful publishing insights.

Thanks to the highly creative and dedicated Charlie Dardis for his early work on cover design and his proofreading too. For his graphic design and website development, additional thanks to Brian O'Mahony.

Thanks to the Centro Cultural in Playa San Juan in Tenerife for their welcome and for the use of the library space during an extended stay.

For their advice on publishing through digital channels, my sincere thanks to prolific authors of poker books, Dara O'Kearney and Barry Carter.

For assisting in the interior design and layout of the book, and for preparing the many required electronic formats for modern publishing standards, my thanks to Carlos G. Barletta and his team from BCG Editores.

A huge thanks to Gavin Daly, for his important structural advice and an important edit at an advanced stage. Gavin 'got' the business and my voice.

For their endless patience and encouragement through the recording and editing of the audiobook, my thanks to Conor Reid, in particular, but also to Marisa and Amy and all the team at the Podcast Studios in Dublin.

Finally, my thoughts go to those we lost along the way, all of whom played a part in the journey: Alf Dwyer, Gerry Scanlan, Nicholas Coen, Jenny Taaffe, Pat Shine, Douglas McArthur OBE, Henry McDonald. Rest in peace. Henry was our tutor at the Irish Writing Centre's Memoir Writing course in the autumn of 2015. Just weeks before publication, I learned of Henry's untimely death at just 57 years of age in February, 2023. He and my classmates gave me great encouragement, tips, and motivation to publish.

Thank you, one and all.

From the Arena:
The Gallery

Colour photos and more are available on the companion website:
www.FromTheArenaBook.com

Chocolate Kimberley – the first tin in 1991 - by artist Orla Walsh

Scribbles on the Indo in Nov '99

The big Outdoor Ads from 2000 2 Weeks of Tease, then this Reveal

Pig Coverage in *Cara* Magazine, Oct 2000
Cara is the popular Aer Lingus in-flight magazine

Ella being welcomed home by Kerry (right) and Nicky, 2001
These three were much of my motivation and distraction

Johnny Mc in Rock Star Mode at an early Pigsback Gig

Rory, Gareth and Alan on a cheeky Team Trip to Disneyland, Paris

**Savouring the "Skittle Brew" with James Green and Stephen
Lennon aka Ste**

With the OG Family at our London Launch, 2005
(l-r) Harry, Valerie, John, Elma, me, Alf
(Geraldine absent)

With Karen at the London Launch

The Pigsback Fleet of Fiat 500s in 2012

A Pigsback Branded Bus in 2012

Harry, John and Michael (l to r) at the World Series of Poker, 2012

At the Poker Table with Daniel Negreanu (left) in Barcelona, 2014
(Photo: Danny Maxwell via PokerNews)

Nick Coen to the fore, 2014 with Funds raised for the Marie Keating Foundation

Piecing the Acquisition Jigsaw together

Working on the Journals 2017

With Artist and Friend John Nolan at the SeaRooms in 2019
We collaborated on *Gallery* for Dublin's Millenium in 1988

With Gavin Daly, Editor, in 2022 at the SeaRooms

Yin and Yang 2020

My Girls, July 2012
L–R: Ella, Nicky, Karen, Kerry

Messages

The many messages I received following the sale of Pigsback meant a huge amount to me - the themes were recurring and of no surprise….

Printed in Great Britain
by Amazon

28805816R00172